It's Not Fair

It's Not Fair

why it's time for a grown-up conversation about how adults treat children

Eloise Rickman

SCRIBE
Melbourne | London | Minneapolis

Scribe Publications
18–20 Edward St, Brunswick, Victoria 3056, Australia
2 John St, Clerkenwell, London, WC1N 2ES, United Kingdom
3754 Pleasant Ave, Suite 100, Minneapolis, Minnesota 55409, USA

Published by Scribe 2024

Typeset in Garamond Premier Pro by the publishers.

Printed and bound in the UK by CPI Group (UK) Ltd, Croydon CR0 4YY

Scribe is committed to the sustainable use of natural resources and the use of paper products made responsibly from those resources.

978 1 911617 17 4 (paperback edition)
978 1 761385 74 2 (ebook)

Catalogue records for this book are available from the National Library of Australia and the British Library.

scribepublications.com.au
scribepublications.co.uk
scribepublications.com

In solidarity with children everywhere

Contents

'Where, after all, do universal human rights begin? In small places, close to home — so close and so small that they cannot be seen on any maps of the world. Such are the places where every man, woman and child seeks equal justice, equal opportunity, equal dignity without discrimination. Unless these rights have meaning there, they have little meaning anywhere. Without concerned citizen action to uphold them close to home, we shall look in vain for progress in the larger world.'

Eleanor Roosevelt, 1958

A child-friendly summary

- Children are often treated unfairly by adults.
- Some people call this unfair treatment adultism.
- Children and adults can challenge adultism. Some people call this fight for fairness children's liberation.
- Children's rights are very important.
- One way of protecting children's rights is to turn them into laws.
- Children belong to themselves, not their parents.
- Adults should listen to what children have to say.
- All children should feel loved and safe.
- Too many children live in families without enough money. I think that governments should do more to help them.
- Most children cannot choose what and where they learn. I think that schools should let children learn about what they are interested in and listen to how children want to be treated.
- Climate change and pollution are making the world more dangerous for children. I think adults must fix these things now before they get worse.

- Children are the only group of people who can't vote. I think that children should have the right to vote.
- Adults need to do more to make the world a fairer place for all children.

Introduction

It started over pizza with friends.

We were talking about our childhood experiences when one of the group started telling a story about her younger brother going through a biting phase. I grimaced sympathetically: my daughter was a toddler at the time, and I knew first-hand how sharp those little teeth could be. Her mother solved the problem though, my friend continued, by biting him back so he could feel how painful it was.

'I'm sorry — how unfair,' came my response. 'That must have been horrible for him.' I didn't give it much thought; I expected everyone sitting around the table to agree that, however children might act, adults shouldn't bite them. What I did not expect was the heated discussion that would follow. Biting him, my friend told me in no uncertain terms, was the right thing to do. He needed to know that biting hurt so that he could stop doing it! Others either agreed or went silent.

I was shocked. This happened some years ago, and I was the only person at the table who was a parent. But surely that didn't matter? It seemed clear to me that the solution to a child's inability to control their actions was not to repeat the same violence. How was it possible that people I loved and respected could think it was okay to bite a young child — even if it was to teach them that biting hurt?

I went home after the meal feeling angry and disappointed — in my friends and myself. My friends were self-described feminists who cared about social justice; I imagine they'd all be horrified if I'd just described being bitten by my husband. If they couldn't see why using violence to teach children a lesson was wrong, what hope was there for wider change? And why was it that I, despite feeling so strongly that this was unfair, didn't have better language to describe why it was so unjust? Why couldn't I convince them?

Looking back on the situation, I can offer us all grace. My friends were in their twenties, and they didn't spend much time with children; I don't think they'd thought about parenting or children's rights all that much at the time. (Most of them are now parents themselves and they are all brilliant, loving, and gentle parents — none of them have ever bitten their children.) Like me, they had been raised in homes where parents were very much the ones in control. Most of them had experienced being smacked by parents who loved them deeply; all of them had experienced being punished and having to obey the adults around them at home and in school. Although they were primed to spot other forms of injustice — sexism, racism, classism, ableism — no one had ever pointed out to them that the way we treat children isn't fair.

No one had ever talked to me about this either. When I was trying to articulate to them why I felt so passionately that children shouldn't be bitten, I struggled to find the words to describe the double standards we hold adults and children to. Nor did I have a clear vision of the alternative. The thought that the problem was bigger than changing individual parenting practices — that children might need their own liberation movement to dismantle the discrimination they face — hadn't crossed my mind. All I knew is that I was horrified by the thought of ever intentionally hurting my daughter.

Since that meal, I've been interested in understanding how we treat children as a social justice issue, rather than as a question of individual parenting preferences. Parenting, I've come to realise, is political. And the unfair treatment that children face every day has a name: *adultism*.

Thankfully, I'm no longer at a loss for words.

It's not fair

How we treat children isn't fair.

Collectively, children are the most discriminated-against group in our society. Because of adultism, children are more likely to live in poverty, more likely to experience and witness violence, and are much more likely to have their lives significantly controlled by other people, from what and when they are allowed to eat to how they spend their time. They suffer from a lack of property rights, barriers to facing legal representation, and a need to go through caregivers to access certain types of services or healthcare. They earn less money for doing the same job as adults, and under many jurisdictions, children are the only people who can legally be hit. They can be threatened, punished, and shamed by their caregivers and coerced into doing things they don't want to do. They routinely have their bodily autonomy violated, for example by being forced to wear clothes they don't want to wear or by being made to go to bed when they're not tired.

Children know they are being treated unfairly, and they tell us often. I remember telling my parents that it wasn't fair when I was grounded for leaving my room messy and using the language of fairness to push back when I got into trouble at school; these days, I'm more likely to hear 'it's not fair!' from my daughter when I do something that she disagrees with. But how often do we really listen to children when they call out injustice — and how often do we make changes to our behaviour based on what they are telling us?

We can't pick and choose which people get to be treated with dignity and compassion. If we don't believe children when they tell us they are being treated unfairly — if we don't think children's rights are as important as other social justice movements — then it makes it hard to claim that we care about justice for everyone. If we think that women should be listened to when they report sexual harassment and violence, that we should believe people when they tell us they have experienced racism, then it's time to start questioning why we don't extend the same willingness to listen to children when they speak out against the way they are treated. What's more, the roots of much of the violence we see in society can be traced back to the domination, humiliation, and powerlessness so many of us experience as children. Right from the start, we are taught that those with more power can use that power to get others to do what they want — or else face the consequences. Adultism is the first injustice we experience, and it paves the way for all the rest.

Just as we look back on the blatant sexism and overt racism of the recent past with a mix of horror, shame, and bafflement, I believe that when our descendants look back on how we treat children today they will feel similar emotions. But it doesn't have to be that way. We could be remembered as the generation that changed things for the better, paving the way for a better, kinder, fairer future for all.

Why this book?

I've been working with families since 2018, running courses on parenting, education, and children's rights that help parents to notice the adultism around them and support them in creating a rights-respecting culture in their homes. As a parent-educator — and as a parent myself — I have read a lot of books and materials on raising and educating children. But the more I read, the more I noticed that virtually no books outside of academia were talking explicitly about power, which seemed strange given that the parent–child dynamic can feel so unequal. Even 'gentle' parenting books, which encourage readers to move away from outdated parenting practices like punishments and making babies 'cry-it-out', stopped short at analysing power relationships or calling out adultism, instead assuming that it is normal for adults to hold more power and set the rules. These books seemed to rely on and support a vision of parenting as something private, happening between an individual adult and child, without significance for society at large.

Much of what I read seemed focused on the idea of raising children who would grow up to be good people — polite, kind, helpful, invested in justice — with many references made to the impact parenting and education practices can have on children's future development and outcomes. At a time when more children than ever are struggling with their mental health, when families are living in poverty and struggling to put food on the table, when young people are growing up with the threat of the climate crisis looming over their shoulder, it seemed strange to ignore these things — and unfair to heap all of the responsibility for 'fixing' children's problems onto individual parents. Few of the books I read had anything to say about children as capable, brilliant, complete people (with some notable exceptions: see the recommended reading list at the back), much less about children's capacity to make meaningful decisions about their lives. I began incorporating more reflections on adult–child power relations in my work, prompting my clients to think about where they might be able to make changes in their own lives, but I was frustrated that I didn't have many resources to recommend if they wanted to find out more.

Still more surprising to me was the complete absence of any mention of children's rights. When I first started reading about the UN Convention on the Rights of the Child, years after becoming a parent, I was baffled: why was I only just reading about this now? Why weren't the parenting books I was reading shouting about children's rights from the rooftops — or at least mentioning them? I soon realised I wanted to go deeper, and signed up to do an MA in the Sociology of Childhood and Children's Rights at UCL's Institute of Education. It's no exaggeration to say that my mind was blown. It turned out there were decades of research and academic writing exploring children's rights, adultism, and ideas surrounding children's liberation. I discovered a whole new world, where suddenly the ideas I'd been boring my friends with for years fitted into a framework of rich scholarship.

But while it was exciting to engage with a wealth of radical, exciting, even revolutionary ideas, it was also disheartening to realise that so few of them were making it through to parents, teachers, journalists, or policy makers. Academics exploring these issues don't always feel the need to consider how they might translate into a shift in policy or practice. Ideas are important, but we need action too if we want things to change. And most parents, teachers, and policy makers — those people whose actions can most easily impact children's daily lives — don't have the time, energy, or desire to wade through stacks of technical writing.

This book is an attempt to bridge the gap between theory and practice. In it I want to help you understand adultism and the effect it has on children's lives as well as offering some practical suggestions for how we can move towards children's liberation. It is the book I wish I had had when my daughter was tiny, and I was starting to rethink everything I thought I knew about parenting. Writing and researching it has been life-changing for me. I hope it will be similarly impactful for you as a reader.

What you will find inside

This is a book about children and childhood, but it is not a parenting book, and I don't assume you are a parent. While there is plenty in here about the individual parent–child relationship, I also discuss issues that may not directly affect the children in your life, but which do affect children as a social group. Similarly, although individual parents and teachers have an impact on children's lives, every aspect of adultism is tied into larger social structures and economic systems. If we are to work towards children's liberation, we need to be thinking bigger than the family unit and considering how collective action and widening our circles of care can make life better for all children — not just our own.

Although my focus isn't on practical tips, each chapter includes ideas for how to support children's liberation — at home, at work, in your community, and through political engagement and activism — as well as offering material for deep reflection. My starting point when writing this book was that social change happens when we are able to challenge existing structures, and this requires the time and space to reconsider some of our commonly held beliefs and assumptions. I hope that this book will help provide you with some of that space to think.

To understand why we treat children unfairly, we need to understand how we think about children. Chapter one looks closely at how we see children and the beliefs we hold about them, how social constructions of childhood come to be, and why questioning our collective view of children matters so much.

Central to our understanding of children is *adultism*, the structural discrimination faced by children. Chapter two provides a full explanation of the concept, showing how adultism shows up in children's lives and our laws and policies, why adultism must be understood as an important social justice issue, and how moving towards children's liberation is crucial if we are to make the world a better place for children — and everyone else.

Understanding children's rights is vital if we are to make progress in protecting them and supporting children to advocate for themselves. Yet many adults I have spoken to, including parents and teachers, are not familiar with what is covered by children's rights declarations. Chapter three provides a brief introduction to children's rights: what they are, how they came to be agreed upon, practices that go against them, and where these rights don't go far enough.

How we treat children's bodies tells us a lot about how we view children and their social status in society. Chapter four explores how everyday medical, parenting, and education practices — such as scanning for 'abnormalities' during pregnancy, deciding whether to sleep train, or scoring children's development or academic progress against a baseline — are in fact deeply political, rooted in ideas of how 'normal' children behave and develop. Thinking about children's bodies is especially interesting as they are at once sites of adult control and children's resistance, and can provide us with concrete examples to consider questions of consent, autonomy, and privacy.

Although children's liberation is about more than what happens in the home, parents play an enormous role in their children's lives, as well as collectively shaping attitudes towards children among the public at large. Parenting can be a radical act of hope and change, and chapter five asks what rights-based, liberatory parenting might look like, what challenges stand in the way of a shift away from authoritarian and outdated practices, and what support is needed from wider society to get us all there.

Parents are not the only ones who care for children, and childcare arrangements form an important part of many families' support systems. Chapter six explores some of the tensions between feminism and children's rights under capitalism, and asks how we might fund children's care in a way that supports all children and their families, whether they are cared for at home or in a dedicated setting. This can only happen if caring for children is valued as important work, which in turn requires us to value children and see them as whole people whose preferences and experiences matter.

Supporting parents to return to work with properly funded, high-quality childcare is an important part of tackling child poverty, but it's not the whole picture. Chapter seven shows that childhood poverty and the growing inequality between those whose families can afford the basics and those whose families cannot is a deliberate political decision, with devastating consequences for children. The good news is that policies can be changed; if poverty is a political decision then it is one we can loudly and strongly argue against.

School is often put forward as the answer to questions of inequality and children's rights, and good education can certainly be a transformative force in children's lives. But the education system doesn't always achieve what it sets out to do, and for some children school can be a nightmare. Chapter eight investigates whether the current school system is fit for purpose, and what changes can be made so that it truly reflects children's needs and lives in a rapidly changing world.

The biggest challenge faced by children today is undoubtedly the climate crisis. Chapter nine looks at how children's rights are put at risk by global heating and pollution, and how children all over the world are making their voices heard in the fight for their futures. It's easy for discussions of the climate crisis to leave us feeling scared and overwhelmed, but the science is clear that the worst outcomes are preventable. Action is the best antidote to hopelessness, and there has never been a more important time to start. Every tonne of carbon saved is one our children — and theirs — will not inherit.

The fight to end adultism can be won. It will require individual action from all of us, as well as a commitment to radical political change. One change that would have an impact straight away would be to embrace truly universal suffrage by giving children the vote. Chapter ten explores the reasons for doing so, as well as showing that — far from being incapable of political thinking and action — children around the world are already acting in ways which are explicitly political, including organising themselves in children's parliaments to create meaningful change in their communities and forming coalitions to fight for better pay and working conditions.

My perspective has predominantly been influenced by the twin academic fields of childhood studies and children's rights, though I also borrow from the work of other disciplines, notably philosophy. I owe an enormous debt to the hundreds of authors, activists, and academics whose work I have relied upon while writing this book, and I've suggested further reading linked to each chapter for readers who would like to go deeper into the themes raised in the book. You can find this list at the end of the book.

Some notes on the text

Scope

A book exploring children's liberation from a truly global perspective would necessarily be much longer than this one. Because of this I've chosen to focus predominantly on WEIRD countries — an acronym devised by Joseph Henrich standing for Western, Educated, Industrialised, Rich, and Democratic — in particular, the UK, where I live, and the US and Australia, where many of my clients are from. When we think of problems of children's rights, it can be tempting to look far from home; to children enslaved on cocoa farms on the West coast of Africa, to Bangladeshi child brides, or to the Afghani girls banned from attending school. These are all issues worthy of deep care and attention. But it would be wrong to assume that children's rights are secure in higher-income countries. Adultism is a global phenomenon — it just looks different from place to place. Those of us living in places with higher rates of children in education and stricter laws on child labour and violence against children may feel like our work on children's rights is done, but as this book will show, we still have a long way to go.

Language

Language is always changing. In this book I have used the word adultism to refer to the age-based discrimination that favours adults over children, following the work of many scholars of children's rights including Harry Shier, John Wall, and Manfred Liebel. For a detailed discussion on the importance of language when talking about the discrimination children face, see chapter two.

I hope that this book will be helpful to readers of all genders, and I make no assumptions about who is reading. This is why I use the word parent, apart from in certain situations when I discuss mothers specifically and the struggles they face, such as the lack of adequate maternity leave, the risk of poverty in single-parent families, and unpaid caring responsibilities, as well as the tensions between children's rights and women's rights. It's important to note that these issues will also be experienced by some trans and non-binary parents, alongside the additional prejudices and discrimination they face based on their gender identity.

For brevity I use the term parent to describe all of those with familial caregiving responsibilities, including step-parents, guardians, and foster carers.

Numerous academics and activists have written at length on

race as a social construct rooted in white supremacy, an idea that is now widely accepted.[1] It may be more accurate to talk about someone being 'racialised as Black' than being 'Black', though the former describes 'the phenomenon that is happening to them' rather than their community or identity.[2] For ease of writing, I endeavour to use the language that best reflects children's identity and is as specific as possible, e.g. Black, white, Jewish, or African American, rather than umbrella terms. I recognise that the term BAME (Black and Asian Minority Ethic) can homogenise people with very diverse experiences, though at times I have used it because that's the language used in the research that I'm referencing.

Names

All of the names of children and their parents mentioned in this book have been changed to support their right to privacy, unless they are already in the public eye.

CHAPTER ONE

How we see children

What is a child?

In answering this question, you might first refer to age. Perhaps you'd say that a child is a person under the age of 18. If I gave you longer to think about it, maybe you'd say something about the term 'child' being a legal definition, with childhood entitling people under a certain age to some protections and preventing them from taking part in certain institutions, such as marriage, voting, or joining the armed forces, or participating in certain acts like drinking alcohol or having sex. You might also say a child is someone who is in a period of physical or biological growth and development, someone who has not yet reached full puberty or whose brain hasn't reached maturity yet. Perhaps you'd also talk about childhood as a set of practices, such as playing, attending school, learning, growing socially and morally, living with parents, and respecting elders. Or maybe you would talk about the word with reference to generations. I am still my parents' child, even though I am an adult with a child of my own; here the word child has nothing to do with age, and everything to do with my place among immediate and wider family.

You might even talk to me about children's status in society. I, for one, cannot think of a single culture across time and space where children have not held a lower social status than adults. Children are subject to more controls and restrictions over their lives, are more likely to experience violence and poverty, and are seen as less rational and developed than adults. Because of this, you might also hold assumptions about a child's capacity: what they can or cannot do, where they should live, how they should spend their time, what they should be protected from and what they should be exposed to, and whether they can make certain decisions relating to their own lives.

How you would answer the question would also be influenced by where you live in the world, what your life is like, and the fact you are alive in the 21st century. In some communities, a good childhood will be one spent working for money in order to ensure the family's survival, with school attendance a luxury; in others, it will mean spending every available hour studying for school to ensure future employment opportunities.

When I first considered how to define childhood, I found that the longer I thought about it the harder I found it to come up with an answer. After all, do we really believe that people are 'fully developed' when they hit 18 or 21? What about societies where childhood ends with social markers such as marriage or parenthood, rather than with reaching a certain age? What does it mean when the age of criminal responsibility (ten in the UK) is lower than the legal age of majority (18), or when people access different rights and responsibilities at different ages? I think we are aware of the term 'child' being inadequate to describe the huge variety of people under the age of 18, even if it's not a conscious thing: we tend to use clarifying words such as infant, baby, toddler, or young child to refer to children at the lower end of the 0–18 range, and words like tween, teen, youth, and young person to describe those at the higher end. When I asked a friend's 13-year-old daughter to define the term 'child' she was quick to point out 'I'm not a child, I'm a teenager'.

When I look back on my own life it certainly doesn't feel like there was one clear shift from childhood to adulthood that took place on my 18th birthday. While I was glad I could legally drink in pubs without worrying about needing a fake ID, and I was excited about moving away from home to attend university, not much else changed. The move from child to adult felt less like a leap and far more like a gradual process of growth, independence, and learning from experiences and mistakes. Some of the markers we think of as belonging to adult life — earning money, responsibility for others — were present during my teenage years, as I juggled part-time work, caring for younger siblings, studying, and carving out my own friendships and support systems outside of the home.

People don't change significantly overnight. Research suggests that, rather than being 'fully developed' at age 18 (or even 25 as has been suggested), human brains continue changing throughout our lives: we don't suddenly reach a static point when our development is 'done'.[1] The age of 18 as the cut-off point for childhood is arbitrary; clearly it's not a natural or biological shift that we are marking, but a cultural one (further evidenced in the UK by the fact that the legal age of majority decreased from 21 to 18 in 1969).[2] Collectively we have long agreed that childhood exists, but when it comes to considering what it looks like, most of us would say that it exists on a continuum of developing maturity, responsibility, and capability. (There are even some areas where children are more capable than adults, such as in learning new languages.)

Although at first what a child is seems to be self-evident, the difficulty in precisely defining the label shows it isn't a wholly biological or natural category. Instead, the terms child and childhood are *socially constructed*.[3] The period we think of as childhood isn't set in stone, but rather has changed and developed in different ways in different societies and cultures, alongside specific institutions, laws, structures, and ideas about personhood.[4] But to say that the label of child is socially constructed is not the same as saying that children are the same as adults and that there is no differentiation between people of different ages, or that children do not need special protections or exceptions. Thinking about children as a social group is important, not least because they face certain struggles and challenges, and being able to state clearly what is happening to whom is important. But when we step back, we can see that 'child' is just one of many identities a person may wear, and we can begin to question the rigid boundaries and social norms associated with childhood.

Rachel Rosen, associate professor in childhood at IOE, UCL's Faculty of Education and Society, points out that 'young humans are reliant on others for their very survival ... however, this early dependency has been increasingly taken to describe the institution of childhood, in its entirety, overwriting children's potential capabilities with social ascriptions of vulnerability, need, and dependency'.[5] Children are capable of being both vulnerable and full of agency at the same time; one does not cancel out the other. If the idea of the child is at least partially socially constructed, then it stands to reason that what we believe about 'good' parenting, 'good' education, and what it means to be a 'good' child can tell us a lot about the society or culture we live in — but not very much about children themselves. It's these cultural views that we need to unpack if we are to understand and resist the oppression of children.

Human beings, human becomings: children as future adults

'We understand the world in its becoming, not in its being,' writes physicist Carlo Rovelli.[6] I think the same is true for how we tend to understand children. If we were looking for a very simple answer to the question 'what is a child?' we might just answer: not (yet) adults.

Much of our language and practice around children is focused on them as adults in training. In fact, children have been perceived as immature, irrational, and somehow incomplete throughout the intellectual history of the West.[7] Despite the new ways of thinking ushered in during the Enlightenment, children were seen as progressing in a linear fashion towards the civility and rationality of adulthood. English philosopher John Locke wrote his key works in the late 17th century and in many ways his ideas about childhood were progressive. He cautioned against using corporal punishment too freely and encouraged parents to engage children in conversation and nurture their curiosity. Yet he still viewed children as incomplete, arguing that humans were born as if a tabula rasa (blank slate) and that knowledge, skills, and learning come through sensory experience and education.[8] 18th-century French philosopher Jean-Jacques Rousseau had similarly modern ideas about children. In his treatise *Emile*, he suggests that children need access to nature and should be given time to play freely, with education in the earlier years focusing on experience rather than book-learning. But still, he stressed that children are inherently incapable of reason, only progressing towards rationality in the later stages of education: 'The noblest work in education is to make a reasoning man, and we expect to train a young child by making him reason.'[9] We might call this treating children as *human becomings* rather than full and complete *human beings* here and now.[10]

We can also see the idea of children growing towards a rational, adult self in the influential work of Swiss psychologist Jean Piaget. Writing in the 20th century, Piaget sought to present a specific view of children's development, identifying four stages that children pass through as they actively construct a model of the world around them: the sensorimotor stage (0–2 years old), where children primarily learn about their environment through their senses and motor activities; the preoperational stage (2–7 years old), where children start to use mental abstractions, such as by picking up a stick and pretending it's a sword; the concrete operational stage (7–11 years old), where children are more capable of solving problems because they can consider numerous outcomes and perspectives; and the formal operational stage (11 years old through adulthood), which is characterised by abstract, systematic, and reflective thought. These stages were seen as unchanging, with all children moving through them in the same order, though not at the same speed, and with each stage representing a jump forward in rationality and sophistication. Piaget also believed that children and adults think differently, seeing the world in different ways.

In the West, a lot of our thinking about children and childhood has roots in Christian doctrine. The idea of original sin suggests that children are born bad and in need of firm discipline and education, this time to shape them into godly adults who will respect divine authority and not stray from the word of God. This belief in children's inherent sinfulness and untrustworthiness has been used to justify oppressive parenting practices such as corporal punishment, on the basis that children need to learn to obey their parents, and through their parents, God. Advocates of this style of parenting can be found on social media turning to scriptures such as 'Children, obey your parents in the Lord, for this is right' (Ephesians 6:10) and 'Whoever spares the rod hates their children, but the one who loves their children is careful to discipline them' (Proverbs 13:12) to support their actions. Of course, not all Christians believe in harsh parenting; some see Jesus as the ultimate model in gentle parenting.[11]

I spoke to Adele Jarrett-Kerr, who runs a self-directed education setting in the UK alongside unschooling her three children (more about both these things in chapter eight) and who grew up attending an evangelical church. She explained to me that growing up, she was taught that her mind was sinful and that she was born evil.

'I was raised believing that I couldn't question things because my mind was inherently untrustworthy, and that I couldn't trust myself to make good decisions,' she tells me over Zoom from her home in Cornwall. 'As I got older, I was encouraged to always see friends of other faiths as "projects", looking for ways to evangelise to them. I think this view impacts on how children are treated too — instead of seeing them as people, we're treating them as projects in need of training to make them "good".' Adele has since left evangelicalism, having embarked on what she terms a 'faith-shift', and her children are having a very different childhood experience to the way she was raised.

This sense that children are inherently untrustworthy has been picked up by writer and unschooling advocate Akilah Richards, who argues in her TED talk 'Raising Free People' that we need to stop telling children that freedom is something to earn. 'Deciding that an entire group of people is untrustworthy until we fix them to be trustworthy is madness ... we haven't quite developed the language and practice that roots our parenting and education in trust instead of fear.'[12] Educator and children's liberationist John Holt wrote along similar lines: 'Trust children. Nothing could be more simple — or more difficult. Difficult, because to trust children we must trust ourselves — and most of us were taught as children that we could not be trusted.'[13] If we look at some of the language used to describe young children, we find words like attention-seeking and manipulative; the sense that children are trying to wrap caregivers around their little fingers, and that to 'give in' would be to 'create a rod for your own back'. Interestingly, studies suggest that far from being born 'evil', it's much more likely that we are all born with the instinctive drive to be cooperative, sympathetic, and helpful.[14]

We can also see the view of children as 'human becomings' reflected widely in modern discussions around childcare, schooling, and parenting. If we look at popular parenting writing, there is currently much focus on raising children to be polite, hard-working, cooperative, and self-disciplined. Although I'm sure advice is shared with the best of intentions, it still feeds into the sense that children are 'becomings' who can be shaped into good people in the future if we just do the right thing now. In practice, parenting with optimal development in mind will often look like parenting with children's rights and needs in mind, which is, in part, why we are seeing an explosion of gentle and respectful parenting advice online from psychologists. But it is interesting to take a step back and think about why we are doing what we are doing — and whether we are holding up 'typical, rational' development as the end goal, rather than our children's happiness, autonomy, and wellbeing.

Although the sense that children are to some extent adults-in-training is widespread and far-reaching, there have long been dissenting voices. Writing in the Victorian times, educator Charlotte Mason stressed that children were 'born people' and should be treated with respect.[15] Since the late sixties and seventies, alongside other social justice movements such as the Women's Liberation and Civil Rights movements, resistance has been picking up speed. As I write this now, there is a broad and varied coalition of academics, educators, activists, writers, parents, and scientists — and children themselves, of course — arguing that children are competent social actors who are enthusiastic agents of their own lives from birth. We need only look at research done with street children who live in groups without adult caregivers to see that children are more capable of caring for themselves and each other than we tend to assume, sourcing food, shelter, and coping with extreme violence while supporting each other emotionally and practically.[16]

Who counts as a child?

Another important question we can ask about the social construction of childhood is who counts as a child, and when. Where certain children are afforded the 'innocence' of youth, Black children are subject to *adultification*, where they are treated as if older than they are, usually in order to justify their bad treatment or punishment.[17] A groundbreaking study by the Georgetown Law Center on Poverty and Inequality found that people perceive Black girls as needing less nurturing, protection, support, and comfort, believing that they are more independent, and that they know more about so-called adult topics, including sex.[18] Meanwhile, Black boys are more likely to be mistaken as older, be perceived as guilty, and face police violence if accused of a crime, according to research published by the American Psychological Association.[19] Sociologist Katherine Brown Rosier writes: 'Just as middle-class and white children are increasingly "infantilized" and their dependency is often effectively extended into their twenties, the disdain many Americans feel for "other" children is evidenced in the public's support for increasingly harsh sanctions for the "bad" behaviour of children ... who are held responsible.'[20] Class and poverty are factors in how much blame and responsibility we place on children, too. Rosier writes that children who are held responsible for their 'personal choices' and behaviour tend to be from poorer backgrounds, and are much more likely to be suspended or expelled, while their middle-class peers are given the benefit of the doubt because they are still seen as children.

Who gets to be seen as a child, and under which circumstances, matters a great deal — particularly when adultification can lead to children being detained, incarcerated, and even killed. While we might think of children in general as innocent, vulnerable, and deserving of care, refugee and migrant children occupy a deeply marginalised space in society, unseen by most and rendered doubly silenced: for being children and for seeking asylum. Every year children die trying to reach Europe in small boats or through other unsafe routes. And when children do make it to dry land, their horrors don't end. Children in the asylum system are at great risk of living in deep poverty. The UK's immigration system issues asylum seekers accommodation — which can be horrific, with infestations, large rats, and collapsing ceilings — and a payment of £45 for each family member each week (though small additional payments are made for pregnant mothers, newborns, and very young children), which would leave a family of five trying to survive on just £11,700 a year, little more than a third of median household income in the UK.[21] It is no surprise that cases of malnutrition among both children and adult asylum-seekers have been reported in asylum 'hotels' across the UK, with *The Guardian* newspaper finding that parents have been found rummaging through bins to find food for their children.[22]

At least these children are still living with family members. The same cannot be said for unaccompanied migrant children — those without their parents or caregivers — who are especially at risk of poor treatment. Housed in unsuitable lodgings, children routinely disappear from the places where they are supposed to be kept safe, often in quick succession. These children are kidnapped or 'scooped up' by gangs and criminal operations and moved all over the country, where they are trafficked into the drugs trade and sent to work in county lines (moving drugs from one part of the county to another) or coerced into other criminal activity like money laundering and burglary. Some traffickers exploit the UK's hostile attitude towards asylum seekers, telling children they will be deported if they stay where they are. Many of these children — who have already endured so much in their lives — endure appalling violence at the hands of these gangs.[23] And this is preventable: sources claim that the UK Home Office has ignored warnings that children will be targeted by criminal networks.[24]

The lack of care felt towards these children by the government can be summed up by the instructions given by the UK's then immigration minister, Robert Jenrick, that murals of cartoon characters on the walls of a centre for unaccompanied child asylum-seekers should be painted over because they were 'too welcoming'.[25] When asylum-seeking and refugee children do make it to school, they are significantly more likely to be bullied and excluded from school than non-migrant children.[26]

It's easy to see these children as 'other' when their lives seem so removed from our own. Sometimes our idealised view of what childhood should be like — a time for innocence, care-free play, schooling, and family — can obscure the experiences of children whose lives look very different to that rose-tinted vision: children who are in the care system or who have been abused by caregivers, children who work for a living, children who have caregiving responsibilities (including children who are parents themselves), child soldiers, children in the sex trade, profoundly disabled children, and so on. Because these children challenge our ideas about what childhood should be like, it can be easier to ignore them altogether. But just as children are all different, childhoods can be vastly different, with some children inhabiting very 'adult' worlds and facing challenges we have never had to cope with.

How conceptions of childhood are used as tools for wider oppression

The ways in which we have historically positioned children as incomplete, irrational, and wild — and thus in need of controlling, shaping, training, and taming — has not only had consequences for children but for other groups who have experienced systemic oppression. Toby Rollo is a professor of political science at Lakeland University in Canada, where he researches childhood, colonialism, and the state. Rollo has argued that the way we see children has directly contributed to the violence which Black people have — and continue to — experience. This is because colonial projects worked to associate Blackness with childhood.[27] Colonial Europe's self-imposed task of educating the 'sinful and ignorant' non-European subjects of empire through force was made possible in part by linking of people of colour with notions of childhood — and the inherent sinfulness and ignorance children were thought to possess. This is not just a historic issue, Rollo writes, but something that 'persists today as Black people (and Black children in particular) are disproportionally exposed to violence in education, policing, and carceral systems'. Even in the late 18th century, he writes, colonialism was not really a racial project, but rather one that constructed a view of Indigenous people as children, painting them as a populace lacking intelligence and reason, and in need of civilising. In this world view, 'children are not simply human beings with different ways of interacting with the world ... they are a lesser, deficient, or otherwise incomplete form of human being'. In the colonial framework, both children and Indigenous populations are 'understood as the beneficiaries of violence', which is justified as a necessary part of the transition from an inferior state to a mature, adult one. The characterisation of Indigenous people as children made possible 'the dispossession of lands, removal of children from native communities, forced schooling ... as well as the host of institutions designed to assimilate and destroy Indigenous cultures'.[28]

The language we use, and assumptions we make, about children also crosses over with ableism, where disabled and neurodivergent people are treated as if they are less capable than other non-disabled or neurotypical adults. A 2006 study showed that people tend to associate disability-related words with words connoting childhood or child-like features, and further studies have shown that people change how they speak to adults with visible disabilities, utilising a voice and language similar to how they speak to children.[29] Other research has shown how people with intellectual disabilities are treated as children both by professionals as well as in their care settings and local surroundings, creating an inescapable daily reality of 'eternal childhood'.[30] Disabled and neurodivergent people want to be treated with dignity and respect, the same as all people.

Why the social construction of childhood matters

Just as we now understand that rigid understandings, stereotypes, and prejudices around gender, disability, race, ethnicity, and sexuality are socially constructed and can be harmful, so too can we begin questioning received wisdom about what it means to be a child and what it means to care for a child. How often have we heard that it is a parent's 'natural' responsibility to discipline their children in order to raise adults who know right from wrong, or that 'giving in' to children's needs and desires will create a generation of spoiled adults who won't be able to fend for themselves due to all the coddling they received as infants?

Exploring the construction of childhood — and how we might challenge some of the dominant messages we are fed about children — also provides us with space to start thinking about adulthood as something which is equally constructed. When we see adulthood and parenthood as concepts that are malleable rather than hard-set, we begin to see how the ways in which we think about ourselves might have been limited and restricted by the messages we have soaked up about what adulthood should look like. Through my work I have spoken to people whose parents did not feel capable of playfulness, joy, or silliness, and who still struggle to loosen up and get on the floor and play or be silly with their own children. The spectre of the sensible, authoritarian adulthood looms over their shoulder.

Jo is a mother to a young child, and she shared the following reflection with me after we'd been exploring ideas around childhood on a course I was running:

> When I think of a child, age and social status definitely come into play, but I also feel like the main idea in my head is this unfettered time of creativity and freedom from a lot of the societal pressures, stresses, and responsibilities of adults. Some of these are inherent to our culture, but many of these are just things we put on ourselves because of these ideas of how we 'should' act. Running around outside in the rain seems like such a 'childish' thing, but I think it's something many adults could benefit from doing every once in a while. Or having a dance party to shake out some rage or anxiety — things that seem like something a child could do but adults just don't do — this is the beauty of childhood to me. It's a time before all these silly norms are really a part of our consciousness.

The term 'child' is a label that can suggest many things about a person's experience, but — as with other labels such as 'woman' or 'Autistic' or 'working-class' — cannot tell us everything. There is not only one way for children to have a good childhood, just as there is no one way for adults to live a fulfilling life. Rather, there are as many ways for children to be happy and thrive as there are children. Every human has different needs, interests, ideas, relationships, responsibilities, and constraints, and every child will grow up in a cultural context that is unique to them. Our ideas around childhood are specific to the time and place we live in. But thinking about our preconceptions when it comes to what a child is, what they need, what they can do, and how they should be treated can only help us in figuring out which ideas are helpful to children — and what we want to challenge and let go of.

The child in front of us

How we think about childhood is intensely bound up in our ideas and understandings of time. To be a parent is to be always looking forward, both in our children's lives (celebrating milestones as they acquire new skills, chalking up lines on the door frames to measure their growth, imagining what the next stage of parenting will bring) but also in how we think about ourselves, situated on a family tree stretching back into the past and onwards towards future generations. Yet while we might have long-term dreams and fears for the children in our lives, we also live alongside them in the present. When my daughter falls down and scrapes her knee, I respond to her in the here and now, not because I'm thinking about how this will affect her in the future, but because I love her and want to support her through her discomfort. I see her as the person right in front of me, not her future self.

To acknowledge a child's personhood without invoking their potential as an adult does not mean that their future ceases to be important. We would do the children in our care a disservice to never be thinking about the years to come, just as we as adults think about our own futures too.[31] This is why we might still insist on teeth being brushed, even when the child in front of us doesn't feel it's high on their priority list! But we can speak to children about their hopes for the future and how we can support them to meet these, rather than making assumptions about what a 'good' future life should look like. It is their lives, after all, not ours.

I find it useful to remember the distinction between being and becoming in my parenting. It's easy to feel pressure to prepare my daughter for the future, especially when messages — implicit and explicit — about the challenges children will face in the future surround us. But even if I could shape her adult self through my parenting now — something I highly doubt, seeing how very much herself she has been since she was a tiny baby — I'm not sure I should. Central to my understanding of children's liberation is the idea that children do not belong to their parents any more than a wife belongs to her husband. Just because children are overwhelmingly financially dependent on the adults who care for them, this doesn't mean that we get to control them (and as we shall discuss in chapter seven, there are good arguments for putting money into children's pockets so that they are not totally dependent on their caregivers). When we move towards seeing children as people who belong only to themselves — who wear many labels and social identities, as we all do — then it becomes easier to notice when they are treated in ways we would not tolerate ourselves, and to think about how we can better protect and support their collective rights while honouring and respecting their individual needs and preferences.

Although it might seem contradictory, I think that we can all understand that children are both full and complete people in their own right, and that collectively they have a different set of needs and vulnerabilities to adults, especially when they are very young. Loris Malaguzzi was the founder of the Reggio Emilia education movement, an educational philosophy based on an understanding of children as subjects with rights, who play an active and capable role in constructing their lives. As he puts it, 'The child is already from birth an active co-habitant asking to be treated and recognised as such.'[32] Even the youngest of children are people with feelings, needs, opinions, ideas, knowledge, and rights who deserve to be treated with respect and taken seriously. Rather than seeing children as empty vessels to fill, we can recognise them as competent and able to do and decide things for themselves, even if there are certain things they find hard due to their physical size, their relative lack of experience in the world, and their being in a stage of life where they are still learning a lot of things that adults take for granted. This shift can help us to see children as people who are actively participating in and co-constructing the world around them rather than simply passively soaking up information.

When it comes to social change, my tendency is usually to seek out concrete actions — things I can read, do, or change now — to help move towards the sort of world I want to be living in. Actions are clearly important; without people who are committed to changing things for the better and taking action to support this, social change would be impossible. But I wonder if the most important action we can take towards children's liberation is to slowly start changing our way of thinking. I'm not sure that meaningful change in how we treat children is possible without recognising where and how the language of childhood, development, progress, rationality, and infancy has been used to oppress children and others. An exercise I sometimes suggest to my clients is to look through a newspaper and notice how stories about children are reported. What sort of language is used? Which assumptions are being made? Whose voices are included, and whose are left out? If you substituted the word 'child' or 'children' for woman, disabled person, or gay person, would the tone of the article still feel right? Only when we become aware of these narratives can we start to disrupt them, which is why shifting to a liberatory lens that focuses on children as people feels so crucial.

*

The power dynamics we might have grown up with, where the adults are in charge and the children are expected to obey, are a choice — even when they feel deeply ingrained and instinctive. To truly see children as full and complete people here and now is to demand a shift in the widely accepted childcare and education practices and policies we so often take for granted. When we see children as future people it positions them as less than fully human, even if that isn't our intention. When we assume that they are incapable of complex, rational thinking, we assume that they cannot make important decisions about their lives and that it is down to adults to take control 'in their best interests', without ever questioning our focus on rationality as a marker of humanity in the first place. When we start to question our long-held — and perhaps previously unexamined — assumptions about what it means to be a child (and what it means to be an adult) we see that there are many ways to be in a relationship with the children in our lives. And to be able to challenge and interrogate the power relations between adults and children, we need better, more precise, language.

CHAPTER TWO

Adultism

Throughout history, those with power have used it to infringe upon those who have less. Many political movements around the world have sought to redress these social injustices, although there is still a long way to go. As men infringe on the rights of women and girls, as those racialised as white oppress and mistreat those racialised as Black, as disabled people are excluded from opportunities and the care they need to thrive, people speak out and fight back. Unlike misogyny, racism, or ableism, however, we lack the language to adequately talk about how adults use their power over children.

Philosopher Miranda Fricker has developed a useful concept that she calls *hermeneutical injustice*: injustice that occurs when people don't have the language to talk about, describe, or understand what is happening to them. This can lead to our individual and collective experiences being obscured through a lack of shared language with which to interpret them (the word 'hermeneutic' simply means to do with interpretation). Fricker highlights that unless we can name an injustice it's difficult to call it out and stand up against it, even if we have the strong feeling that something isn't right. The example she gives is of sexual harassment in the workplace, something that women didn't have the language to describe until the 1970s, despite knowing they hated it when their boss stared at their chest or slid a hand over their knee. Naming things is important: being able to say 'I am experiencing sexual harassment' matters a great deal, both for the person who is experiencing harassment and also so that their harasser can know without question that their actions are unacceptable.[1]

Viewing children's experiences through this lens of hermeneutical injustice shows us why we desperately need shared language to talk about the harm that children face. If a synagogue is vandalised, we are able to name it as an act of antisemitism; when a Black person is stopped and harassed by the police, it's important that we can call this out as racism. Just think about how hard it would be to discuss and challenge antisemitism or racism if we didn't have the specific language with which to do so. But when children are oppressed, abused, or harmed by adults, we lack the language to describe that this is an attack by a member of a powerful group (adults) against a member of a group which suffers prejudice and discrimination (children).

Naming the injustices children face is an important first step in challenging those injustices, so let's find the language we need. The power imbalance between adults and children can be summed up by the term *adultism*, which I use to refer to the structural discrimination and oppression children face from adults, and society's bias towards adults. Though the term was first utilised by educator Patterson Du Bois in 1903, it didn't become popular until the 1970s. In a groundbreaking article published in the journal *Adolescence* in 1978, psychologist Jack Flasher argued that adults have extra power over children, and that 'adultism is related to the tendency to believe that all adults are superior in all skills and virtues to all children'.[2] The word adultism has been used since then, with activists, writers, and academics developing their own definitions over the decades.

Harry Shier, an independent scholar who has been researching children's rights, liberation, and participation for over 25 years, defines adultism as 'the belief that the adult human being is intrinsically superior to or of greater worth than the child'.[3] In adultist societies, children are defined by their lack of adult abilities, lower level of physical, intellectual, and socio-emotional development, and perceived irrationality. Childhood is perceived to be a deficient state inferior to adulthood; as we saw in the last chapter, children are often seen as 'adults in training' or 'future citizens'.

German Sociologist and Children's Rights scholar Professor Manfred Liebel offers four separate categories of discriminatory measures faced by children all over the globe:

- *'Measures against and punishment of undesired attitudes of children, which are tolerated or seen as normal in adults.'*
  A so-called 'good' child might be imagined as obedient — someone who does what they are told even if they don't want to do it or don't think it's the right thing to do — yet these are not qualities we would seek in adults. For example, children may be punished at school for 'talking back' to teachers, who in a different situation would congratulate an adult friend for sticking up for themselves. The very idea of punishment as a typical tool of parenting or teaching is adultist; we would not think it suitable in any other relationship based on respect, trust, or love. If a friend told me that her husband wouldn't let her go out and see her friends because he hadn't liked the way she had spoken to him, or had shut her in a room because

she was feeling overwhelmed, I would direct her to a domestic violence service. Yet we do not recognise parents who ground their children, or teachers who send students to isolation rooms, as acting in ways that are inherently harmful or cruel.

- *'Measures which are justified by real or assumed children's special needs for protection, but which in the end lead to further disadvantages towards children, on the one hand because their scope of activity is limited, on the other hand because they are excluded from specific practices and areas of social life.'* Here Liebel is talking about age limits, which can be important but need to be treated with care. In seeking to protect children, adults can end up causing more harm than good. For instance, fears around children's safety have led to them spending more and more time indoors, despite a wealth of research showing how important time outside is for their health and development. Language that paints children as excessively vulnerable or focuses on ideas of innocence has also been used to justify adult goals in the name of keeping children protected. We only need look at the so-called 'parental rights' movement in the US, which exploits the rhetoric of safeguarding children to promote regressive far-right aims, including criminalising the parents of transgender children and banning books that are deemed 'harmful'.[4]
- *'The limited access, in comparison to adults, to rights, goods, institutions and services.'* When we compare laws, we see that children have fewer rights than adults when it comes to protection from physical and emotional violence, as well as less access to certain spaces. During the week, our local swimming pool is only open to adults, something that is hugely frustrating as my daughter and I love to swim together.

Children are regularly barred from certain restaurants, cafes, and holiday resorts. Children also suffer from a lack of property rights, barriers to facing legal representation, and a need to go through caregivers to access certain types of services or healthcare.

- *'The lack of consideration of the social group of children in political decision-making which might have negative consequences in the later life of children and that of following generations.'* An ageing population combined with children's lack of voting rights can be seen as a gradual shift towards *gerontocracy*, or the rule of the oldest. The relative weight of older age groups in the electorate incentivises politicians and political parties to shape their manifestoes and policies to suit their preferences, rather than tackle the problems young people care about. We only have to think of the lack of action on tackling child poverty or securing a liveable climate for younger generations to see this in action, as we shall discuss in more detail in later chapters.[5]

We could add one other key aspect: *the assumption that adults are better capable of estimating children's needs and their best interest than children themselves.* Jelena Vranješević, associate professor of philosophy at Belgrade University, writes: 'If an adult believes that the child's decision is not in his/her best interest, the adult will most probably conclude that the child is incompetent, unable to decide.' When children use different decision-making criteria to adults, adults may assume that the child's ability to make decisions is less developmentally sound than theirs, and that they can — and should — override the child's decisions.[6] This ranges from minor points — a child deciding to eat dessert first rather than their main course, on the basis that they are less likely to be full up by the time their favourite part of the meal is available, and their parent vetoing their decision because it's not perceived to be a 'good' choice — to major decisions, like when children are ordered by courts into family relationships they do not want.[7] When children are very young, it's normal that adults have to take some decisions on their behalf, trying to decide what's in their best interests. But as children get older, we are not always so good at taking a step back. Children could make so many meaningful decisions about their lives, yet we continue to believe that we know best because we are adults. This is so normalised that we rarely pause to question whether this is ethically justifiable, let alone desirable.

Untangling adultism

Adultism shows up in things like 'no children' signs in shops and the Mosquito alarms used as 'teenager repellent'. Marketed at residents and small-business owners who want to prevent teenagers from gathering in public, these dystopian-sounding devices work by emitting a high frequency tone that adults cannot hear but which is unbearable to young people.[8] Can you imagine it being socially acceptable for something like this to be sold targeting any other group of people?

Adultism can also be seen in many things we consider normal behaviour: adults feeling free to say 'I don't like children' when they would never dream of saying this about another marginalised group; children being barred from social occasions such as weddings despite the rest of their families being invited; the rise in airlines offering 'adult only' flights; the normalisation and legality of smacking; sending children to educational institutions where they are publicly shamed and heavily controlled; the inaccessibility of public spaces such as art galleries, where children can find themselves reprimanded for making any noise; and harsh maternity leave policies that separate babies from their parents at a few weeks old.

It's considered totally normal to use disparaging language when describing children, with terms such as brats, monsters, the 'terrible twos', and 'threenagers' (this last one managing to critique both teens and young children at once; both groups get an especially rough deal in the way they are talked about). We also see children's lower social status reflected in the language we use when addressing other adults: 'That was pretty childish of you,' we might say to a friend acting inappropriately, or even 'don't be such a child'. And when we feel our autonomy is being ignored: 'Don't infantilise me.'

Children are often spoken about as a problem to solve, as if they are disruptive to adult life, particularly in conversations about childcare (as we shall explore further in chapter six).[9] Many of us live in societies where having a child does make life harder, with inadequate support for parents and a lack of social networks with whom to share the work of parenting. But our focus and criticism should lie squarely with these systems, not on children themselves.

Adultism affects all children, although it intersects with children's multiple identities and shows up in different ways for different children. Because 'child' is simply one part of a person's identity, we need to take an intersectional approach when looking at the effects of adultism. All children will experience adultism, but some children will experience other forms of oppression including classism, racism, misogyny, ableism, or xenophobia. Others will be born in a place where children face greater challenges. A Black child is likely to have a different experience at school than their white peers, and a disabled child may find the experience of accessing public spaces far more challenging than peers who are not disabled. As we saw in chapter one, there is no one universal narrative or global experience of childhood, and it's vital that we see adultism as just one thread when we are unpicking the harm children face, albeit one which gets tangled up with many others. Tackling adultism cannot be done if we are not at the same time dismantling classism, racism, misogyny, xenophobia, and other harmful systems of oppression — just as ridding ourselves of other forms of oppression cannot be done unless we are also fighting against adultism.

It's important that we are able to clearly understand adultism as a social justice issue, based on unequal power relations and supported by the systems that surround us. Like other forms of discrimination, adultism is a structural issue. This means it goes deeper than individual action (though individuals still have a responsibility to tackle adultism), with discrimination embedded in social structures, systems, and institutions, and often passed down from generation to generation. However, adultism also occupies a unique space as all adults were once children, and most children will become adults; children generally move from the oppressed class into the oppressing one as they move into adulthood. This is further complicated by the fact that most of us who are given a public voice to speak out against adultism are themselves adults — like me! So we have a situation where the vast majority of the arguments, debates, research, writing, and decision-making about children is in the hands of adults. (This is not to say that adults are not impacted by adultism. We are, both directly through, for example, overpriced and underfunded childcare options, and indirectly through witnessing the impact on the children we love.)

We would rightly not accept the conversation around women's rights to be led by men, nor all of the published writing on racism to come from white people. Yet this is the situation we are in when it comes to adultism.

Why use the term adultism?

Language matters a great deal and is always changing, something that I find exciting as a writer but which can sometimes be confusing as a reader. Why use the term adultism, rather than ageism, childism, or another word?

Society is geared towards adults — their needs, preferences, and values — and it's adults who make laws, decide policy, and run our institutions. Much as the term ableism focuses our attention on how society prioritises and favours those who are non-disabled, I use the term adultism to refer to the structural prioritising and favouring of adult needs, knowledge, and power. It's also the preferred term in the children's rights movement and in the sociology of childhood — two disciplines that are inherently concerned with making things better for children and listening to children's voices — and it's becoming widely accepted both in academia and, increasingly, outside of it.

Instead of adultism, we could use the term *adult supremacy*: 'the worldview that children are inferior, adults are superior, and that children must comply to adult expectations and environments.'[10] I like that expression a lot, as it so clearly captures the problem, though because it's a less widely used term I've decided to stick with adultism in this book. We could also use the term *misopedy*, literally meaning 'the hatred of children'. This is similar to the word misogyny, the hatred of women. But it's not always an accurate descriptor: someone can be adultist in their behaviour towards children without hating them or wishing to cause them harm.

You may have also seen the same thing referred to as *childism*, a term coined by psychiatrists in the 1970s and popularised by psychoanalyst Elisabeth Young-Bruehl's book of the same title in 2012. But — just to complicate things further — in the fields of philosophy, childhood studies, and children's rights, the words childism and childist are used in a positive sense. To quote philosopher Tanu Biswas, 'Growing out of the field of childhood studies, childism in its broadest sense refers to the critique of social norms and structures in response to what is marginalized in the experiences of children.'[11] As the Childism Institute at Rutgers University states, childism is 'like feminism but for children':

> [Childism] has emerged in the academic literature as a term to describe efforts to empower the lived experiences of the third of humanity who are children through the radical systemic critique of scholarly, social, and political norms. Beyond including children and young people as active social participants, childism challenges and transforms the historically ingrained adult-centered assumptions that underlie children's systemic marginalization in the first place.[12]

Childism has a lot in common with feminism, as both women and children suffer under patriarchy; the systems of dominance that feed into and support adultism and sexism are patriarchal systems. Because of this link, using the word childism to describe the positive movement for the rights of children makes a lot of sense to me. It's also the term used in other languages; in France, academics and activists are beginning to use '*l'enfantisme*' (childism) to describe the fight against '*l'adultisme*' (adultism).[13] But because of the dual-use of the term as both a positive and a negative, to avoid confusion I've chosen to use the terms *children's liberation* and *children's resistance* to denote the positive push-back on adultism.

Of course, these are all adult terms to describe what is happening to children; I've not heard many children use this language. Although my own daughter has no problem in telling me when I am being adultist — a word she has heard me using for a long time — I've noticed that she tends to use the words 'ageist' and 'ageism' when referring to the discrimination children face (by contrast, I use these words to refer to the structural discrimination faced by older people). And as we shall see in chapter four, children's resistance often doesn't involve calling adults out on their behaviour with technical language: their opposition can show up in 'bad behaviour' and bodily resistance, among other things.

It's tempting to think that the language we use to talk about the harm and discrimination children face doesn't really matter as long as we are trying to make things better for them; that lingering over language is an indulgence. But I don't think we would say this about any other term describing the harm faced by a marginalised group. We wouldn't argue that language doesn't matter when writing or campaigning about racism, classism, or ableism. Why should it be any less important to find precise, careful language to discuss children's experiences? How powerful would it be if we routinely saw harm against children reported as adultist violence, in news bulletins and on the front pages of the papers? If we were able to talk about the adultism we experienced as children in therapy sessions? If we were able to recognise and name the adultism our own children are experiencing, and give them the language to make sense of their own frustrations and experiences?

Finally, while adults certainly have an important part to play in helping children understand their experiences through language, academics and activists need to work with children to find language which resonates with them. I choose to use the word adultism, but I'm an adult. Much as it's not for men to define feminism, it's not for adults to police or define what language children use. As language is constantly evolving, I'm excited to see how this discussion continues in years to come.

Adult privilege

Because of adultism, all adults enjoy something called *adult privilege*. Privilege can be defined as 'systematically conferred advantages individuals enjoy by virtue of their membership in dominant groups with access to resources and institutional power that are beyond the common advantages of marginalised citizens', the marginalised citizens here being children.[14] This doesn't mean adults have stress-free lives, and it doesn't ignore adults who experience oppression or discrimination. Rather it simply means that adults do not experience adultism because they are no longer children.

Recognising this privilege is important, as when people are unable to do so they are also unable to recognise their role in keeping other groups subordinated, argues Bob Pease, Adjunct

Professor in the School of Social Sciences at the University of Tasmania. 'Members of privileged groups believe that they have a right to be respected, acknowledged, protected, and rewarded, and that they deserve whatever benefits and status they attain because they have struggled for them.'[15]

When I was researching the idea of adult privilege, I came across a brilliant checklist that highlighted basic privileges adults take for granted:

- Others cannot restrict what I can do in my own home, short of breaking the law. If they try, I can object and others will see my objection as valid.
- I can speak on my own behalf in public forums, and it will be treated as valid.
- I can demand that (my) children treat me with respect, which can consist of anything from tone of voice to unquestioning obedience, because I am an adult/their parent.
- Asking me personal questions, telling me how to dress, and viewing my computer activity is considered invasive to privacy.
- My mental capability to make informed decisions, regardless of what is informing them, is respected.
- I can actually vote on the laws and legislators that dictate what I can and can't do.
- My body is legally my own to do with as I see fit. No one else can restrict the things I do to my own body. No one else can do things to my body without my permission.
- There are no laws telling me that I must remain in an enclosed area under the supervision and guidance of authorities I must obey for the majority of my waking life. My future does not rely on doing work without recompense.

- The phrase 'no taxation without representation' applies to me.
- My access to food and shelter does not rely on pleasing others regardless of what I want.
- The vast majority of people whose views are represented in public media are on my side of the 'adult' age line.
- Almost all fictional representations of and nonfictional guides to the experiences of people in my age group are actually written by people in my age group, so I can expect a certain degree of accuracy or at least respectfulness in their depictions.
- It is considered assault to inflict physical pain on me without permission. I have clear avenues of legal recourse to pursue that will help protect me from assault.
- The people I live with cannot restrict where I go and when, who I talk to, what I spend my time doing, or my access to the outside world.
- I cannot be sent to any prison-like institution without breaking a law (as is the case for children sent to 'troubled teen' camps).[16]

Of course, some of these points only apply to certain adults, and only to a degree. The point about adults being free from restriction over what they do to their bodies won't apply to women who cannot access a safe and legal abortion, or to gay men who cannot hold hands publicly for fear of persecution. Conversely, some of these points may apply to some children; in some countries it is indeed considered assault for children to be hit. But these nuances aside, it's clear that children as a group experience far more restriction and control — and far less representation and access — than adults.

It's important to stress that adults can hold adult privilege and act in ways which are adultist while still loving the children in their lives and wanting the best for them. No one is perfect! Working to end adultism is a practice we can all be involved in, imperfect as we are. In order to move forward, we first need to be able to recognise that the parent–child (and teacher–child, grandparent–child, doctor–child, social worker–child ...) relationship involves one person having more power than the other, and that this power is often codified into law or formal agreements. This doesn't invalidate the love and care adults feel for the children in their lives, or the fact that most adults are trying hard to do the best they can for them. Understanding how adultism and adult privilege works isn't about pointing the finger at individual people, but about starting to recognise and disrupt patterns of behaviour, belief, and policy that disadvantage children compared to adults.

Adultism in action: The response to Covid-19

During the Covid-19 outbreak many policy decisions were taken that prioritised adult safety, at cost to children. There were lengthy public discussions around how to protect businesses and corporate interests in the face of lockdowns and restrictions, but comparatively little thought given to the impact that shutting schools, removing vital services, and reducing the amount of social contact and support would have on children's lives and development.

Before we go any further, I want to stress that I'm not here to argue against lockdowns, but rather to think about them from an adultism perspective. There was a rise in children turning up at hospitals with injuries, yet initial reports showed a reduction in violence against children because it was simply not being picked up: children were not being seen face-to-face by teachers, social workers, or even family and friends. It is always very difficult for children to report abuse — especially if they are young, do not understand the law, or do not have access to their own mobile devices to call for help — but lockdowns made it even harder for children to seek help or advice from others. Researchers have called this violence against children a 'silent pandemic'.[17] Children were also affected by witnessing increased violence against their mothers, with the UN using the similar term of a 'shadow pandemic' to refer to increased violence against women during lockdown, highlighting how adultism can both coexist with and be intensified by other forms of oppression.[18]

In the UK, as with many other countries, the pandemic also saw a rise in families struggling financially, with many finding it difficult to put food on the table. After significant media pressure and campaigning from footballer Marcus Rashford, the government agreed to offer free meals to certain children, but these were often shockingly meagre.[19] Influential commentators argued that feeding children is the responsibility of parents, and that if parents couldn't afford to feed their own children they shouldn't have them; a senseless argument in a country with high rates of in-work poverty, and one lacking in care and compassion for the children who can do little to provide for themselves.

The closing of schools led to children as young as four accessing schooling through a screen, something I think we can all intuitively sense is not ideal. Many children couldn't follow along with lessons, finding them confusing or boring, and struggled to connect with their teachers or with other children online. This was just about okay for those children who had parents with the time and energy to push back; at the time, I spoke to a number of families who had told their child's school that they would do their own thing instead, focusing on crafts, history projects, and kitchen science experiments rather than forcing their children to fill in worksheets or join Zoom calls. But for those children whose parents were busy trying to work from home or who didn't have the ability or resources to offer a tailor-made education, things were often lonely and hard.

Although the lockdowns negatively affected a lot of children, some suffered worse than others. Children who were already vulnerable bore the brunt of the impacts of poverty, violence, and lack of access to outdoor spaces and technology, not to mention the effects of the virus itself on their and their families' health.[20] School closures and online learning exacerbated existing inequalities in education.[21] Pupils at private schools were more likely to have regular contact with a teacher outside class during lockdowns, and the move to replace GCSE and A-level exams with teacher-assessed grades in 2020 and 2021 saw privately educated students' grades sky-rocket.[22] Wealthier families were more able to offer a quieter and more comfortable space for children to play and learn, with increased adult support and involvement with both home learning tasks and other activities.

Arguably those most affected by the closure of services were disabled children and their families. Many services — including access to specialist schools and respite care — were reduced or withdrawn altogether, which meant that children with complex needs missed out on receiving essential therapies and support at school. In a statement on this issue, Gina Wilson, Head of

Strategy for the Children and Young People's Commissioner Scotland, said 'For children with the most complex needs school often provides an important respite to parents, carers and siblings who during periods of lockdown have been caring for their disabled children on a full-time basis with limited support.'[23] Parent-carers found themselves supporting children with significant disabilities 24 hours a day without respite or support, with the Disabled Children's Partnership finding that the consistent delay of services has had a 'massive' impact on the physical and psychological development of children, and grossly impacted the mental health of parents.[24]

When there was a widespread return to school, there was seemingly little thought given to children who were medically vulnerable or who had medically vulnerable family members and needed to stay home longer. Some families were threatened with fines and attendance orders for choosing to keep their children home.[25] Because of the closures, a lot of children struggled when they returned to school. While parents and teachers alike called for more support for children's social and emotional wellbeing post-pandemic — time to play and reconnect with friends, support to process the grief of isolation and the death of loved ones, outings to museums, cinemas, and theatres — government responses narrowly focused on extra lessons and tutoring to help children catch up on 'learning loss'.[26] The priorities of politicians — getting children doing as well as possible in exams so that they compare favourably to other countries — can be wildly at odds with children's needs and desires, a common phenomenon in the education system, as we shall see in chapter eight.

Again though, it's important to note that children are not a homogenous group. While many children experienced the lockdowns as negative, for some the restrictions were a welcome reprieve from the stresses of school. There has been a rise in parents deciding to home educate their children after trying it out during lockdowns and seeing how their children were more relaxed, less anxious, and learning more when they were able to take a more active role in their education. For children who had experienced bullying, or for whom school had been intolerable due to neurodivergence, it's no exaggeration to say that being home was a lifeline. Lots of children enjoyed spending more time with their families and their pets and found they had more time to rest, enjoy hobbies, and spend time outdoors. In a way, the lockdowns exposed the adultism present in these children's lives too: freed from the usual norms and rules that usually controlled their lives day-to-day, they flourished.

A way forward: Children's liberation

Understanding what adultism is and being able to start spotting where and how it shows up in children's lives is the first crucial step towards dismantling it and working towards what might be termed *children's liberation*.

Children's liberation is not a new idea. It first took shape as a movement in the 1970s, with a series of books by writers such as John Holt and A. S. Neil that argued that 'the rights, privileges, duties of adult citizens be made available to any young person, of whatever age, who wants to make use of them'.[27] Some of the ideas in these books are as challenging and problematic today as they were when first published. I'm guessing few people would agree with Holt that children should be allowed the same sexual freedoms as adults; that children should be allowed to access all the information that adults can (including movies and TV shows); that children should be free to live independently, apart from their parents; and that children should have the right to the same legal and financial responsibilities as adults.

By contrast, other ideas have been embraced. 'Gentle' parenting has become a popular way of raising children; many countries have made corporal punishment illegal; and children's rights are more widely understood and put into practice. There is a growing movement fighting for children's right to vote (as we will discuss in chapter ten), while the rise in unschooling families who choose to live without school, giving their children control over their own learning, is testament to the power of Holt's view that children should never be forced to learn. Calls for children to have a basic income or to be allowed to work have less traction, yet at a time when poverty is damaging the lives of so many children — as we will see in chapter seven — these ideas are worth exploring.

The children's liberation movement of the seventies contains ideas and questions that we should still be engaging with now. What it lacked was an acknowledgement that a movement for children must be different from other liberation movements, because children are fundamentally different to most other social groups: they *do* need more protection, care, and guidance, and are more vulnerable to exploitation and harm from adults. Rejecting adultism doesn't mean rejecting the principle that there should be things adults can legally do which children should ideally be protected from doing.

Instead, what I am suggesting is a children's liberation movement that:

- Acknowledges that all children are complete people here and now;
- Actively works to challenge and disrupt adultism;
- Argues for children's equality as rights-holders and children's equality of human dignity, rather than total legal and practical equality;
- Demands radical change across the 'institutions of childhood', notably the family and the education system;
- Is committed to centring and uplifting children's ideas, needs, desires, voices, and goals, with children as leaders and adults as supporters and facilitators;
- Notes the tension between children's rights to participation, access, and autonomy and their rights to extra protection and support from adults;
- Recognises children's agency, capacity, competence, and knowledge;
- Seeks to expand children's access to public life, including giving children the right to vote;
- Takes an intersectional approach to exploring and tackling the challenges children face, and is committed to challenging and disrupting all other forms of oppression, including exploitative economic systems; and
- Understands that the relationship between adults and children is a political one.

It's important to note once more that I'm writing this as an adult, based on my own experiences and research, and my conversations with children. But children are not a monolithic social group, and different children will have different views on what they want and need. I hope that my ideas act as a spark for discussion, and in no way want to suggest that this is the final word on the topic: this is a constantly evolving subject, and one where we need children's input and leadership.

*

One thing we as adults can do to challenge adultism and to make life better for children is to work to protect their rights. But we can't fight to protect something we don't know about, so developing a good understanding of children's rights is an important step in being able to speak up in solidarity with children. All adults — particularly parents and those who work with children — should be aware of children's rights and their implications, and more needs to be done to support children themselves to understand and meaningfully engage with their rights. As well as providing a set of minimum standards for how children should be treated, a children's rights framework can help us weigh up conflicting decisions and make sense of our own responsibilities towards children.

CHAPTER THREE

Understanding children's rights

Children's rights are a crucial tool in dismantling adultism. If your basic rights are not being met, then it's hard to thrive. But it's not enough for these rights to simply exist. Instead, governments and state institutions need to be serious about protecting them, with international bodies able to step in if governments are failing to do so. On an individual level, people need to be aware of them, understand them, and know what they can do when a right is not being met.

I was curious about how well parents understood their children's rights, so last year I carried out a short survey. Over half of the 550 respondents did not know what the UN Convention on the Rights of the Child was. When asked how familiar they were with children's rights, a third said that they were not sure they could name any single right.[1] I wasn't surprised by these responses; until I started researching this book, I wouldn't have been able to name many either. I certainly don't remember being taught about my rights as a child, either at school or by my parents. Nor did any health professional talk to me about children's rights during my antenatal or postnatal appointments with my daughter. Children's rights weren't mentioned in the many parenting books I read, nor did they come up in conversations with friends.

This matters, for purely practical reasons if nothing else. Children usually rely on adult support to ensure their rights are protected, and so as adults we need to be aware of what these rights are, and ready to speak up if we witness them being ignored or violated. If we are unaware of children's rights, we also might unwittingly be going against these in our own interactions with children. For example, many of the parents I surveyed didn't know that children have a right to have their views heard and taken seriously, or to choose their own beliefs.

Although not all the rights in the CRC will feel directly relevant to the children in your life, it's still worth being aware of what the Convention says to be able to start spotting when governments and institutions are working in ways that go against these rights. A knowledge of rights can also be useful to refer to when deciding which political party you might vote for, and can help make sense of news stories and policy announcements that have to do with children's lives.

A brief history of children's rights

The path towards children's rights was not always obvious. Slowly, children have been recognised as rights holders and people in their own right, but not to the same level as adults. It wasn't until the 18th century that children started to be seen as a separate social group in political texts, when Enlightenment thinkers presented children as vital to the health and prosperity of society. In this view, children were future citizens who needed proper care and education so that they would grow up to be rational, reasonable, and responsible. Despite this thinking, the ways in which many children were treated left a lot to be desired.

The 19th century saw the beginnings of child protection laws and compulsory education, for the first time separating children from their parents as individuals who could enjoy legal protection.[2] In the late 1800s, the Society for the Prevention of Cruelty to Children (later the NSPCC) led the charge in England. It played a key role in the campaign for legislation known as the Children's Charter and was part of a wider movement that sought to make children's protection a major social concern.[3] This movement built on the work of reformers such as Charles Dickens, who used his writing to speak out against widespread child abuse and poverty. He famously used his novel *Oliver Twist* to criticise the Poor Law legislation of 1834, which made relief for the elderly, sick, or poor the responsibility of workhouses. These were places where desperate people, including children, were housed and forced to do hard labour.[4] In the story, when a starving boy threatens to turn to cannibalism unless he gets more food, the orphan Oliver draws the short straw and must ask the workhouse for a second helping of gruel. The Master's retribution is swift: Oliver is starved, caned, publicly beaten, threatened with death, and kept in solitarily confinement before being sent off to work at an undertaker's, where he is fed on scraps and forced to sleep among the coffins.

In the early 20th century, Eglantyne Jebb — a teacher turned campaigner against poverty and class divides — founded the campaigning charity Save the Children after seeing photos of children starving due to blockades in Austria and Germany during the First World War. Following years of work delivering relief to children in Macedonia, Russia, and other countries affected by war, in 1924, Jebb attended the League of Nations convention in Geneva and presented her Declaration of the Rights of the Child. The Declaration stated that children should be cared for sufficiently, both materially — with adequate food, healthcare, and shelter — and 'spiritually', with concern that 'backward' children should be given help and 'delinquent' children helped to become good citizens. It stressed that all children should be able to earn a livelihood one day, suggesting universal education and training, and that they should be protected from exploitation. The Declaration was adopted a year later, becoming the first ever intergovernmental human rights document.

Jebb's declaration went on to be adopted in extended form in 1959 by the United Nations General Assembly as the Declaration of the Rights of the Child, which spoke of the child's right to a happy childhood, freedom from discrimination, social security, education, and a minimum age for employment.[5] In the Declaration, children were clearly positioned as in need of 'special safeguards and care' due to their age, and the rights focused on protections that would keep them safe, and provisions, or services they were entitled to access.

In recognising children as in need of special protection and care, these incremental changes paved the way for a further important document, which would shape the landscape of children's rights for decades to come.

The Convention on the Rights of the Child

Children's rights are part of human rights. Children have rights that apply to everyone in the world, such as those enshrined in the UN Universal Declaration on Human Rights (UDHR). But they have their own rights, too: those enshrined in the Convention on the Rights of the Child. The CRC was adopted by the UN in 1989 and came into force a year later. A convention is the strongest form of international treaty, signifying that this was a document with big intentions; indeed, the CRC is the most widely ratified human rights document in history.

The CRC is split into two sections: the Preamble and the 54 Articles, 41 of which identify specific rights.[6] These rights are:

- universal (they apply equally to every person under the age of 18, everywhere in the world — in theory at least);
- inalienable (they cannot be taken away, though as we shall see they are not always enforced);
- indivisible (they can't be separated from each other, and are all important and essential, although we might argue that in some situations certain rights are more important than others);
- and interdependent (the rights rely on each other, for example the right to the best possible health rests on the right to an adequate standard of living, though again, as we shall see, sometimes different rights can be in tension with one another).

They are also supposed to act as minimum standards, though in reality we have a long way to go before these standards are met for all children.

Every right in the CRC includes corresponding *duties*, the things adults owe to children (for example, the right to education places a duty on governments to provide free, accessible education). The main duty bearers in the CRC are governments, states, and institutions, but many of the rights also ask things of teachers, parents, and other adults who work with or care for children, both in terms of ensuring rights are upheld and pushing for justice when they are not.

The Preamble sets out the principles and beliefs that underpin all the Articles within the document. Some of the core messages included are:

- Children are entitled to special safeguards, care, and assistance;
- Families should be afforded protection and assistance;
- Children should grow up in a family environment, in an atmosphere of happiness, love, and understanding; and
- Children should be brought up in the spirit of peace, dignity, tolerance, freedom, equality, and solidarity.

This is quite strong language coming from a UN document; when I first read it, I was pleasantly surprised to see a commitment not just to children's safety but to their understanding and happiness, and the emphasis on raising children in a spirit of peace and solidarity, even if these things are hard to enforce in practice.

The rights in the CRC can be understood as broadly fitting into three overlapping categories: provision, protection, and participation.[7] A full summary of the rights can be found in the back of this book.

Provision rights

This group sets out access to necessary goods, services, and resources that all children have the right to enjoy. It includes the right to the best possible health (Article 24); the right to have their treatment reviewed when living in care (25); the right to social security (26); the right to an adequate standard of living (27); the right to an education that supports children to develop to their full potential and where discipline is consistent with their dignity (28, 29); the right to play, relax, and take part in cultural and artistic activities (31); and the right to know about the CRC (41).

In many ways, this is the most straightforward set of rights. But looking at some of the topics contained within it, we can see how debated they are in many policy issues and legal questions that dominate today's news. For example, the right for children to enjoy the best possible health may encompass a lot of things, including tackling air and water pollution and taking effective steps to tackle the climate crisis. London, where I live, has become what is known as an Ultra Low Emission Zone (ULEZ) in a bid to tackle the high levels of air pollution that has contributed to the ill health and even death of children in the city. But this right to clean air has to be weighed against the need for people and businesses to get around, and the policy has had staunch opponents despite the clear benefits to children's health.

To take another example, children's right to play and relaxation may sound basic — surely all children have plenty of opportunity to play? — yet across England, playgrounds are crumbling or being locked up due to council budget cuts. This won't really affect the children who live in homes with big gardens, or whose parents can drive them to the nearest beach or wood, but for children who live in small flats and whose families have fewer resources these spaces can mean the difference between playing outside with other children or not. The head of the charity Play England has said that the decline in playgrounds is causing children's mental health to suffer and has criticised the 'shameful' lack of protection for children and play in local planning.[8]

The right to education is particularly interesting, because it states that primary education should be both free and *compulsory*, language which doesn't show up anywhere else in the CRC. What education should look like is left extremely vague, although the CRC stresses that it should help children develop to their 'fullest potential' and prepare them for a responsible life in free society, as well as developing respect for human rights and fundamental freedoms, and respect for the natural environment. Whether this right is even close to being met fully — even in high-income countries — is debatable, particularly when we look at provision for children with special educational needs and disabilities, children from low-income families, and children living in under-served communities. As for children reaching their 'full potential', this has generally been interpreted as something like 'increasing children's future earning potential' or 'giving children the skills they need to enter the workforce' rather than a broader, more generous interpretation that might include each child living a life which is as fulfilling and joyful as possible. Some efforts to help children reach their 'potential' have ended up causing harm, such as in South Korean *hagwons*, or cramming schools, which can see children as young as six attending extra classes every day after school, sometimes until 10.00 pm, with restricted access to toilets and food.[9] Where do we draw the line between a useful education that helps children succeed in a competitive job market — and one which infringes on their right to health, play time, and rest?

Protection rights

This group of rights covers protection from neglect, abuse, discrimination, and exploitation. It includes the right to protection from discrimination in their enjoyment of the CRC rights (Article 2); protection from interference with their privacy and unlawful attacks on their reputation (16); protection from harmful information or media materials (17); protection from all forms of violence, abuse, neglect, exploitation, and bad treatment from anyone who cares for them (19); protection from economic exploitation and work that is dangerous or might harm their health, development, or education (32; note that this is not an outright ban on children working); protection from using, producing, or distributing illegal drugs (33); protection from all forms of sexual abuse and exploitation (34); and protection in the judicial system (40). It also includes a commitment that children who have experienced neglect, abuse, exploitation, torture, or who are victims of war should receive special support to help them recover (39).

Despite clearly set out protection rights, these have not always translated into practice. Recent reporting from Australia found that children in youth detention centres had been kept in solitary confinement for up to 20 hours a day, with one disabled teenager locked in solitary for more than 500 days. In some cases, children were becoming so distressed that they were self-harming just so they could leave their rooms and go to hospital.[10]

And of course, harm occurs outside of institutions too. By the age of 18, at least one in seven children in the UK — four in a classroom of 30 — will have been affected by domestic violence, either directly or through the trauma of witnessing a parent or sibling being attacked or threatened. This statistic is very likely to be substantially underestimated; one study calculated the maltreatment rates for children in the UK were 7–17 times greater than official numbers suggest.[11] And some violence against children remains perfectly legal: in England, Australia, and numerous US states, parents are allowed to hit their children in the name of discipline, despite Article 19, which states that children should be protected from *all* forms of violence. This lack of protection directly goes against the large body of research that shows how damaging smacking is to children's present and future wellbeing, leading to a whole host of issues including poor mental health and behavioural problems (we will look at this in greater detail in chapter five).[12] Banning smacking might also reduce other forms of violence: New Zealand banned smacking in 2007 and has since recorded a steep fall in both severe and minor assaults against children, with views around the acceptability of using physical punishment changing.[13]

If governments were interested in the evidence, there would be simply no justification. The lack of protection in some countries stems from an ideological, adultist position that still sees children as inferior and belonging to their parents; arguments against banning smacking have tended to revolve around not wanting to create a 'nanny state'.[14] But do we really need evidence to tell us that using violence on children is a bad idea? If we replaced children with any other social group — women, disabled people, the elderly — we would be horrified if their partners or carers could use violence as a 'reasonable punishment' to induce compliance. When asked about smacking, children say over and over again that it makes them feel sad, frightened, angry, and ashamed.

Protecting children from physical violence has been an important issue since well before the CRC was written. But one of the biggest children's protection issues of our time is one those involved in the drafting of the CRC in the late eighties could not have foreseen: the internet. The tension between protecting children on the one hand and honouring their right to privacy and need for autonomy on the other, can be clearly seen in the issues arising from young people's access to the digital world. Most of the parents I work with and speak to tell me that they are worried about what their children are, or could be, exposed to online, and these fears are not baseless. A recent two-year investigation by *Guardian* journalists found that social media sites like Facebook and Instagram are enabling the targeting and contacting of children by traffickers, who will comment on children's profiles or send them messages, gradually gaining their trust and manipulating them through a process known as grooming.[15] While Meta, the company that owns both social media sites, says it is doing 'all it can' to prevent child sex trafficking, the investigation paints a picture of a company that is often slow and unwilling to take action, and unaware of the scale of the problem.[16] Many of the children involved are young — 11 or 12 — Black, Latinx, or LGBTQ+, and from vulnerable backgrounds. This problem is only getting worse, and so far we are pitifully lacking in solutions to protect these children from harm.

Exploitation isn't always sexual, and it doesn't always come from strangers. There is an increasing number of discussions about whether children whose parents make them participate in online 'influencing' through photos, videos, and having information shared about them with strangers online are being exploited, and whether they should be afforded the same protections as children who act in traditional adverts. In 2023, Illinois became the first US state to ensure children appearing in social media ads are compensated for their work, following successful lobbying from local teenager Shreya Nallamothu.

'I realised that there's a lot of exploitation that can happen within the world of "kidfluencing"', said Shreya, 'and that there was absolutely zero legislation in place to protect them.' Shreya raised her concerns with her senator when she was 13, and the changes mean that earnings for children who appear in social media ads will now have to be held in a trust account for them. Children whose parents fail to do this will be able to sue.[17]

Although trafficking and exploitation are serious problems, they only affect a small minority of children. The same can't be said of other online harms. According to recent research by the Children's Commissioner for England, Dame Rachel de Souza, one in ten children have watched pornography by the time they are nine.[18] Eight out of ten of those surveyed had seen pornography involving violence by the age of 18 (with a third actively seeking out depictions of sexual violence). In her introduction to the report, Dame de Souza wrote, 'I truly believe that we will look back in 20 years and be shocked by the content to which children were exposed ... I will never forget the girl who told me about her first kiss with her boyfriend, aged 12, who strangled her. He had seen it in pornography and thought it normal.' The effect of this on children's lives — particularly girls — is chilling. In an interview with *The Guardian*, author and feminist campaigner Laura Bates reflected that girls are experiencing the 'impossibility of escaping from harassment, revenge pornography, deepfake porn — just a whole bombardment. I was talking to a 14-year-old girl at a book event the other day. She said ten boys had messaged her, pressuring her to send them nude pictures, in a single night. That landscape of what teenage girls are navigating is completely new.'

Alongside the access to, and influence of, pornography, children experience online bullying and harassment, and can access damaging and inaccurate information. But I don't think the answer to this is more adult control over children: our lives are increasingly lived in the digital world, and to ban children from using the internet is to cut them off from accessing useful information, tools, services, and connecting with their friends. Digital technologies are vital to both their current lives and their futures and are becoming ever more important. In 2021, the UN Committee on the Rights of the Child released a statement on children's rights in relation to the digital environment, which affirms that meaningful access to digital technologies can support children to 'realize the full range of their civil, political, cultural, economic and social rights'. In order to ensure that the digital sphere is a space where children's rights can be met rather than violated, the committee recommends that 'States parties should identify and address the emerging risks that children face [online] … including by listening to their views on the nature of the particular risks that they face'.[19] We shall have to see if this translates into meaningful action.

If there are some areas of children's lives where protection doesn't go far enough, I also have concerns around how a focus on protecting children from (real or imagined) harm can lead to the restriction of their autonomy. It's widely accepted that children now have less freedom to go out by themselves, with a study finding that British children now go out to play alone two years later than their parents' generation did and that children often reach the end of their primary-school years without having had enough opportunities to develop their ability to assess and manage risk independently.[20] A report from Play England stated that: 'Children are telling us that they want to spend more time in their local area, but are frequently being given the message that they, and their play, are not welcome. Together, we need to listen to what they are saying, and to act.'[21]

The less children are given the opportunity to go out by themselves, the less socially acceptable it becomes, and the less responsibility we assume for children. Priscilla Alderson, professor emeritus of childhood studies at UCL, writes: 'Who benefits from this anxious vigilance? The murder rate of young children outside their homes has hardly changed ... whereas inside the home, each week one or two children die from abuse and neglect, and they need neighbours and friends to listen to them before it's too late.'[22] Perhaps the key is moving away from a highly individualistic view of families and children, which places the sole responsibility for the child on their parents and caregivers, towards a collective form of community care where we all watch out for each other's children. I would definitely feel more confident about my daughter travelling around by herself if I knew that other adults would look out for her.

Participation rights

The newest set of rights, first appearing in the CRC, focus on respecting children as active participants in their own lives, with voices that are worth listening to and taking seriously. This is a big deal and poses a challenge to many beliefs around children that position them as irrational, immature, and incomplete, or 'adults in training'. These rights include the need for parents to show respect for their children's evolving capacities when providing direction and guidance (Article 5); the right to express their views freely in all matters affecting them, and have these views taken seriously [this includes at home and at school] (12); the right to freedom of expression, including to seek, receive, and impart information (13); the right to freedom of thought, conscience, and belief (14); the right to freedom of association and peaceful assembly (15); the right to access reliable information (17); and the right for children from minority groups to enjoy their own culture, language, and religion (30).

These participation rights are particularly important for parents and those who work with children because they set out a clear commitment to children's views and opinions being heard and, where possible, acted upon. Philosopher Miranda Fricker talks about something she dubs *testimonial injustice*, which is when certain groups of people with less social power (i.e. children) are seen as less credible than others, and are less likely to be believed and have their experiences taken seriously.[23] This can show up in children's daily life, for example when a caregiver tells them to eat more even though they've clearly stated they are full up, or when a parent ignores them saying they feel ill and sends them to school anyway — until it becomes apparent they need to be sent home because they really are sick. This form of injustice can have far more serious consequences. An NSPCC study found that when children did disclose sexual abuse, many disclosures were either not recognised or understood, or they were dismissed, played down, or ignored, which meant no action was taken to protect or support them.[24]

Honouring children's participation in daily life might look like acknowledging children's feelings, listening to them and being responsive to their communication, and taking their ideas seriously, even when we think we know better. Research has shown that valuing children's unique knowledge and involvement in decision-making processes can lead to all sorts of benefits for children and their communities. Even very young children — including newborn babies — can meaningfully participate in the world around them, communicating their preferences, needs, and feelings. Dr Emmi Pikler, founder of the influential Pikler approach, famously said that world peace starts on the changing table. By this, she meant that routine caregiving tasks — like changing a nappy — should be carried out in collaboration with the child, rather than done 'to' children. In 'The Art of Diapering', a beautiful, short YouTube video inspired by this approach, we see a caregiver waiting until a baby, Noelle, has finished playing with a toy so that she can 'fully participate, without distraction' in the changing process. The caregiver warns Noelle before she picks her up, talks to her all the way through the change about what is happening, and asks for her participation to raise her legs to put on the fresh diaper. All the way through she demonstrates a deep respect for Noelle, who in turn is engaged, making noises and moving her body.[25] It's easy to dismiss this deliberate, slow care as a luxury most modern parents and childcare workers don't have time for, but in truth I'm not sure we really value children's participation in these everyday moments, seeing them instead as another chore to rush through — and distract children through! — rather than as an opportunity for connection and communication.

Like adults, children want to be listened to and taken seriously. In 2001, *The Guardian* newspaper launched a competition called 'The School I'd Like', in which young people between the ages of five and 18 were asked to imagine their ideal school. They received thousands of responses. The research was written up, and the authors found some overarching themes in the responses: '"Respect" was the word that occurred most; it was what the children wanted, but felt they didn't get ... They were expected to fit into a structure and a curriculum that seemed to have been created without the first reference to what they might enjoy or respond to. Most of all, they were sick of not being listened to. Sick of being treated like kids.'[26] When the project was repeated ten years later, the same themes came up. Kathryn, age 12, wrote that she would like to go to a school 'where everyone's equal, and everyone's respected and their voices are heard'.[27]

Children's participation in decision-making is not always the be all and end all. Many scholars have raised concerns that participation can sometimes be tokenistic, involving listening without taking action or allowing children to 'play' at participation rather than having their voices truly valued. While the *Guardian* project did have an impact — it influenced (and continues to influence) students and academics within the field of education — how much more powerful might the project have been if it had been designed by children and taken note of by the Department of Education? One way to ensure children's meaningful participation might have been to follow a pioneering approach developed by Professor Laura Lundy at Queens University Belfast.[28] This approach includes giving children a safe and inclusive space to express their views, providing information and support for children to express their views, ensuring children's views are taken seriously and acted upon, wherever possible, and making sure their views are communicated to the right people. And it works. The Lundy Model, as it's become known, has been used effectively by national and international organisations for a decade, including the United Nations, European Commission, Council of Europe, UNICEF, World Vision, Save the Children, and national governments and agencies in Ireland, Taiwan, Belgium, Scotland, Iceland, and New Zealand.

Harry Shier, quoted in the last chapter, has been researching and writing on children's participation for over 25 years. His Pathways to Participation model describes the five stages of child and youth participation, leadership, and decision-making in organisations and communities:

1. Children are listened to. This means that when children express a view, this is listened to with due care and attention by adults.
2. Children are supported in expressing their views. This means that adults must actively enable children to overcome barriers (such as shyness, low self-esteem, negative self-beliefs, language barriers, cultural differences, or prejudice and stereotyping) that may prevent them from expressing their opinions and ideas, and create the conditions — such as a school culture free from bias or a home culture where children don't fear speaking out — for children to feel safe expressing themselves.
3. Children's views are taken into account. This doesn't imply that every decision must be made in accordance with children's wishes, or that adults are bound to implement whatever children ask for; however, it does mean that they are taken seriously and considered carefully.[29]
4. Children are involved in decision-making processes. At this stage, children are not simply consulted, but they participate

in decision-making processes alongside adults. This can improve service provision; increase children's sense of ownership and belonging; increase self-esteem, empathy and responsibility; and lay the groundwork for citizenship and democratic participation.

5. Children share power and responsibility for decision-making. Whilst at stage four adults might have the final say or veto, at this stage adults do not, or cannot, unilaterally overrule children and youth in a decision-making process.[30]

One of the biggest challenges for adults aiming to facilitate meaningful participation, Shier argues, is to ensure that children are not manipulated into serving adult agendas, and that participation is an ongoing process of education and personal development rather than a one-time project of getting children to take part in an activity or decision.

Using the example of CESESMA, an independent NGO working with children in the coffee growing region of Nicaragua, Shier describes how children as young as six are able to join a number of groups run by other young people, including environmental action groups, youth theatre groups, and girls' groups.[31] As the children's confidence and self-esteem increases, many of them decide that they too want to share their skills with the other children of their community, and can sign up for specialist training programmes. In their teens they might take over the running of community groups, or start their own groups, as part of a wider supportive network of children and young people.

Although most of the children work on coffee plantations, on family small-holdings, or in domestic work (or all three), alongside attending school part-time, their involvement in their community is seen as valuable. There is a deep-rooted belief that 'children are capable and competent. They have expert knowledge about their lives, their families, their communities, their hopes and fears. The tools they have available for analysis of this information may be limited to start with, but this is due to lack of educational opportunities, not lack of capability, and their local knowledge is no less valid and valuable.'[32]

Participation is not just about institutions or community groups, however. The CRC advises parents to pay attention to the 'evolving capacities' of the child, ensuring their parental direction and guidance is appropriate. As children get older, they are likely to be able to make more decisions for themselves (even if they make mistakes!) and parental control can loosen in line with their growing capacity and their need to develop responsibility. I might tell a five-year-old which TV shows she is allowed to watch, in order to protect her from content that might harm or upset her, but I wouldn't try to exert the same level of control over a 15-year-old. Children will all have different needs and abilities; some children may need more support than others, and those who care for children will need to consider the tension between protection, independence, and care, as well as navigating those situations where adult and child disagree about what constitutes the 'best' interests of the child. We can imagine a situation — perhaps this is your reality at the moment! — where a ten-year-old wants an Instagram account like her friends and feels that this would help her feel less excluded at school, but her parents believe she needs protecting from the harmful effects of social media and that she is too young to have a smartphone. This is not a problem with an easy solution, with different rights coming into play. Despite the complexity of putting this Article into practice, the principle of stepping in to direct and guide only when needed is a useful one when thinking about the wider movement towards children's liberation. Taken alongside Article 12 (children's views should be listened to and taken seriously) I believe it provides a robust critique of authoritarian parenting and education approaches, which too often rely on the belief that adults always know best.

Criticisms of the CRC

Although the CRC is the most widely ratified human rights' instrument in the world, and has been positive for children in many ways, it's not without its problems. Perhaps the most challenging aspect of the CRC is that, although Article 12 affirms a belief that every child has the right to express their views on matters affecting them, children were not consulted as part of the CRC development process. The rights were formulated by adults in an adultist world. If an international convention on the rights of women was drafted without women being involved, we would rightly ask some searching questions about its validity.

The fact that children are young and less experienced need not be a barrier to them being involved in drafting these sorts of documents, and a growing field of research co-created with children demonstrates that young people can be meaningfully involved in complex policy work. Wanting to understand children's experiences of life under Covid-19, researchers carried out a ground-breaking survey that was co-designed with children, using a children's rights-based research methodology developed by the Centre for Children's Rights at Queen's University Belfast. The survey captured the experiences of over 26,000 children in 137 countries, providing unprecedented insight into children's lives over this time.[33]

Children are not the only ones whose participation in the CRC has been limited. Its creation was led predominantly by countries traditionally described as 'developed' or 'Western' who have inserted their own culturally informed views around childhood into the Convention. This process can be termed cultural imperialism, says Dr Afua Twum-Danso Imoh, senior lecturer at the University of Bristol, who writes that 'the cultural bias inherent both in [the CRC's] drafting and content has led many to question its relevance to non-Western communities'.[34] At the heart of the CRC lies the concept of people as individuals who form the core unit of society, a worldview that originated in the 18th century in Europe and North America. 'The CRC assumes that children are universally the same,' writes anthropologist Rachel Burr. 'It can be argued that its provisions are weighted in favour of a modern, western sense of the individual.'[35]

It is interesting to compare the CRC to the African Charter on the Rights and Welfare of the Child. While very similar, the African Charter stresses the responsibilities children have towards their families and societies, including a duty to respect their elders, and to preserve and strengthen cultural values.[36] In some communities, children may not be seen as individuals but as assets belonging to the clan or kinship group, with the collective good taking precedence over individual rights and wellbeing.[37] The way the CRC is worded may bear little resemblance to the way that childhood is understood and experienced in places such as these, although understandings of childhood are changing in the context of globalisation.

As with many international agreements and conventions,

the drafting of the CRC was difficult, involving many drafts and tensions. It needed to appeal to such a broad range of countries — each with different cultures, beliefs, budgets, and priorities — and so it focused on broad principles to be interpreted according to local traditions and values. Because of this, the language used in the CRC has been criticised as being intentionally vague. For example, although a commitment to raising children in a spirit of dignity may sound laudable, who gets to define what this looks like?

Article 3, which states that all decisions should be made with the best interests of the child in mind, can result in an adult-centred interpretation of what is 'good' for children. Indeed, many people use this to justify harsh punishments or draconian rules; I wonder how many of us heard the words 'it's for your own good' as children? This can cause tensions in states that are based predominantly around religions which place children under their parents, or that are structured hierarchically with adults. This can also raise problems when charities or organisations try to improve things for children in cultures that are not their own. For example, most people would agree that female genital mutilation (FGM) is something which girls should be protected from, but without understanding the context in which these practices arise, pushes to stop or reduce FGM have had unintended consequences, in some situations actually strengthening a local commitment to the practice.[38] Rights are not a separate thing that exist in isolation; they are embedded into the daily fabric of children's lives. Without understanding the varied contexts children live in, it's hard to ensure that their rights are meaningful, let alone being protected and enjoyed.

Despite its broad scope and language, and 'Western' ideology, there remains one country in the world still holding out: the US. Despite signing the Convention in the mid-nineties, the US has never ratified it, sidestepping the process that ensures a country's laws and policies are in line with the CRC. This is a problem for the 74 million children who live there. Two main arguments have been made against the CRC by its opponents: that the CRC undermines parental rights — for example, to use corporal punishment, opt out of their child receiving sex education, or to prevent their child from choosing their own religion — and that it undermines national sovereignty by setting a precedent for the US to base its laws on international agreements rather than the US Constitution. As the writer Kevin Moclair puts it, 'Being the only country not to ratify the UNCRC and having an obscenely high child poverty rate are things that can only happen if lawmakers simply do not care about the rights of the child as much as other issues.'[39] This is perhaps unsurprising from a country where guns are the leading cause of death for children, but where gun reform continues to be vehemently opposed by powerful lobby groups. 'One in 25 American five-year-olds now won't live to see 40, a death rate about four times as high as in other wealthy nations. And although the spike in death rates among the young has been dramatic since the beginning of the pandemic, little of the impact is from Covid-19. Firearms account for almost half of the increase,' writes journalist David Wallace-Wells. 'The horror is that in the average American kindergarten at least one child can expect to be buried by his or her parents. Probably we should be much more focused on protecting our young.'[40]

Children's rights mean little if they are not implemented and protected. Violations of these rights clearly happen all over the world, despite widespread lip service to the CRC, and there is often a sizeable gap between stated policy aims and children's experiences. Some scholars have suggested that states have signed up to the CRC for appearances' sake, with little intention of committing to meaningful change.[41] States have to report to the Committee on the Rights of the Child (CORC) every five years on their progress, and the CORC replies with comments identifying what the government needs to do. Even though governments are expected to act on these recommendations, it's all too easy to ignore them. Just because a country has ratified the CRC it doesn't mean that it's legally binding, despite the state's obligations under Article 4.

The UK gave the CRC formal consent in 1991 but still has not incorporated it into domestic law, so most of the rights in the CRC cannot be enforced by domestic courts. When the Scottish Parliament unanimously passed a Bill in 2021 to incorporate the CRC into Scots law — a move thst would give Scottish children and their representatives the ability to use the courts to enforce their rights — it was struck down by the Supreme Court of the United Kingdom.[42] This is despite the UK's Equality and Human Rights Commission recommendations made in 2020.[43] What this means in practice is that many children's rights are unenforceable. Despite robust criticism from the UK's Children's Commissioners around issues such as child poverty, violence, and the use of restraint and isolation in educational settings, there is no mechanism by which policies can be forced to change.

Australia faces the same issues, with John Tobin, professor of law at Melbourne Law School, describing the situation as a 'patchwork system of legislative measures that reflect differing levels of commitment to and opportunities for engagement with the Convention'.[44] This does not mean that the CRC has no impact in Australia, but the pick-and-mix approach can lead to those who are most vulnerable — refugee children, Indigenous children, disabled children — having their rights routinely ignored.

So far, around a hundred countries have fully incorporated the CRC into law, allowing children to challenge laws and practices that violate their rights.[45] Robust legal protection for children can be achieved if the political will exists to do so. As adults, this is where we can show solidarity to children by petitioning our political representatives. Imagine if every politician received a dozen letters every week from their constituents telling them how important enshrining the CRC in law was to them as voters, and that it was an issue they would be taking to the ballot box.

Even when children's rights are enshrined in law, access to justice is still an issue. According to UNICEF, children from poor family backgrounds receive 'less information than others about their rights, are less likely to seek redress, and have greater difficulties in paying for lawyers, court fees and transportation'. The same applies to children with disabilities, who might lack the communication aids and support that would make it possible for them to participate in justice processes, and for children from ethnic minorities who experience stigma.[46] A lack of independence also creates a serious barrier to children accessing justice, as most children rely on their parents and other adults in their lives to ensure they are able to enjoy their rights (a feature of adultism). As the Child Rights International Network puts it: 'Access to justice is a human right, but it is also what makes other rights a reality. For children's rights to be more than a promise, there must be a way for those rights to be enforced.'[47]

There is another area we can all help with. Children have not been adequately informed of their rights, despite the obligation under Article 42 that governments must work to make sure children know about the CRC. If children have any hope of being able to fight for their rights, then they need to be able to understand them and the benefits they bring, as has been found in children's experiences of abuse and violence. A 2015 report carried out for the NSPCC researched the experiences of deaf and disabled people who had experienced abuse as children. 'I didn't know it was illegal,' said one participant. There was no information ... When you're immersed in an abusive environment as a child, you don't realise that it's abuse.'[48]

Children's rights need to be communicated to them clearly, in an age-appropriate way that makes sense to them within their daily lives and cultural settings. This is something that needs to happen in all areas of their lives.

- Parents can help children understand their rights by discussing them when they come up in conversation (many children may be interested in their right to the best possible health with regards to pollution and climate change, for example) or by proactively starting up conversations about the CRC. There are some beautiful picture books that have been published in the last few years which families can read together, and there are simple posters that can be downloaded for free which depict the rights in the CRC — perfect to stick next to the kettle or toilet!
- New parents could be given information on the CRC at antenatal appointments, birth classes, and at their children's medical check-ups.
- Every school could commit to becoming a Rights Respecting School, the UNICEF accreditation for schools that have

ensured all their pupils are able to enjoy their rights (see chapter eight for more discussion on this). As well as sharing materials on rights with teachers and students, they could pass information to parents in order to work towards a joined-up approach.

- We could embed discussion of rights across the places where children spend time, both on- and offline. There could be signs in playgrounds talking about the right to play, TV shows exploring themes children's rights, and even songs. (If Snoop Dogg can record a children's song about positive affirmations, there's nothing stopping him making a song for them to learn their rights!)

Adults can also speak up when we notice children's rights being violated, including in news reports on the media. Again, writing to our representatives can show them that this is an issue we take seriously, and are taking into consideration when casting our votes.

In their book *Rethinking Children's Rights*, Phil Jones and Sue Welch write that 'The level of awareness [of children's rights] by children and adults alike is affected by a number of factors, including the ways that a society sees the position of children from political, economic, cultural, and religious perspectives.'[49] How we see children and their role in society impacts on everything: how they are treated, which institutions and services they have access to, and how effectively their rights can be safeguarded. This is why tackling adultism must go hand-in-hand with safeguarding and enforcing children's rights.

Children's rights: necessary, but not sufficient

Children's rights as currently implemented may not be perfect, but I don't think we should dismiss them as unimportant. Rights are undoubtedly useful, both in terms of setting out a clear vision of what children should be able to expect from the world around them, and placing a duty on governments, institutions, and adults to see that these rights are met. They provide a framework for children to seek justice when their rights are being violated, including the language to clearly describe what their rights are and to ask for their rights to be met.[50] In this sense children's rights are necessary for children's liberation: they set out the minimum standards that all children around the globe should enjoy if they are to have a decent quality of life. But just because they are necessary, it doesn't mean that rights alone are sufficient if we are to tackle the adultism which affects children's daily lives.

First, children's liberation requires deep structural change, which in turn calls for critical engagement with the power imbalance between adults and children, and — crucially — demands that children have a seat at the table and are involved with decision-making processes which affect their lives.

Second, if we can understand children's rights as laid out in the CRC as a 'top-down' approach — coming from international bodies and decided upon by politicians — then children's liberation requires 'bottom-up' working and thinking.[51] Children's rights don't exist in a static vacuum, but are always being negotiated, interpreted, and at times weighed against one other. For example, do we give more weight to a child's right to education or their right to an adequate standard of living when their family relies on them working in order to meet their basic needs? Sarada Balagopalan, professor of childhood studies at Rutgers University, argues that countries can claim to be committed to children's rights while simultaneously remaining unwilling to create the equitable institutions and structures through which these rights can be enjoyed. Knowing, for example, that you have a right to go to school doesn't automatically mean that you can access a quality education — or indeed any school at all — especially when you also have to work, as is the case for many children living in India and other post-colonial settings.[52]

Third, although children need legal protection, for example to protect them from violence, there is a question of how we can uphold children's rights and their safety at a community level — protecting them from genuinely abusive or negligent care — without adding further fuel to the fire of the carceral state. Children's liberation doesn't exist in a silo, and any policies or practices we put forward to advance children's rights must be intersectional, rooted in grassroots work and community care as well as the wider social justice movement to ensure they don't do more harm than good.

*

Restricting discussions of liberation to narrow legal frameworks and definitions obscures much of children's daily lives: their intimate relationships with their family, caregivers, teachers, and friends; the physical space around them; the broader structural inequalities — such as poverty, sexism, or racism — they may face; tensions between children's autonomy and adult control; and the resistance and negotiation that children take part in as they push back on adultism. If we are to move from a place of adultism towards children's liberation, then we need more than just a knowledge of the CRC. We need a radical shift in the ways in which we think about, understand, involve, and treat children, including understanding that all aspects of children's lives — and our relationships with them — are political.

CHAPTER FOUR

Body politics

A useful tool for thinking about adultism and how it affects children's lives is the feminist idea that the personal is political.[1] For decades, feminists have argued that the spheres of life that were once considered private and thus outside the scope for debate, discussion, and legislation — the family, the body, the home — are in fact deeply political matters. To write these areas of life off as private can conceal the patriarchy and misogyny at work in women's lives; in their marriages, domestic duties, sex lives, childcare arrangements, and even doctors' appointments. Instead, women's bodies can be considered battlegrounds; sites of control and resistance where political fights are fought, such as over the issues of abortion rights, marital rape, and domestic violence.

Children face different struggles to adult women, but the idea that the personal is political is crucial when we're thinking about children's liberation. Wherever there is an imbalance of power within a relationship, such as between a teacher and pupil, or a parent and a child, it could be said that this is a political relationship. This can take some getting used to: you may find it strange to think about the relationship you have with the children in your life as a political one, when caring for children so often feels intimate, private, and intensely personal. But if we want to end adultism, starting off by looking close to home can not only help us understand where adultism shows up in children's lives and where their rights may not be being realised, but also what we can do to change things. You can't get much more personal than your own body, and that's where I want to focus my attention in this chapter.

Bodies are particularly interesting to think about when it comes to children because so much of early childhood is lived out in an embodied, physical, and immediate way. How we treat children's bodies tells us a lot about how we view children and their social status vis-à-vis adults, as well as reflecting societal values and political tensions. Throughout time and across the world, children's bodies have been sites of violence, abuse, and control, but also of deep tenderness, affection, and care. Parenting and childcare, especially when children are very young, is necessarily preoccupied with children's bodies and physical needs: eating, sleeping, toileting, keeping warm, soothing cries, and keeping them physically safe from dangers. Some child-led parenting styles promote care that follows children's own bodily rhythms and needs — letting babies feed as often as they want, following their natural sleep patterns, comforting their cries as quickly as possible — while certain adult-centred approaches expound the benefits of getting babies onto schedules for milk, sleep, and play time, and 'training' them to fit these routines if necessary, even if this causes children distress. If anyone doubts that how we treat children's bodies is a political issue, I suggest they look no further than an online debate between parents on the topic of sleep training. Even though the specific language of rights and politics doesn't tend to be used in these arguments, the themes that come up are fit for a philosophy seminar: What should be placed higher on the scale of needs, a parent's need for adequate sleep, or a child's need for comfort? Would we ignore the cries of an older child, or an adult? How do we untangle the pressure for parents to separate from their babies and go out to work as soon as possible from the needs of the babies themselves? These aren't questions with easy answers; they are complex, ethical dilemmas that require examination of the power relations between parent and child, and between parents and the wider structures of family support.

As children get older and their bodies require less immediate input from their caregivers, even the most child-led adult's attention will often shift towards the management, training, and disciplining of children's bodies: keeping them from harm, yes, but also managing their time and activities; training them to control their behaviour and bodily reactions through praise, punishments, and rewards; learning good manners and social norms; and always keeping an eye on what is developmentally 'typical' — and what's not. There can be intense anxiety in adults when children's bodies aren't 'normal', and adult control over children's bodies is often portrayed as caring behaviour — for example, in the case of fat children whose parents put them on restrictive diets or send them to 'fat camps', despite evidence to show that dieting in childhood can cause long-lasting harm and trigger eating disorders, sometimes lasting generations.[2] Controlling children's bodies can start off as a form of adult control, but quickly becomes something children learn to do to themselves. We're not born hating or judging our bodies or ignoring their needs; these are things we are taught.

The normative child

One of the first experiences of a child's life is being measured. It's so normal that it's one of the standard questions new parents are asked: 'How much did she weigh?' My daughter hadn't even been born for an hour, and I already knew her exact weight (and which centile this put her in), head circumference (ditto), and whether she'd been born 'early', 'late', or 'on time'. Before we left the hospital the next day, my daughter had had her hearing tested, her eyes, heart, and hips checked, and been declared 'perfectly normal and healthy' by the midwife on duty.

This measuring, monitoring, and categorising starts in utero. During my pregnancy I had at least four scans, alongside regular midwife appointments where my growing bump was measured. And monitoring and measuring don't end after the prenatal and newborn checks. Throughout childhood, there is a clearly defined set of standards — around body size, development, behaviour, and intellectual, social, and physical ability — that children are supposed to meet by certain ages. We can call this ideal standard the 'normative child'. Practically every aspect of the child's body is held up for monitoring and assessment, with suggestions made for children who don't fit the standard developmental norms. Some monitoring is undoubtedly helpful: as a parent, you want to know sooner rather than later if your child has a serious illness or will need some extra support to help them thrive. Many children benefit from interventions such as speech and language therapy (SALT), occupational therapy (OT), or an assessment that shows them to be neurodivergent. But it's not realistic to expect every child to follow the same developmental path — and if we know that, then is framing children who differ from the normative child as 'behind' or 'delayed' really the best we can do?

Measuring children against the norm or statistical average is not just carried out at the behest of health professionals; most parents I know have spent tens if not hundreds of hours on online forums and health websites trying to find out if such and such a behaviour is 'normal' — and second-guessing their own parenting, and their children, in the process. The popularisation of models such as attachment theory and widespread access to simplified articles on developmental psychology means that parents can now assess whether their child is developing as they 'should' be. The thousands of parenting books that paint their own picture of the normative child all add to the enormous pressure parents can feel to make their children fit a particular mould, and to the isolation, guilt, and sadness of parents whose children are following their own path. It's a lot.

The very idea that there can be universal standards of development — which so happen to have been mostly developed by white Europeans in the 19th and 20th centuries — ignores much of what we know about the rich variety of children's lives. Measuring children against a set of standards is a blunt tool if we are really seeking to make their lives better — and surely, this should be the aim of all this assessment, otherwise we have to ask ourselves what the point is. Instead, perhaps we would be better off looking at the wider social structures that disadvantage children as a group, and certain children in particular. Finally, in creating a picture of the normal — 'good' — body, this in turn defines which bodies are deviant, abnormal, and 'bad', contributing to the marginalisation of certain groups of children.

Which bodies matter?

All children are discriminated against because of their age — this is adultism, as we discussed in chapter two. However, as Kimberlé Crenshaw's theory of intersectionality shows, some children will be further discriminated against because of other identities they hold.[3] When it comes to listening to children, disabled children's voices are more likely to be left out or ignored.

The ableism that disabled children face can start before they are even born. Disabled parents have written about how, during pregnancy, their doctors worried there would be something 'wrong' with their children; wrong, in this case, meaning inheriting their disability. In an essay about being a disabled parent, Nina Tame writes that she was offered a termination at each of her antenatal appointments right up until the birth of her third son, simply because he had spina bifida like her and might not be able to walk. (Nina uses a wheelchair.) 'A termination of my very, very wanted baby, purely because he was like me ... Because a life like mine isn't worth living? He currently does walk, but even if he didn't, a non-walking life is no less of a life.'[4] Before her son was even born, he had already been judged to be less valuable, less precious — less worthy of life.

In the UK, it's common for parents of babies who will be born disabled to be offered terminations right up to birth, like Nina, when the limit for abortion is otherwise 24 weeks. In 2022, Heidi Crowter brought a Court of Appeal challenge arguing that the law was discriminatory and stigmatised disabled people. Crowter, who has Down Syndrome, said that the law made her feel as though she 'shouldn't be here'. The appeal was dismissed, and at the time of writing the law remains unchanged.[5]

Perhaps the starkest example of how little disabled children's lives are valued can be seen in the responses received by 18-year-old disability rights activist Isabel Mavrides-Calderón, who asked disabled students in the US to share their experiences of emergencies and drills in the classroom. One child who uses a wheelchair was left alone in a classroom during an active shooter scare, and another child was left inside during a fire. 'Naïvely, I thought that if disabled people were able to set up plans with schools, they would be safe,' Mavrides-Calderón wrote. 'But these stories showed that even when disabled people advocate for themselves, even when plans are made, disabled people lives are still not valued enough to save.'[6]

Disabled children are some of the most vulnerable in our society and have long been stigmatised. In 1987 it was discovered that two of Queen Elizabeth II's cousins, Katherine and Nerissa Bowes-Lyon, had not died in 1940 — as had been publicly recorded — but had been living in a mental health institution. Born with learning disabilities, the sisters had been admitted to the hospital in 1941, their existence treated as a dirty secret. Nerissa died in 1986 and was buried in a grave marked with a plastic name tag and serial number.[7] This sort of burial seems desperately sad regardless of context, but when we know that she was a member of the Royal Family, the contrast with other royal funerals hits especially hard — and says a lot about how disabled people are valued.

Human Rights Watch estimates that globally between two to eight million children are living in institutions, a disproportionate number of whom have disabilities. Many are held in nightmarish conditions, separated from their families and communities, deprived of education and freedom, violently abused, and neglected.[8] In many cases, these are children who could be cared for at home by loving relatives, but for various reasons — insufficient support and lack of community-based services, stigma, lack of awareness of alternative options, and coercion by medical and other professionals — are forced into institutions. This abuse doesn't just happen in 'other' places; in the UK, care homes for disabled children have often been found to be anything but caring. In 2023, an investigation alleged that children living in for-profit care homes run by the Hesley Group had experienced torture and abuse — with one staff member likening the children's treatment to that of prisoners in Guantanamo Bay.[9]

Even at home, children are not always safe. Research by the NSPCC found that children who are d/Deaf, disabled, or neurodivergent are 3.7 times more likely to experience violence than their non-disabled peers, including physical and sexual violence. However, the abuse is less likely to be noticed by professionals, another example of the testimonial injustice identified by philosopher Miranda Fricker.[10] Globally, nearly a third of disabled children have experienced violence, with economically disadvantaged children especially vulnerable.[11] They are also at higher risk of being killed by their caregivers. The Disability Day of Mourning takes place every year on 1 March to commemorate disabled people murdered by their parents, and works to counter attempts to excuse these deaths. From the organisers: 'We see the same pattern repeating over and over again. A parent kills their disabled child. The media portrays these murders as justifiable and inevitable due to the "burden" of having a disabled person in the family. If the parent stands trial, they are given sympathy and comparatively lighter sentences, if they are sentenced at all. The victims are disregarded, blamed for their own murder at the hands of the person they should have been able to trust the most, and ultimately forgotten.'[12] All children have a right to life, but almost half of deaths among people with learning disabilities (including Autistic people) are avoidable — double the rate seen in the general population.[13]

Caring for a disabled child requires a lot of support — financial, practical, and emotional; support that families often struggle to access because the political will is not in place to properly fund it. A 2023 report by the Childhood Trust found that, in the UK, a family with a disabled child has to pay £581 per month extra to have the same standard of living as a family with a non-disabled child — yet disabled children are far more likely to come from low-income households, especially when their parents are full-time carers and cannot take on work. The cost-of-living crisis is having a disproportionate impact on disabled children, both on their family budgets and in terms of the professional help they are able to access: 96 per cent of social workers reported that the cost-of-living crisis has negatively impacted their ability to support children with additional needs.[14] We need to focus on ensuring that parent-carers are properly paid and they have access to robust (and well-funded) systems of support and respite to help them keep going.

Different brains

Often, we will sooner label neurodivergent children as 'badly behaved' or 'naughty' than address the structural barriers and stereotypes that make life harder for them. Mainstream parenting and schooling advice reinforce this. For example, despite the NHS website stating clearly that people with ADHD 'can find it difficult to suppress impulses, which means they may not stop to consider a situation, or the consequences, before they act', it offers the following advice for parents of children with the condition: 'Make sure everyone knows what behaviour is expected ... be clear, using enforceable consequences, such as taking away a privilege, if boundaries are overstepped and follow these through consistently.'[15] Can you imagine if this was the advice given to carers of older people? As someone with ADHD myself, I was constantly in trouble at school for talking too much in class, swinging on my chair, being late, and forgetting my homework; all of which make sense now that I know more about how my brain works, but which was put down to 'misbehaviour' by my teachers. Thankfully, we are now gradually seeing some better, rights-based information and training for parents and educators on how to support neurodivergent children, though this is not consistently applied across the education sector and much progress still needs to be made.

I spoke to author and academic Kerry Murphy, whose research focuses on how education policy and practice can better support and value neurodivergent children. She believes that we need to shift from a deficit model that focuses on milestones and what children can't do, to something much more positive that embraces all children as capable, competent learners.[16] Rather than thinking about children through the lens of 'delays' or challenges, we can instead recognise that all children learn and play differently and will have unique needs and preferences. And this starts with parents.

'Lots of parents aren't aware of the joys and benefits of neurodiversity,' Kerry told me. 'The first thing parents can do is to use social media and see what life is like for neurodivergent adults

— tags like #ActuallyAutistic are great to follow. Parents need to be able to see that neurodivergent people can do well.'

With their play-rich, child-led pedagogy, early years settings generally lend themselves more naturally to inclusive practice than the rest of the education sector. The challenges can start to show when children move up to primary school, which makes greater demands on children's time and exerts more control over how they behave. Kerry, who is Autistic with ADHD herself, told me that parental advocacy is essential in getting neurodivergent children the support and adaptations they need, even if this risks coming across as pushy. For some neurodivergent children, she continued, school can be so detrimental as to constitute an adverse childhood experience (ACE), with children as young as preschool age learning to mask their autism or soaking in the message that there is something 'wrong' with them or the way they play or interact with the world around them. ACEs are highly stressful and potentially traumatic events or situations that occur during childhood and/or adolescence; according to the charity Young Minds, these can be 'single events, or prolonged threats to (and breaches of) the young person's safety, security, trust or bodily integrity'.[17] In other words, these are not things we should be taking lightly.

'Trusting your gut as a parent is vital,' Kerry concluded. 'Sometimes as a parent you might need to ask yourself honestly: if I have to fight for my child to be included [in a school or early years setting], are they safe there?'

It's an uncomfortable question, but one we can't dismiss. A 2021 survey of thousands of Autistic people, including children, found that around 70 per cent of respondents did not think their school experience was positive.[18] Interestingly, when parents of Autistic children were asked if their child's school knows/knew how to support them, only 46 per cent disagreed or strongly disagreed, suggesting that the parents of Autistic children don't always recognise how hard things are for them at school. We need to be listening to children's experiences and taking them seriously; if all children have a right to education, then all children deserve to enjoy that right, not just those whose bodies and brains allow them to fit into strict school timetables and unforgiving behaviour policies. Many neurodivergent children communicate how unhappy they are at school, either through their behaviour in the classroom or by refusing to attend at all. I've worked with a lot of families for whom school has been a disaster for their Autistic or ADHD children, and who have felt forced into home education or been plunged into lengthy negotiations to try and access better support — or both. Even the allocation of specialist support — such as one-to-one teaching assistants who can facilitate regular breaks — can be focused on helping them get through the school day without disturbing the rest of the class, rather than on creating a tailored learning environment that plays to their strengths and helps them feel safe, calm, and heard.

Body policing

From the moment children are born, society holds certain expectations about how they are supposed to act, look, and dress — and who they are supposed to be. Nowhere do we see this more than with the expectations placed on children based on their gender. From the clothes children are given to wear and the books we read them, to the toys they are bought and the assumptions we make about their interests, adult actions can build up to reinforce strong stereotypes: girls are sweet, submissive, and love nature, and boys are tough, dominant, and scientific. We can see this clearly by looking at the children's clothing section of any shopping centre, where you will find flowers, hearts, and cute animals on pink and other pastel colours for girls, and dinosaurs, trucks, rockets, and predatory animals on blue, dark, and neutral backgrounds for boys. 'Pink and blue themselves are not the problem — the problem is what they come to represent,' writes Kirstie Beaven, the founder of *Sonshine* magazine. 'Making something pink means you want to sell it only to girls. And the things that get made pink are not just selling an idea of femininity, they're selling an idea of female inferiority. They are selling domestic roles in a society that massively undervalues domestic labour, caring roles in a system that refuses to pay fair wages to those who take on caring as a profession, magic instead of science, looks instead of thoughts, sexual power instead of earning power.'[19]

From birth, we are raising children within a patriarchal system that prepares them for different societal roles and polices their choices and expression. This harms all children, regardless of gender. A report by the Commission on Gender Stereotypes in Early Childhood set out how gender expectations significantly limit children, causing problems such as lower self-esteem in girls and poorer reading skills in boys. Stereotypes contribute towards the mental health crisis among children, and are at the root of issues including girls' problems with body image and eating disorders, higher male suicide rates, and violence against women and girls.[20] One children's social worker I spoke to told me that girls as young as 11 and 12 are being assaulted — physically and sexually — by their male classmates; child-on-child violence cases now take up a large proportion of her time. She's noticed a steep increase in boys who are turning to misogynistic 'influencers' such as Andrew Tate. They might start watching his YouTube videos on the importance of exercise, but quickly end up viewing content where he is talking about how women need to be controlled and threatened to keep them in their place. Encouragingly, some schools are starting to organise workshops on positive masculinity to counter these harmful influences, covering topics like aspiration, communication, role models, and how women are perceived, but it's too important for this to be left to chance — or to be the sole responsibility of schools.

Children are aware of the differences in how they are treated: one UK study found that nearly two thirds of girls — and more than half of boys — believed they were not treated the same by their classmates. Oliver, aged ten, told researchers: 'Once I heard a boy say to another boy, "Don't be such a wimp, you are more like a girl!" when they backed out of a task.' Ciya, also aged ten, said: 'There are set things that girls are expected to do, and it isn't fair. I love football but our school is a girls' school, so apparently we can't play football. I've been told to act more ladylike, and often questioned it. Why do girls have to be like this?'[21] Some parents of boys I've spoken to have told me that, while they don't care what their son wears, they are worried he will get teased if he goes to school dressed up as Elsa from *Frozen* or goes to the playground wearing a skirt. I can understand this fear; we know bullying is a common problem, and children can be ruthless in policing each other's appearance and gender expression if this has been modelled to them by others. But rather than putting the onus on our children to conform, why not tell them instead that we have their backs? Parents can talk to classroom teachers, asking them to keep an eye out for teasing and suggesting that they make use of inclusive books and imagery in their lessons if problems arise. We can also surround children with diverse images that challenge stereotypes: men with long hair, women with shaved heads, masculine people wearing dresses or working as nurses and teachers, and feminine people working as firefighters and truck drivers. Happily, the media landscape is starting to change, with more books, films, TV shows, and games that feature characters who don't fit into gender stereotypical norms or who feature gender neutral or non-binary characters; it's never been easier to show children a range of gender expression.

As well as normalising diverse ways of dressing and presenting ourselves to the world, we can — and should — normalise a range of sexualities. LGBTQ+ children regularly face pressure to conform and fit in with a model that denies who they are; from a young age, the language we use around children can assume they will grow up to be straight. We make jokes about two babies of different sexes growing up and getting married, or talk about boys who will grow up to 'break girls' hearts'. In a move that is both misogynistic and adultist, it's not uncommon to see fathers of girls joking about how they will never let their daughters have boyfriends. It's normal for even young children to be asked if their friend of the opposite gender is their boyfriend or girlfriend. We might do it without thinking, saying things like 'when you have a wife one day ...' or 'you'll see when you have a boyfriend'.

This can be embarrassing for children and risks sexualising them. It also creates an atmosphere where children feel that the norm is to be straight. My husband and I have always been mindful to make no assumptions about our daughter's sexuality, and if she talks to us about the future, we're careful to use gender-neutral language such as 'if you have a partner one day ...'. As well as ensuring we use inclusive language, we've also made an effort to buy books that depict same-sex relationships, including books that talk about assisted reproduction and adoption, so she knows there are many ways of making a family. We want to create a home environment where, if it turns out our daughter isn't straight, she never has to 'come out' to us — she can just be who she is, safe in the knowledge that it's totally normal. This is good for her, and it's also good for her friends, some of whom have same-sex parents.

Creating home environments where children are safe to be who they are feels increasingly vital, with right-wing movements around the world seeking to ban books that deal with LGBTQ+ themes.[22] In Florida, a controversial piece of legislation has been signed into law that prevents schools from teaching students about sexual orientation and gender, with teachers opening themselves up to lawsuits should they broach these topics.[23] Florida is a particularly tough place to be an LGBTQ+ child, with further legislation passed that would allow the state to remove transgender children from their parents if they are 'at risk' or 'subjected' to gender-affirming health care such as puberty blockers or hormone replacement therapy. Drag performances and Pride parades are also under threat for posing a danger to children. Guns, however, remain free to purchase without a permit, license, or registration; an average of 185 children die by guns every year in Florida, whereas to my knowledge no child has been killed by watching a drag show.[24] Florida is also the capital of child beauty pageants, which require young girls to parade in front of adults who will rank them on their looks, sometimes wearing make-up, skimpy clothing, or swimwear. This, however, is not deemed sexualising or dangerous.

Florida is not an outlier; similar bills and laws have been

introduced in other states that hold a devastating power over LGBTQ+ children's lives. Banning children from learning about what it means to be gay or transgender won't stop children from being who they are, but it will stop them from feeling safe and included. Writing about how trans people's experiences of shame and discrimination often start early in life, author and journalist Shon Faye states: 'If the existence of adult trans people has in recent decades become increasingly accepted, the same isn't true for trans children, whose existence is more often disputed and who risk censure, even punishment, from adults for expressing their trans identity.'[25] LGBTQ+ youth face greater violence, bullying, and prejudice than their peers in all spheres of life. A survey of LGBTQ+ school pupils in the UK by the charity group Just Like Us found that four out of ten had experienced bullying in the past year alone, and that they were at higher risk of experiencing mental illness, loneliness, and isolation, and of self-harming or having suicidal thoughts. Many of them had received little or no positive support or messaging from their school, despite the duty of education providers to prevent bullying.[26] Figures from akt, a UK charity supporting homeless queer and trans youth, report that 24 per cent of homeless young people identify as LGBTQ+, with three quarters of them believing that coming out at home was the main factor in causing their homelessness.[27] But this is not inevitable — there are many children living in supportive households who are loved and affirmed for being themselves, something that can be life-saving.

Body positive?

It's not just children's gender expression that is monitored and policed: it's their bodies full stop, especially when it comes to their weight. In her brilliant book *Fat Talk*, anti-diet journalist Virginia Sole-Smith writes: 'We do not question "fat is bad" because that is the premise built into everything we do. It is also, increasingly, a premise of how we parent ... Our kids' weight has become a measure of their current and future health and happiness, as well as our own success or failure as parents.' The relationship between body size and health is much less clearcut than we generally assume — being fat doesn't automatically equate to being unhealthy — yet parents can feel as though they have failed if their child has a bigger body. As Sole-Smith makes clear, there is a wealth of research showing that restricting children's food intake or pressuring them about their body size is unlikely to make children healthier: going on diets and experiencing weight-related teasing as a child are the strongest predictors of both weight gain and eating disorders.[28] Yet in the UK, school children are weighed twice, once between the ages of four and five, and again between the ages of 10 and 11, as part of the National Child Measurement Programme. This programme runs despite recommendations from the eating disorder charity Beat, who argue that weighing children in school increases the risk of developing eating disorders.[29] It also runs counter to research that suggests that increased weight gain during childhood is associated with parents viewing their children as overweight. The researchers wrote: 'One possibility is that parental identification of their child as being overweight results in that child viewing his or her body size negatively and attempting to lose weight, which eventually results in weight gain.'[30] We are putting children through something we know leads to eating disorders and a disturbed relationship with food and their bodies because of this fixation on measurement and norms, and our unwillingness to challenge deeply fat-phobic beauty standards that tell us that being fat is the worst thing we can be.

A 2022 survey found that three quarters of children were dissatisfied with their body by age 12, and that nearly half of those surveyed were regularly bullied or trolled online about their physical appearance. Social media was found to be exacerbating these issues, something that has been admitted by Meta, the company that owns Facebook and Instagram.[31] This isn't surprising when you consider the content children are shown by online algorithms. In an investigation into TikTok, journalists created a fake profile, setting up as a 14-year-old girl; after just eight minutes of scrolling, they were shown a promotional video for a plastic surgeon.[32] Social media is full of influencers promoting 'detox' teas, weight-loss programmes, exercise subscriptions, and cosmetic surgery, as well as fast fashion and beauty brands. All of these share the same subtle message, even when adopting a 'body positive' stance: with this product or service you could be a better, more aesthetically pleasing, version of you. It's not just online accounts who are trying to sell you something: friends, acquaintances, and celebrities may use filters or apps to change their body shapes, giving themselves bigger curves, smoother jaws, and smaller waistlines. When 60 per cent of eight- to 11-year-olds have at least one social media account, the impact of being constantly bombarded with images of 'perfection' is something we cannot dismiss.

What can be done? It's tempting to think that consuming different content and learning more about how social media works is the antidote to the shame and anguish young people feel over their bodies. Unfortunately, research suggests that following 'body positive' pages and accounts isn't particularly effective when it comes to protecting body image, particularly for girls, nor is exposing the artifice — the airbrushing, photoshopping, and 'face-tuning' — of social media content.[33] The best solution might be the most drastic one: a recent study found that teens who cut their social media use in half for a few weeks felt much better about both their weight and overall appearance.[34] Talking to children openly about the risks associated with certain social media sites and the pressures of diet culture, while staying curious and non-judgemental about their feelings and the way they spend their time online, might not directly lessen the damage of the content they are accessing online, but it could support more children to take regular mental-health breaks from these platforms — or even join the growing number of young people who are choosing to ditch social media altogether. Of course, this isn't much of a solution for young people who rely on social media networks to communicate with friends and connect with like-minded people. What we really need is for social media companies to take responsibility for their own algorithms, and proactively shut down harmful content that is targeted at children and young adults.

We can also make sure our homes are safe spaces for our children no matter what size their body is — especially if they are fat. 'What fat kids need is to know that we see them, we accept them, and we know they are worthy of respect, safety, and dignity,' writes Virginia Sole-Smith. 'They need to know that we believe this unconditionally; that we would not love them more if they weighed less because our love already has no limit. And they need to know that we trust them to be the experts regarding their own bodies.'

Control and resistance

Humans have a hard-wired psychological need for autonomy.[35] Children communicate this need to us early on — most parents will recognise the sound of a toddler saying they will do something 'by my own self' — yet children's lives are heavily controlled by the adults around them. The food they eat, the clothes and toys they have access to, what they are allowed to touch, whether they go to nursery or school or not, what time they go to bed, what they are allowed to do with their free time — all these things will be impacted by adult control to a greater or lesser degree.

We can make a distinction between two types of adult control over children's bodies and behaviour:

1. External control is open and overt, for example including reward charts, punishments, or shouting. At its most benign, it might look like a sticker chart to help a child learn to brush their teeth twice a day; at its extreme, it looks like the infamous US troubled teen industry (a children's rights nightmare, with children kidnapped from their beds and taken to 'treatment' camps where they face extreme harsh treatment and abuse).[36] This external control has at times played out directly on children's bodies, with left-handed children being forced to write with their right hands, children being beaten as a punishment both in schools and homes, or children being forced to work long hours for little pay.
2. Internal control is more subtle and may not seem outwardly harsh or controlling but may trigger feelings of shame and guilt in children. (How many of us grew up hearing the words 'I'm not angry, I'm just disappointed'?) It might involve not

listening when a child is telling us something from their point of view and being less warm or affectionate when a child does something 'wrong', even including facial expressions.[37] This is control that relies, eventually, on children controlling themselves. Through common education and parenting practices, children learn what behaviour is expected of them, and many will learn to control themselves, shaping their own behaviour to better reflect what adults are looking for. This can be mistaken for genuine motivation, but it is different from the autonomous desire and self-direction that can be the root of so much deep learning and joy.

Most children will experience both external and internal control regularly, and this has an impact on them — and on wider society. Research consistently finds that children of parents who are more controlling suffer negative effects, including being more controlling and dominant in their relationships with their peers.[38] But I'm wary of any discussion of control that paints children as passive recipients of adult behaviour. Newton's third rule of physics tells us that when we push against something, that thing pushes back with equal force, and I think that works well as an analogy for power relationships. As well as children's bodies being the object of control and discipline, they are sites of powerful resistance. We don't usually see children's resistance as such, though. Think about a child refusing to eat dinner, or throwing themselves on the floor because they don't want to leave the playground, or refusing to answer questions about how their day at school went. Seen in a certain light, the children's behaviour can be read in a straightforward way: labelled as 'naughty', 'rude', or 'tired', brushed off as a sign of children's irrationality or youth, and depending on the adults around them could lead to them being punished or told off. Yet all of these are tactics used by activists: think of prisoners on hunger strike or climate activists going floppy and having to be carried off by police. When adults do these things, we recognise their actions as political, pushing back against oppressive forces and regimes. Why don't we do the same for children?

When children use their bodies to refuse to cooperate with adult demands, they shine a light on adultism and highlight the unequal power relations between adults and children in daily life. One of my favourite definitions of political activism is to think about it 'in terms of resistance and challenge to social norms ... a response to that which stifles and suppresses identities and practices which do not conform'.[39] So much of the adult presence in children's lives can be seen as a 'stifling' power. This is particularly obvious in schools, where children are expected to follow adult rules and timetables with very little choice in the matter, but we can also see it in children's home lives, where there can be strict rules and behavioural expectations. Even in homes where parents are conscious of not being authoritarian, many children have lives that leave them feeling out of control and rushed about. Rather than dubbing children naughty or unreasonable or mocking them when they try to regain control where they can — for example, insisting on a certain colour of plate, or refusing to get dressed for school — how might our view of the situation change if we instead saw their behaviour as a form of resistance to adult norms and expectations that may not match their own needs and desires?

Writer Lorna Finlayson speaks of her decision to leave school at 13 as an act of resistance: 'I was a child liberationist. I objected to the notion of compulsory schooling, and to society's treatment of children more generally — the consensus that children's lives are not their own but must be closely regulated by adults.'[40] As a teenager, I regularly and consciously broke the school dress codes, even though this led to punishments like being told off in front of my peers, sent out of class, and given detentions. Objectively, it's hard to argue that the benefits of sneaking brightly coloured earrings into class outweighed the negative consequences. But I hated being told what I could and couldn't do with my body; for me, resisting a controlling uniform policy was a way of asserting my autonomy and standing up for what I believed in, even if I constantly got in trouble for it. It wasn't about the earrings, or the gum I chewed in class, or the excessive eyeliner, or the baggy flared trousers I wore — it was about trying to take back some control in a situation where I felt I had very little. Paying attention to children's acts of resistance helps us to notice power imbalances and where adultism is being felt especially keenly by young people.

Adult control is not always bad. As the CRC makes clear, children's capacities are evolving, and adults have a responsibility to ensure the children in their care are safe and thriving. Being overly controlling isn't good for children, but neither is neglect. Furthermore, all children are different. Some will thrive on a strong, dependable rhythm with clear expectations and instructions, whereas others will find this unbearably stifling. Again, it can be helpful for parents and caregivers to question their own motivations: am I doing this either because I know it will help my child achieve their goals (like when I remind my daughter to do her piano practice) or because it's necessary for my family (like taking a child to nursery when they would prefer to stay home because their parents have to work)? Or is this something I can let my child decide, even if I'm feeling a bit uncomfortable with it (like trusting them when they say they are full up) or worry I'm going to be judged by others (like letting a boy wear a dress to a family party)?

It's too easy to blame individual teachers and parents for being overly controlling. All adults have a role to play in tackling adultism, but caregivers are also under immense pressure, and this can have a huge impact on their interactions with children. Our current political and economic structures position parents as solely responsible for children, and the parents I speak to are feeling the stress of having to get things right. At a time when the future feels more uncertain than ever, I don't blame parents for doing what they think will give their children the best chance in life — and a recent study has in fact shown that when parents are feeling more fearful, they are more controlling in their interactions with their children.[41] I know that when I'm feeling stressed and overwhelmed, I'm much more likely to be less patient and flexible with my daughter.

I'm not advocating that family life revolves entirely around children's preferences, either. Living in a family, or being part of a community, means sometimes doing things you don't especially want to do because it meets the needs of others or makes them happy. This might mean that my family and I visit a beautiful church when we're on holiday because it brings me joy, even though my daughter finds it boring and would prefer to do something else. I don't think this is specific to children though; this give and take is a feature of all respectful relationships. No, my daughter might not love visiting a church, but she can give her consent to it, even if she's not overjoyed at the idea! And we can make adjustments — maybe the church trip will be boring, but we can make it more fun by listening to her favourite podcast on the way and stopping off for ice cream afterwards. When we move from control to collaboration — from a top-down relationship to one of equals — things tend to feel a lot better for everyone, because we all feel heard.

Body autonomy and consent

Under the CRC, children have a right to have their views listened to and taken seriously in all matters that concern them (Article 12) and to have their parents take their growing capacity to decide things for themselves into consideration (Article 5). One of the ways we can put this into practice is by respecting the autonomy that children have over their own bodies, honouring their consent, and actively seeking to let go of the control we so often seek to exert over them.

We may tend to think of consent in purely sexual terms, but it can be applied to all aspects of life — particularly when there is a power imbalance, as is the case with children and adults. Honouring children's consent can be as subtle as asking a friend's new baby 'Can I pick you up?' and returning them to their parent when they start looking uncomfortable or worried, or asking your niece if they prefer to hug, high-five, or just say goodbye. Teaching children from the start that their body belongs to them isn't always easy — I remember teaching my daughter the phrase 'my body, my choice' when she was a toddler and then wondering what I had done after she started shouting it at me whenever I asked her to do something she didn't like. But how can we expect adults to honour our own and each other's consent when it's not something we are raised with?

As adults, habitually seeking to control children's bodies can be so ingrained in us that we don't even really notice it. This might look like a teacher insisting on 'eyes on me', a parent pushing their child to take 'one more bite', or a gallery assistant telling children to be quiet in an exhibit. Starting to pay attention to these moments — and asking ourselves how it would feel for us if our bosses were asking us to sit 'criss-cross apple sauce' when we had a team meeting, or if we'd enjoy it if our partner told us we were only allowed to eat one biscuit — can help us to pay attention to what is truly needed, such as stopping children rushing into a busy road, and which is more of an ingrained habit that reinforces adultist power dynamics.

Just looking at the school day shows how little we tend to value children's bodily autonomy and physical needs: movement is greatly restricted during lessons, despite it being vital to children's wellbeing and ability to learn and recall information; adults decide when children can eat, talk, get up, and even in some cases use the toilet; how lesson time is spent and what is learned is dictated by someone else. Many schools also enforce strict uniform codes, down to hairstyles and make-up, and control what and how much children eat for lunch and snacks. And schooling starts too early in the morning for older children and teenagers.[42] Our circadian rhythms — the internal body clock that manages when we feel sleepy and awake — is delayed by one to three hours during puberty, making it difficult for children to go to sleep and get up early; this biological fact pushes back on the narrative that teens are 'lazy' for wanting to sleep in late when they can. School start times that force teens to start class while their body is still telling them they should be asleep have an impact on their ability to learn effectively, while sleep deprivation impacts on health, memory, focus, and attention spans. Why are we putting our children's wellbeing at risk when we could simply shift to a later start time? This highlights how even institutions we claim to be in children's best interests remain organised around adult needs, timetables, and traditions rather than what would truly help children to thrive. I can understand the logistical need for primary schools to start early, so that parents can drop their children off on their way to work, but for teens who are likely to be travelling to school independently there is no reason class couldn't start at 9.00 or 10.00 in the morning.

We may personally not be able to do much about the school system — though if we have children in school, we can always use our power as adults to advocate for their needs, as we shall see in chapter eight — but if we have children in our lives we can honour their bodily autonomy when they spend time with us. Some aspects of honouring my daughter's choice around her body have felt relatively straightforward for me: I breastfed her on demand until she was two, let her co-sleep with us until she was ready to sleep in her own bedroom, and never left her to cry if I could help it. From a young age my husband and I taught her that she didn't need to hug anyone if she didn't feel like it, and we've tried not to interfere too much when it comes to food, leaving it up to her whether or not she finishes the food on her plate or goes for third helpings. We've always let her pick out her own clothes, choose whether to cut her hair or not, and reinforced that all bodies are good bodies, no matter their size or shape.

Admittedly, there are some aspects of supporting my daughter's body autonomy that have felt much trickier to navigate. At times I've struggled with how to handle bedtimes, particularly when my daughter was younger. On the one hand, I wanted her to be able to listen to her body and sleep when she is tired, but I also needed some time to myself in the evenings — particularly as I knew I would be a grumpy parent otherwise — and I wanted to make sure she got enough sleep to stay healthy and enjoy whatever activities we had planned the next day. This is where thinking about children's rights is both useful and complex. Supporting children to have the 'best possible health' (Article 24) will generally include nutritious food, regular toothbrushing, and sufficient sleep. But because all children are different, their needs are different too; if you have a child who only feels safe eating a limited number of foods, or whose nervous system simply cannot handle the sensory experience of brushing their teeth, then the conversation around what is 'best' for them starts to look complex. It feels like there can be a real tension between keeping children well and safe, and respecting their right to be involved with decisions that affect them.

Looking at instances like these through the lens of power really helps me as a parent: am I pushing this because I'm confident it's in my child's best interests? If yes, are there ways of making it easier, such as watching a funny video during tooth brushing or working hard to create a restful bedtime routine to help her wind down? And if there isn't a solid reason for me asking her to do something that has to do with her body — to wear a coat when she doesn't feel cold, or to eat another bite of vegetables — then why do I feel like I need to be interfering?

There is definitely a balance to be found between being overly controlling of children's bodies, and the role adults have to play in supporting children to stay safe, be healthy, and learn the norms and values of their community. Sometimes as a parent I've felt judged when my daughter hasn't wanted to sit down at a table for a whole meal, or has started loudly singing as we've been walking through a quiet museum. It can be hard when social pressures encourage adults to control children — and children to control themselves. But in these moments I try and remind myself that I want to raise a child who feels confident in communicating and advocating for her own needs — and I remember how stifling I found so many adult rules when I was her age. I think a lot of conflict could be removed from children's lives if we listened to what they are trying to tell us and tried trusting them more.

*

Childhood can be death by a thousand cuts when it comes to our relationships with our bodies. We learn when we can speak out, what we can eat, what our bodies should be doing, and what we should look like, and — too often — we learn that we can't trust ourselves or listen to our instincts. But it doesn't have to be. We might not be able to change laws and institutions directly — though we can campaign, write to our representatives, and agitate for change in children's childcare settings and schools, join PTAs, and be active within our communities — but we can make a difference to how the children in our lives view their bodies. The messages children receive from the world around them can either be challenged or reaffirmed by the adults around them, and having just one or two positive role models and allies in their lives — a teacher who uses their preferred pronouns, a parent who never brings up dieting, an aunt who sticks up for them at family dinners — can make a huge difference. As adults we can all choose to be a kind and supportive force in children's lives, especially when they don't fit the norm because they will already be getting messages from all around them that there is something 'weird' or 'bad' about who they are. We can't protect children from these messages, but we can build bubbles of safety and validation for them in homes, classrooms, libraries, and doctor's offices, sourcing books, media, and toys that reflect and celebrate their bodies, cultures, and identities, and be willing to fight for their rights and equal treatment.

Body liberation is intimately tied into children's liberation; there can't be one without the other.

CHAPTER FIVE

Parenting as a radical act

Adults have always had strong opinions about what constitutes good parenting. Throughout the centuries physicians, philosophers, and religious leaders have all weighed in with views on what they perceived to be best for children, from Plato — who believed in censoring Homer lest the impressionable youth copy the behaviour of characters in *The Iliad* — to John Watson, a behaviourist who exhorted parents in the 1920s to greet their children in the morning not with a hug or a kiss but with a handshake.[1] Much of this advice was rooted in the idea that by landing on the perfect set of parenting strategies we could raise a generation of morally upright citizens and improve society.

If past generations of parents felt pressured by child-rearing advice, the situation for parents today can only be described as intense. We have access to more research, more science, more ideas, more knowledge than ever. The noise can make it difficult to take a step back and think about what our role as parents should be, and how our parenting can align with the rest of our values. Whether we think of it as such or not, parenting is deeply political. The very act of parenting can be a radical, empowering, world-changing act. How we treat children and raise children can either work to disrupt or to maintain the status quo, and our homes can become microcosms of the world we want to live in. If we want to live in a fair world, that starts by building a fair home.

Treating children well is good simply because it respects their rights and wellbeing and honours their humanity. Yet if our parenting can be liberatory and supportive of children's rights, it can also be the opposite. Too often parents are their children's first bullies, not only ignoring children's rights but actively violating them. From violent punishments to belittling children or pushing them too hard to succeed, our homes are not always safe places for children.

The problem with punishments

Were you punished as a child? Perhaps that looked like being smacked on the bottom as a young child, not given an ice cream because you pushed your brother, or grounded as a teen for 'talking back'. If you're a parent, have you ever punished your child? Perhaps you'd never dream of hitting them, but you've used time-outs or banned watching TV for a week?

If you answered yes to either question, you're not alone. For many children, punishment (or the threat of it) is a core part of daily life. But is this a natural part of childhood, or a symptom of adultism? Can adult-child punishment ever be compatible with children's liberation?

Save the Children differentiates between two types of punishment, the first of which is termed physical or corporal.[2] This is any act of physical violence applied to a child's body, whether mild or severe. Although most of these 'punishments' are in fact classed as child abuse, some form of corporal punishment is still legal in many countries including the US, England, and Australia, with children the only group who remain legally unprotected from physical violence.

'You'll thank me later' is the justification heard by children for being hit, but according to the evidence this is highly unlikely. Countless studies show that hitting children harms them on multiple levels, both in the future and in terms of their development, for example by lowering their self-esteem and significantly raising their risk of depression and anxiety.[3] Even a 'mild' smack affects children's brains in ways similar to more severe forms of violence.[4] What feels especially cruel about physical punishment is that it also makes children much *more* likely to behave in exactly the ways their parents are trying to avoid, and is linked to increased antisocial behaviour, aggression, and risky behaviour, so it's pointless as well as actively harmful.[5] It teaches children that using violence is an acceptable way to exert power over someone else and get them to do what you want, so it's unsurprising that harsh and violent parenting practices are linked to boys growing up to perpetrate domestic violence.[6]

Although smacking rates are decreasing, they are still high: in the US around four in ten children experience corporal punishment, rising to around six in ten Australian children and seven in ten children in the UK (although the UK figure is from asking 18–24 year olds if they had experienced physical punishment; changes in the law in Scotland and Wales mean I would expect the current figures to be lower).[7] Corporal punishment isn't a dusty relic of parenting's past: it's a grim reality for millions of children.

In 2022, the US state of Missouri reinstated 'paddling' in schools, allowing children to be hit with a wooden board.

Humiliating or degrading punishment is the second type of punishment identified by Save the Children. This can take various forms:

- Psychological punishment, such as yelling or telling children Santa won't bring them any toys because they've been naughty.
- Verbal abuse ('You stupid idiot, look what you've done.')
- Ridicule ('You're acting like a little baby with that whining!')
- Isolation such as 'time-outs'
- Withdrawing love, for example acting coldly with a child or ignoring them ('I won't answer you until you can speak nicely.')
- Threatening them or an object they care for ('If you don't stop that I'll put your tablet in the bin.')

On the surface this appears less serious than physical punishment, but this kind of behaviour can quickly escalate into abuse. The NSPCC states that emotional abuse includes humiliating or constantly criticising a child, threatening, shouting, or name-calling, making the child the subject of jokes or using sarcasm to hurt a child, and blaming and scapegoating.[8] Parenting writer Alfie Kohn describes these kinds of punishments as 'love withdrawal'. When children are punished, ignored, shouted at, or have their privileges removed, their lived experience is that their parent is removing their affection as a direct consequence of their behaviour — they feel that when they act a certain way, they are loved less (even if they are very loved). Similarly, when they are rewarded and praised for certain behaviours, their lived experience is that they are approved of — and loved — more when they act in a way which pleases others.[9]

Although many parents would draw a clear distinction between the two types of punishment, both have the same intention: to cause pain or discomfort in order to 'teach the child a lesson' and change their behaviour. 'Where kids were once routinely subjected to harsh corporal punishments, they may now be sentenced to time-outs or offered rewards when they obey us,' writes Kohn. 'But don't mistake new means for new ends. The goal continues to be control, even if we achieve it with more modern methods.'

The emotional distress felt by a child when they are told their behaviour means they can no longer attend a friend's birthday party is just as real as the physical pain of a smack on the arm. Some brain imaging suggests that the experience of relational pain — like that caused by rejection, for example during a 'time-out' — looks similar to the experience of physical pain in terms of brain activity.[10] And shouting at children has been shown to have similar effects to physical punishments. A 2014 study found that harsh verbal discipline can have the same negative impacts as physical punishments, with the authors writing that 'even in a warm and loving parent–child relationship, harsh verbal discipline reinforces the child's misbehaviors and depressive symptoms, which are often the very behaviors that parents aim to ameliorate'.[11]

Parents who use punishments usually do so because they genuinely believe they are acting in their child's best interests, wanting to change their behaviour so that they grow into 'decent' adults who are able to get along well with others and conform in their society. (Of course, there will also be cases where parents wish to avoid punishments but lose their cool and in the heat of the moment act in a way they later regret.) As we saw in chapter one, our view of children compounds this approach: children are often seen as inherently naughty and irrational, in need of being controlled and trained. But most parents don't realise that, far from being effective tools to train children into 'good behaviour', punishments don't work in the way they hope they will.

By turning to punishments, we miss an opportunity to consider why children are acting a certain way, how they are feeling, and what they are communicating through their actions. In short, we miss an opportunity to connect and deepen our relationship. Punishments also focus the child on the wrong that is being done to them, rather than on their behaviour. A child who has been punished will — understandably — feel angry and upset at the adult punishing them. All their thoughts will be about the unfairness and misery of the situation. There is no space or support for reflection on how their actions may have affected others, and punishment can weaken the relationship between children and their parents, including creating feelings of resentment and hostility towards parents.[12]

Insofar as punishments and threats are effective, it is because children do things they don't want to do because they fear retribution from someone more powerful. Do we want to raise children who will do things they don't believe in just because they are scared of the consequences — or who will see that as an acceptable way to get the behaviour they want from others? They also normalise coercion for children, teaching them that it's okay for people to use fear to make them do things they don't want to do. If we want to raise children who can recognise when they are being poorly treated, we shouldn't make it the norm for them. By punishing children at home and at school we teach them that it's okay to punish others, and we know that children who experience controlling and punitive discipline are far more likely to go on to bully others.[13]

Even if punishments were an effective way of encouraging children to follow adult rules and norms, I would still argue against them. To put it bluntly, I don't think punishments of any sort can coexist with a commitment to ending adultism or supporting children's liberation. They are predicated on a parent–child relationship based on adult control, and often stand in direct violation of children's rights. They embed and reaffirm an unequal power relation where one person — the adult parent — has the right to make demands of obedience from another person — the child — who does not wield the same power in return. 'Instant judgement and punishment are practices of power over others,' writes adrienne maree brown, 'It's what those with power do to those who can't stop them, who can't demand justice. This injustice of power is practiced at an individual and collective level.'[14] If we want to live in a society focused on supporting people to thrive in their communities rather than on punitive justice, where all people are treated as equally valuable and worthy of respect and empathy, this must start in the home.

As parents, we don't get the right to control our children, just as our partners or parents or friends don't have the right to control us. This is why I'm also uncomfortable with the widespread use of bribes, rewards, and praising children's 'good' behaviour. Instinctively, many parents feel that rewarding desired behaviour is a good way of encouraging the adoption of positive habits and actions, and I agree that these are much kinder to children than using punishments. However, when we look at this through a lens of adult control, punishment and rewards feel like two sides of the same coin. For me, it's the difference between my husband buying me a gift because he was thinking of me, and my husband buying me a gift because I did a good job of cleaning the kitchen that morning. If, as bell hooks wrote, childhood is 'the original school of love', then we need to think carefully about what children are learning about what it means to love and be loved.[15]

Parenting towards liberation

The CRC states that children should grow up in an atmosphere of happiness, love, and understanding, and be brought up in the spirit of peace, dignity, tolerance, freedom, equality, and solidarity. This language is intentionally vague, but it still paints a vivid picture of the sort of home life all children have the right to enjoy. Parenting that respects children as people and seeks to centre the parent–child relationship is a fundamental part of honouring children's rights and working towards children's liberation.

Raising a child may not sound like a very radical thing to do; we've been doing it since the dawn of time. However, there is something radical about choosing to parent our children in a way that actively seeks to combat adultism. In a society that tells us children should be controlled and disciplined, leaning into connection and joy is an act of resistance. This rights-based, relationship-focused parenting has a positive impact not only on our children but on everyone else our children will encounter throughout their lives, for how we raise children can have a deep impact on their values, beliefs, and actions. Recognising how children should be treated helps us treat ourselves — and others around us — with more humanity and compassion too. The ripples of respectful parenting can spread out across time and space, for generations to come. To parent in this way is an act of hope, an act of trust in our children and in ourselves.

Fran Liberatore is a writer, podcaster, and advocate for consent-based parenting. Over Zoom she told me how things had reached a head in her relationship with her daughter, where she found herself replicating the dynamics she had felt growing up with her own mother. She realised she needed things to change, and decided to take action.

> I got a piece of paper, and I wrote her a letter. I wrote down the things I was going to work on that I felt that I hadn't done, and I told her that I'd been too hard on her in certain ways. I explained that I was going to approach her with curiosity and love from then on, and that I wanted to value our connection over anything else. I wanted her to know that I'm learning, and I'm human — saying things like this isn't the way that I was brought up. But I am going to do my best, and I will always try to apologise and make amends. I still have the letter somewhere; I look at it sometimes just to remind myself of what I promised. I think it was really nice to put it into writing, because once it's written she could see it and be like, 'Well, in this document, you said you would do this!' so that accountability is there.

Fran quickly noticed a change in their relationship: her daughter started opening up more when previously she had been hiding things, and she began pushing back when she was unhappy with something. 'I felt like it was a sign that she could trust me — she could say to me "what you did in that moment, I think that was wrong" — and she hadn't been able to do that previously, because I would get really defensive. We talk about so many things now.'

When I talk to people like Fran, who are consciously working to break away from the parenting patterns they were raised with, I feel deeply hopeful. The progress we're making might not seem apparent in our daily lives, but when we look back even a couple of generations it's clear that we are moving in the right direction, at least when it comes to parenting. We can take my family as an example. If I look at the care my maternal grandparents received from their parents, it was far from what we would consider ideal. My grandfather, Max, was sent away from home at age nine to work for another family in a part of France where he didn't speak the dialect because his own family couldn't afford to feed him any longer. My grandmother, Liliane, fared a little better, but from a young age was made to carry out heavy work duties to support her mother with housework, growing food, and caring for her younger siblings. She was subject to harsh physical punishments if she made mistakes or allowed her siblings to get into trouble. My mother, Agnès, was raised with more material comfort and affection than her parents, and enjoyed experiences like holidays, outings, and music lessons, but still suffered from my grandparents' authoritarian parenting styles and was regularly beaten. The parenting advice of the time was reflected in my grandparents' beliefs about how they should act: as soon as my mother was brought home from the hospital she was put on a tight feeding and sleeping schedule, and was left to scream during the night.

When I was born, my mother was determined to do things differently: instead of sleep training and bottle-feeding me on a schedule, as she had been, I co-slept with my parents and was breastfed on demand. Her parenting style was warm, flexible, and affectionate, with connection and joy highly prioritised — I really have to dig deep to find a memory of her shouting at me. Yet despite their warmth and love, I get the sense that both of my parents struggled to know what to do when I was 'disobedient'. I was punished, which included being smacked as a young child and grounded as a teen. My mother often tells me she wishes she had had access to the gentle parenting books and support that abound today.

Fast forward to now, my daughter has never been punished, by me or my husband. I'm certainly not a perfect parent by any means, but I apologise when I mess up, and am doing my best to intentionally disrupt the adult–child power dynamics of my own childhood. If she ever has her own child, I'm sure she will have a whole list of things she wishes I had done differently, and that she will move even further towards parenting which supports children's liberation and dismantles adultism.

I'm truly excited about the time we're living in right now. It feels like we're on the cusp of widespread change in terms of how we treat children. The old childrearing methods our parents and grandparents were told were effective have been shown to be rooted in adultism and based on outdated views of children and bad science, while books like *Good Inside* by Dr Becky Kennedy and *The Book You Wish Your Parents Had Read* by Philippa Perry — which would once have been considered outrageously radical — regularly top the bestseller charts. There are hundreds of gentle parenting books and coaches — and thousands of parenting accounts on social media — offering support to caregivers who want to move away from punishments and control. Lots of the parents I work with feel isolated because their friends and family don't agree with their respectful parenting style, and have found real comfort and friendship with likeminded parents online with whom they can swap advice and encouragement. And with the internet at our fingertips, we can pull up scripts and tips for tackling tricky moments (show me a parent who has never argued with their child about putting their shoes on when they're already late for an appointment) and access countless resources for understanding ourselves as parents.

It's never too late to change things. If you currently smack your child, you can stop. If you currently use punishments, you can stop. One mother who discovered respectful parenting after a few years told me that she felt much closer and more connected to her child now; another told me that she feels able to see her children for their 'whole selves', even when things felt tricky. Whether your child is six months or 16 years old, you have time.

Ten guiding principles

I don't think it's all that helpful to give rights-based, liberatory parenting a specific name (there are already so many different labels!) or be overly prescriptive with what it looks like in practice. Every family is different, and each child has individual needs and preferences. Because of this, I think it's more useful to think about guiding principles rather than a set of rules or expectations. Here are ten that make sense to me; you may wish to write your own, or create a family manifesto.

1. Centre children's rights

Rights are not the only thing that matters when it comes to children's liberation, but they are a minimum standard all children should be able to expect. Every family can commit to creating a rights-respecting home where each person is familiar with the CRC and its implications for family life: adults know how they can support children to learn about and enjoy their rights, and children know what to expect from their caregivers (as well as being able to spot and call out behaviour that is not okay). What matters is that we are making an open and active commitment to respecting children's rights, and that we recognise that we can create a bubble of peace, dignity, and freedom for children through our interactions with them.

Sometimes centring children's rights in our parenting can be uncomfortable, or mean admitting we've gotten things wrong. Around the time my daughter turned four I realised that sharing photos of her on social media didn't sit comfortably with her right to privacy and my commitment to respect her consent. I gradually went through my Instagram posts and archived any in which you could see her face, and shifted away from talking about her personal details online. Why? Bluntly, I was sharing these photos for my benefit, not hers; her right to privacy trumps any desire I might have to share photos that feature her. I also have grave doubts around how younger children can ever give truly informed consent to having their image shared online without knowing the potential risks. She's still young enough that I don't want to tell her about the risks in detail, like *The Times* newspaper investigation that found that AI is being used to transform pictures of children from the internet into abusive sexual images.[16] This topic is nuanced: some parents who advocate for their disabled children share their faces and diagnoses because they want their stories to be heard, and some children might genuinely enjoy collaborating on creative content with their parents. All I know is that for me, I couldn't reconcile my values with my actions, so something had to change, especially with a growing number of children and young adults now speaking out against 'sharenting' culture.[17]

2. Question adult power

It's uncomfortable to think that we perpetuate adultism, but the truth is that all of us do at times. Luckily, daily life with children provides us with near limitless opportunities to interrogate and interrupt the adult–child power dynamics we might have grown up with. This might look like ignoring the societal pressure to sleep train and continuing to provide responsive night-time care, catching ourselves when we're about to tell our child they need to finish their meal before they can have dessert, or not forcing them to say please before doing something for them. Sometimes we do need to step in as parents — we have a duty to keep our children safe and every family will have rules to help keep their homes in good condition and ensure everyone can thrive — but there are lots of times when we might feel the urge to step in or interfere without good reason. Do children really need our permission to help themselves to a snack? Does their room have to be kept spotless? Is there a good reason they can't watch one more episode of their favourite show (when we might binge-watch half a Netflix series in one sitting)?

Something that has helped me a lot is noticing the difference between vertical or 'top-down' power dynamics, where we have power over children, and horizontal or 'together' power dynamics where we engage with our children as equals, partnering with them in taking decisions and getting things done. As the CRC reminds us, children have a right to our solidarity. This includes using our adult privilege to support and advocate for children where necessary, and might look like pushing back on adultism in our children's school, faith community, or extended family relationships. In an adultist world, I think one of the most powerful things parents can do is to show our children that no matter what, we will be in their corner, that we will believe them when they tell us something is unfair, and that we are not afraid to stand up for them where necessary.

3. Trust and respect children

As we saw in chapter one, the mainstream view of children often paints them as irrational, incapable, and out to purposefully cause us trouble. We can seek out and cultivate a radically different view of children that sees them as people who are inherently good, curious, driven to learn, and capable of participating in society. Similarly, by pushing back on the ideal of the normative child, we can start recognising our children's unique individuality, strengths, and needs, and avoid comparing them to others.

Taking a respectful view of children means learning to trust them, even when this feels uncomfortable. This includes honouring their autonomy over their own body and bodily needs and stepping out of the way so that they can enjoy freedom away from our watchful gaze. 'Lack of freedom to behave independently and unsupervised causes mental anguish,' says psychologist and education writer Peter Gray. 'Put another way, children's and teens' mental health depends on their being allowed increasing degrees of independent activity as they grow.'[18]

Honouring children's independence also involves supporting them to develop life skills to care for themselves. This might take more work in the short term — when my daughter was younger it was much quicker to prepare a meal by myself than have her take part — but in the long term can help children feel more competent and powerful in their daily lives. Perhaps this is one of the reasons the Montessori method of education is still going strong after a century, with its focus on supporting children's independence and giving children the time and space to work deeply on things that interest them without adult interruption.

4. Accept that children belong to themselves

> Your children are not your children.
> they are the sons and daughters of Life's longing for itself.
> They come through you but not from you,
> and though they are with you yet they belong not to you.[19]

I often find myself coming back to these words by the poet Khalil Gibran, a potent reminder that even though we love them and may have birthed and nourished them with our bodies, our children do not belong to us and are not an extension of us. They are their own people with their own beliefs, ideas, preferences, and futures. We should not try to live vicariously through them, use their achievements to bolster our self-esteem, or assume they will have the same ideas of what constitutes a good life.

I can admit that the idea of my daughter one day holding radically different beliefs to me — whether these are political, social, or religious — makes me feel uncomfortable. But then I think about myself and my parents, and the beliefs and principles I hold dear that are different from theirs. I feel grateful that they raised me to live with integrity to myself, even if that means making different choices from them. 'Our job as parents is not to make a particular kind of child,' writes psychologist and philosopher

Alison Gopnik. 'Instead, our job is to provide a protected space of love, safety, and stability in which children of many unpredictable kinds can flourish.'[20] There are as many ways of being a fulfilled and happy person as there are children, and all children deserve the right to fulfil their own potential.

5. Listen to children

Children have a right to have their voices heard and for all decisions that affect them to be made in their best interests. This includes involving children in family decision-making and listening to their views and feelings on anything that matters to them — even when they tell us they don't like something we are doing!

On the flip side, we need to be careful not to overwhelm children with choices; adults aren't the only ones who get decision fatigue. I tend to actively involve my daughter in decisions that directly affect her (such as choosing what she wants for breakfast or discussing where we will go on holiday) but I'm also confident making choices for her, knowing that she will tell me if she's unhappy with my decision because she knows she will be listened to.

Taking children's preferences seriously doesn't mean always saying yes. Before she turned eight, our daughter asked us for a Nintendo Switch for her birthday. My husband and I had a pretty good sense of what our answer would be already, as we'd previously discussed whether hand-held gaming devices were right for our family at that time. But we listened to her arguments, took her seriously, and shared with her our reasons for saying no, telling her it was something we were open to revisiting in the future. She was surprisingly fine with our decision, something I put down to her feeling heard and respected in our conversation. In any case, it turned out she wanted it for one specific game, which we were able to download onto another device. It's not just about legitimising adult decisions, though. There have been other times where, after discussing something with her, my husband and I have ended up going with our daughter's preference. It's easy for parents to think we know better than our children, but when we take the time to look at a situation from our child's point of view, our relationship is strengthened — and we might learn something.

6. Welcome dissent

Children are not passive victims of adultism, and this is just as true in the home as anywhere else in children's lives. They do not owe us compliance — and often they do not offer it to us either! Although children's dissent and resistance can feel frustrating, confusing, or even triggering, it can shine a light on where they are feeling out of control, rushed, judged, and uncomfortable. We can actively make space for dissent by listening to children when they communicate that they are unhappy, even when this looks like screaming or shouting, or acting in ways we might perceive as rude. I've found it helpful to think about tone policing in this context, something adults do to children a lot. 'Tone policing is when someone (usually a privileged person) in a conversation about oppression shifts the conversation from the oppression being discussed to the way it is being discussed,' writes Ijeoma Oluo. 'Tone policing prioritizes the comfort of the privileged person in the situation over the oppression of the disadvantaged person.'[21]

Sometimes it's hard to know if children are pushing back on something that feels unfair or overly controlling, or if they are genuinely just overtired, hungry, or uncomfortable. I can still be guilty of brushing away or downplaying my daughter's resistance by saying things like, 'Oh, you seem tired. Are you hungry?', rather than sitting with the possibility that she might be unhappy with me. I've found that having explicit conversations with her around power and adultism has helped her recognise it in her own life, and she now has the language to call it out. She often says to me, 'Hey, you're using your power over me' or 'I feel like I have no control over my life right now', which immediately alerts me that something needs addressing.

7. Tackle problems together

If something is not working, it's okay to say so. Parenting with children's rights in mind doesn't mean that anything goes, or that there can never be boundaries or conflict. In fact, engaging in healthy and respectful conflict is a wonderful skill for children to learn. Rather than approaching issues in a way that pits adult against child with top-down discipline, we can start from the position that we are a team who love and care for each other and will work together to sort things out. We can do this by talking to our children and asking them to help come up with solutions to problems. Sometimes when I'm struggling to know how to respond to something, I ask my daughter, 'What do you think you'd do if you were the parent in this situation? I'd love to know your thoughts because I'm not really sure how to tackle this right now but clearly something isn't working here.' This reminds us both that we're on the same side — and that I'm still learning how to be a parent. I don't want to present myself to my daughter as someone who is done growing or who has all the answers.

Sometimes people are surprised to hear that I don't use discipline. It's just not a word I would ever think to use in relation to my daughter, just as I'd never use it to describe my relationship with my husband or friends. Children do not act in ways that feel challenging to us because they're bad, naughty, or irrational; their behaviour reflects their needs in that moment, and their attempts to get their needs met, just like our behaviour as adults reflects our needs. Sometimes we have vastly different needs to our children, and these can clash, but that doesn't mean anyone is at fault. For example, my daughter might not see the need to clear craft materials from our dining table after she's finished using them. As far as she's concerned, she might want to use them again soon, whereas I want the table to be cleared in a timely manner before we sit down to eat. Approaching this situation in a confrontational manner helps neither of us. Instead, I can state my need ('Hey love, we're going to eat in 20 minutes so we'll need some space on the table.') and offer a solution ('Do you want me to put your playlist on and see how much you can clear in the space of two songs?'). If I get the sense that she's feeling overwhelmed by the task, I might break it down ('Can you start by putting all the felt-tips back?'), or offer help.

Even more 'serious' issues like lying can be approached as a team. My daughter recently admitted to me that she had lied about something, and that she felt safe doing so knowing that I wasn't going to tell her off or punish her. Instead, I gave her a huge hug and thanked her for telling me the truth, and then we talked about what had made her feel like she needed to lie in the first place. We ended the conversation feeling more connected to each other, not less, and I'm certain that if she's in the same situation again she'll be able to tell me what's really going on from the start.

8. Be warm and loving

We may love our children, but do we show them that they are unconditionally loved through our actions? Parental warmth is crucial to building and maintaining a strong, nurturing parent–child relationship. It also helps children feel emotionally secure and unafraid of making mistakes because they know that their caregiver will always believe in them and always be on their team. Warm parenting might include:

- Regularly telling children they are loved and valued;
- Using kind, positive language to describe them;
- Offering physical warmth in the form of consensual hugs, kisses, tickle fights, and snuggles;
- Spending time chatting, reading, playing, laughing and being silly, and listening to them;
- Telling children we believe in them, that we enjoy spending time with them, and that we value them;
- Being responsive to their needs and communication;
- Recognising their achievements and successes — even when these might not matter to us — but also recognising their growth and efforts even when they don't meet their goals;
- Providing comfort and reassurance when they are hurt or afraid;
- Showing them we are thinking of them, for example bookmarking a page in a magazine with an interview of their favourite sportsperson or leaving a little note on the fridge before heading off on a work trip;
- Offering non-judgemental support — even if this is just listening — when they are facing challenges;
- Being welcoming to their friends; and
- Showing them that they are trusted.

Some of you might be reading this thinking, why on earth do I need someone to tell me to hug my kids? It's instinctive! But these actions — offering compliments, offering hugs and kisses, playing together — don't come naturally to everyone, and can be especially difficult if you were raised by caregivers who didn't show warmth or affection. I have had clients who never heard the words 'I love you' from their parents. If that's the case, I recommend starting small and even scheduling these things in until they feel more comfortable.

9. Get curious

Whatever we choose to call it, this approach is about getting curious about how we show up as adults in relation to the children in our lives, rather than trying to control or change our children. I say this like it's easy, but it can be hard to change our reactions if we were punished, blamed, or controlled (or worse) as children. There are some things I've found especially helpful in figuring myself out as a parent:

- Taking time to reflect on my own childhood and family history, and the impact it's had on me today. There can often be an unconscious desire to idealise our own parents, put them on a pedestal, or to believe that everything they did was for our own good, and it can be painful to realise that our parents actions may have been harmful. Our parents — and their parents before them — may have experienced abuse, trauma, or war, and all these things will have had an impact on how we were raised, and how we parent today. Because our interactions with our children are so tied up with our own experiences of childhood, our children's actions can trigger intense feelings of frustration, powerlessness, even anger. Sometimes it can feel as though feelings like these hit us out of the blue, leaving us feeling shocked and confused, but they are usually linked to some past unintegrated or unresolved emotional experience.[22] I've found counselling sessions very helpful for unpicking some of this, as well as reading books written by therapists and psychologists that include reflection prompts.

- Learning to accept my emotions — even the uncomfortable ones. The work of mindfulness leaders like Thich Nhat Hanh, Tara Brach, and Jon Kabat-Zinn has been invaluable in helping me learn to accept however I'm feeling and be present to it, and in turn to be able to respond calmly and lovingly to my daughter's emotions (sometimes, at least). In *Everyday Blessings*, Myla and Jon Kabat-Zinn write that 'mindfulness hones an attentive sensitivity to the present moment that helps me keep my heart at least a tiny bit more open and my mind a tiny bit clear, so that I have a chance to see my children for who they are, to remember to give them what they need most from me, and to make plenty of room for them to find their own ways to be in the world'.[23]
- Finding supportive tools. I've found having a flexible rhythm to our days and weeks really helpful with managing my own parental overwhelm, and the predictability of the rhythm can help some children feel more secure and in control because they know what comes next. Having a rhythm can also encourage us to make time for the things that bring us and our children joy — something which tends to be underrated as a parenting tool — and can help us meet our own needs as adults, for example knowing that every day we will have a bit

of time to ourselves while our children watch TV, or that once a week we have an evening free to see friends. I've also found communication tools such as Nonviolent Communication (a communication and conflict-resolution approach that focuses on stating observations, needs, and making requests rather than apportioning blame or making generalised statements) incredibly helpful.

- Familiarising myself with some ideas from child development. Although it's sensible to proceed with caution when it comes to 'ages and stages' (there is no one model of child development because all children are different), having an understanding of some common children's behaviour — for example, knowing that a toddler dropping food from their high chair is exploring, or that during a 'tantrum' a child's brain is probably reacting as though there's a threat — can help us remain calm and warm. It can also be reassuring to learn that many go through phases of biting, hitting, and snatching, and that they will grow out of doing so by themselves.
- Thinking long term. 'I have an absolute burning desire not to end up the way my mum and I are now,' one mother confided to me, a message I've heard again and again from clients and in my online community. I've found it useful to keep the big picture in mind, especially when things are difficult. My actions directly impact on my daughter's life here and now, but they also influence what our long-term relationship will look like. Even though things might feel a big deal now, will they still feel like it next year? What about when she's moving out one day? I sometimes try to picture how I'd like her to describe her childhood to future friends or partners, or

consider the relationship I'd like to have with her if she starts her own family one day. This doesn't make the day-to-day frustrations around leaving the house on time disappear, but it puts things into perspective and reminds me not to sweat the small stuff.

10. Apologise often

It's normal to make mistakes. I've been working with parents and writing about parenting for many years now, and I still have regular moments of being controlling, short-tempered, impatient, and reactive with my daughter, despite having a clear idea of the sort of parent I want to be. Respectful, rights-based parenting doesn't require adults to be perfect, but it does require us to admit to our mistakes and actively work to repair the rift that can occur in the parent-child relationship. This doesn't need to be complicated; it can look like saying 'Hey, I'm really sorry that I raised my voice just then, that wasn't cool. I'm hungry and tired and I shouldn't have spoken to you like that. Are you okay?' It can also look like backtracking on decisions we regret: 'So I've been thinking and although I said this morning that you couldn't go to Ella's party at the weekend, I've realised I was wrong. I shouldn't have said that. You can go, but there are some things I'd like to discuss, do you have a minute to chat?' Practicing repair also models what healthy relationships look like to our children, and helps them learn to navigate their own mistakes and difficult moments.

We can also practice self-compassion when we inevitably mess up. Rather than criticising myself if I behave in a way I usually to my best to avoid — like losing my patience with my daughter — I try and offer myself compassionate curiosity, considering what needs of mine might not be being met in that moment or why it's feeling so hard. This isn't about accepting harmful behaviours as okay, but rather about recognising that I'm human and seeking to be kind to myself before I think about how I might be able to stop the same thing happening next time.

In working to build our relationship-based parenting practices, we also safeguard our future relationships with our children, not just when they are older children or teens but into their adult years too. There will be times when our children will really need our help and guidance to get them through a hard time. By reinforcing from a young age that we are on their side and that we love them unconditionally and will help them work though their problems, we open the door for open communication and support for years to come.

Control as cultural norm

Every parent I know wants the best for their children. Even if they've not thought too deeply about children's rights or youth liberation, the parents I talk to wish they were calmer, more patient, and less shouty. I think most of us instinctively recognise that parenting feels good when our relationship with our children is thriving. So why is it that, despite our best intentions, parenting is still so damn difficult? Thinking about children as complete and capable people can help us envisage the sort of parent we'd like to be, but putting it into practice can be much easier said than done. But what if the problem didn't lie solely with us, but rather the societies we live in? What if the systems and structures that impact our lives are making it harder for us to parent our children in a way which feels good for them — and us? I want to look at just three examples: cultural norms, white supremacy, and capitalism.

Parenting based on adult coercion is culturally specific; not all cultures treat children the same way, and hitting children and speaking harshly to them is unheard of in some communities. Research has found that a strong contributing factor of parents using corporal punishment is the belief that it is a normal, expected, or even necessary part of raising a child, so the family, community, and country we grow up in all have a part to play.[24] Because punishment and top-down power dynamics are so normalised in some places, even the most loving parents can sometimes find themselves reaching for 'consequences' when feeling challenged by their child's actions or are feeling at a loss for how to solve a problem. The parents I speak to don't like resorting to these sorts of actions — it makes them feel guilty and disconnected from their children — but they don't know what else to do to get their children to change their behaviour and feel at their wits' end trying to prevent yet another sibling fight. If we don't see alternatives, it's hard to envisage what different parenting practices might look like.

Racism, colonialism, and white supremacy have also played a big part in shaping parenting practices. US statistics show that Black parents are significantly more likely to hit their children, but this is not because Black communities are naturally harsher. Instead, this is a response to white violence. 'Black parents who tended to be stricter and use corporal punishment as part of their parenting style had concerns for their child's safety,' says Mia Smith-Bynum, a professor of family science and health. With high levels of violence against Black children, some parents feel they have no other option but to instil obedience and respect so that they are safer around white adults and stay out of reach of prisons and police officers. Smyth-Bynum continues: 'There is a disproportionate number of Black families living below the poverty line and being led by single parent homes. Combine the wealth gap and the gender wage gap with the impacts of systemic racism and racial violence and you have a lot of stressed-out parents who have less emotional reserves for patience, for thinking through how to approach discipline or to stay calm.'[25] In other words, while Black children are suffering from corporal punishment at higher rates than their white counterparts, it's the fault of white supremacy. And these roots go deep. African Americans adopted the practice of beating children from white slave masters. Stacy Patton, the author of *Spare the Kids: why whupping children won't save Black America*, writes: 'Historians and anthropologists have found no evidence that ritualistic forms of physical discipline of children existed in precolonial West African societies prior to the Atlantic slave trade. West African societies held children in a much higher regard than slave societies in the Atlantic world, which placed emphasis on black bodies as property, not as human beings.'[26] There is now a strong and growing resistance movement of Black parents and educators who are embracing nonviolent, rights-based parenting. The huge success of gentle parenting coaches like Chazz Lewis and Destini Ann are proof that there is an appetite for a new way of connecting with children which is no longer rooted in white supremacy.

Capitalism also makes peaceful parenting harder. 'Under capitalism, the universal stresses and strains of a wage worker's life routine limits the amount of time and energy available for parenting, in turn constraining the attention and interaction necessary for the maximum development of children during early infancy,' argues socialist writer Antonio Balmer. 'Thus, in addition to extracting the unpaid surplus value from our labor, the capitalist deprives us of something more primal — the time, energy, and material resources necessary to fully nurture the next generation ... The vast majority of parents work harder and longer than ever, often working multiple jobs, precisely to provide for their children, and yet millions are unable to meet their most basic needs.'[27] Companies' thirst for profit has led to situations like in the US where not even a fifth of mothers have access to paid maternity leave. An increase in precarious, zero-hours, low-paid contract work and the competition for stable jobs with decent benefits attached can make parenting feel like a race to prepare our children to 'win' at the so-called meritocratic race to the top, and we can feel judged and isolated when our child is perceived to be 'behind'. The neoliberal construction of families as independent, self-sufficient nuclear units can also make it harder to ask for help, further isolating us from support and community.

Towards collective care

The nuclear family — where each parent or couple is solely responsible for caring for their children as well as providing shelter, food, and material goods — is far from a universal norm and yet it has become an expectation for many of us. In an *Atlantic* article charting the rise of this family set-up, David Brooks explores how the nuclear family poses a real challenge for certain socioeconomic groups. If you're well off, he argues, you can effectively buy 'kinship' in the form of childcare, babysitters, tutors, after-school and holiday clubs, therapists, housekeepers, and life coaches, and this allows the nuclear unit to thrive by reducing parental stress and increasing children's life chances. By contrast, if you're on a lower income, family life can be 'utter chaos' because you can't afford to purchase the support that extended family would have once provided.[28]

Many parents feel intuitively that we are not meant to raise children in this way, but have no other choice. As a new parent, you often hear that 'it takes a village to raise a child', but this can be disheartening if you don't have extended family or a close-knit friendship group around with whom to share the load. In an informal poll of parents I carried out, only 4 per cent said they had enough support and didn't want any more, compared to over 70 per cent who said they needed 'a lot' more.[29] Studies have shown that mothers' feelings of wellbeing and life satisfaction are greatly linked to community, and we know that when parents feel okay they are more likely to be able to interact with their children patiently and calmly.[30]

Some are choosing to seek out more support and work to build the community they are craving. Abi Smissen is one of those taking matters into her own hands. After having her first child in England, she and her husband moved to Australia so that they could be closer to family. Since settling her family on Kombumerri country and having a second child, she has been focused on building and nurturing a community of local parents alongside her work as a postpartum doula. I asked her if she had any advice for others who want to build and nurture support systems with other families:

> Be vulnerable. Prepare yourself for potential rejection. Don't be vague — don't say, 'how can I help?', instead say 'I'm making you some soup, when will you be in for me to bring it around?'. Community relies upon the lost art of dependence

> on other humans, and people are far more likely to get what they need from others who have sat in the vulnerable acts of asking for help themselves, so don't be afraid to expect things. If you don't place your expectations out there, then they will never be met. And rewrite what community is and does. It may not look as you expect or imagined, you may not all share in the same beliefs or like-mindedness.

Other parents told me stories about swapping childcare with one another, or the support they get from their local faith, home education, school, and village networks. Some parents I spoke to live with their children and their extended families, including one four-generational household, and I've chatted to others who are in the process of setting up communal housing projects with friends as well as some who already live in these shared houses and love it. Every parent I spoke to who had taken steps to build community told me they felt their children greatly benefited, both directly by having wider social networks and more playmates, and indirectly by having parents who are less stressed and more supported.

I found it encouraging to hear from families who had learnt about respectful parenting practices from watching those with older children in their communities care for their children in a compassionate and loving manner. We may think our influence only extends to our immediate family, but parenting towards children's liberation can have a ripple effect on others who are watching. Being intentional about building community means we can involve children in decision-making and listen to their voices and needs, for example having a children's patch in a shared allotment, or seeking consensus that any shared childcare will always be rights-respecting.

One exciting idea is trialling a new legal framework that would make every citizen of a city an in loco parentis (or part parent), a symbolic gesture of collective responsibility for every child which could increase accountability for how children are treated and kept safe.[31] I wonder if this would give us more confidence as adults to step in when we see things go seriously wrong. Intervening with someone else's parenting feels like the last taboo, yet our discomfort risks children believing that the way they are treated is normal, or that they are alone and that no one will help them. Much in the same way that domestic violence used to be seen as a 'private' affair between a man and his wife, we need to start viewing childhood mistreatment as a public, political concern.[32] Breaking cycles cannot be left down to individuals, particularly when the power difference between children and parents can be so vast, and although this might be challenging to put into action, the idea that we should collectively care for children is a powerful one.

*

Collective living isn't always what's best for children. I've also spoken to parents who have been forced to move back in with extended family due to financial pressures and who have struggled with older generations' views on their children's behaviour and what discipline should look like, including some where grandparents have treated children harshly and made the daily experience of parenting hugely stressful. For some, a traditional nuclear family is an aspirational goal rather than something to escape — a goal that can feel out of reach for many with the high cost of living and the widespread rental crises found in many countries — and I can admit that I'm not sure I would want to go as far as fully sharing a home with extended family or friends (though I frequently daydream about living a short walk away from close friends and family). But what does seem clear to me, from my years of working with parents and families around the globe, is that lots of parents feel unsupported and alone living in little nuclear family units, despite trying our best to fulfil all the roles and functions our children need to thrive. Without family or other close networks around the best many parents can rely on is paying for childcare support, often at huge expense. And that, as we shall see, can come with its own problems.

CHAPTER SIX

Loving pedagogy

If how we raise children is a political issue, then how we care for children — and who exactly is doing the caring — is an even more fraught question. In recent decades, there has been a steep rise in children attending formal childcare settings — nurseries, preschools, and childminding settings — with families' need for childcare rising alongside economic changes that make being a solo-income family more challenging. More children now are enrolled in formal childcare settings than ever before; in the UK, over 60 per cent of children aged 0–4 attend some kind of formal childcare; similarly, in the US the number of children enrolled in full-time early childhood education and care (ECEC) settings has doubled in the last 40 years to nearly 65 per cent. In Australia, half of children under five attend formal daycare.[1] It would be hard to overstate the importance the role of childcare plays in the daily lives of families, particularly for young children, many of whom spend the majority of their waking hours in ECEC settings.

Conventional wisdom tells us that early years care and education is beneficial for children. This is largely based on an influential 1960s US study, the Perry Preschool Project, which set out to explore its role as an intervention for children who were considered 'at risk'. The study took a randomised sample of African American children from low-income families in the state of Michigan, who were provided with a few hours of stimulating classroom education each day. The specially designed curriculum focused on boosting skills such as problem-solving and perseverance, which were thought to be the key to increasing grades and thus breaking the cycle of poverty. Families were also given weekly home visits that were meant to help mothers learn how best to support their children's development by extending the curriculum into the home.

The results of the study were phenomenal. Not only were there clear immediate benefits for the children who participated, such as improved socio-emotional skills, but follow-up research decades later showed that they enjoyed higher earnings and employment levels, and lower participation in crime. The study seemed to demonstrate that high-quality early childhood education could disrupt intergenerational cycles of poverty and crime, supporting children from low-income backgrounds to thrive, and even to pass on these benefits to future generations. What's more, this kind of childcare paid for itself: for every dollar invested into the programme, researchers found a seven-dollar return, an astonishing figure that has been used around the world to justify more investment into early childhood programmes.[2]

But if we look at more recent research into the impact of mainstream ECEC, we see a more nuanced picture emerging. Studies carried out in 2020 and 2021 for the UK's Department of Education (DfE) by Oxford scholars Edward Melhuish and Julian Gardiner set out to study associations between different types of ECEC, child development, and school achievement.[3] They found that high use of formal group childcare (i.e., at a nursery rather than being cared for by a childminder) was associated with some negative effects: children who spent more than ten hours a week in formal group childcare showed lower levels of emotional and behavioural self-regulation. High-quality care did provide some benefits, particularly for children from disadvantaged backgrounds, such as better verbal ability and cognitive reasoning, but the results were not as clearcut as those from the Perry Preschool project. Perhaps unsurprisingly, the authors found that no matter which type of childcare was used, children's home environment and their caregiver's parenting styles had the most influence on their development and wellbeing, something that is often left out of discussions. This suggests that if we genuinely want to make things better for children, we might be better off supporting and empowering parents and tackling high levels of child poverty (as we shall discuss more in the next chapter).

Both the Perry Preschool Project and the recent DfE studies point towards the same thing: for ECEC to benefit children the most, it needs to be high quality, with reasonable hours, and supported by parents who can provide a stable and enriching home life. It intuitively makes sense that, if children are going to be cared for by someone other than their parents, they should feel warm, loved, happy, and safe, and be allowed to learn, play, and thrive with people who value them for who they are, in a place which honours their rights.

Loving pedagogy

It's half past eight in the morning in Bristol, south-west England, and I'm watching as children are greeted by Millie, who runs a small early years setting from her big back garden. The children run into Millie's arms, smiling, and looking delighted to be there. Once they've said hello and put their things away, they're quick to get into the important business of deep play: there's a mud kitchen, a tyre swing, a sandpit, art materials, and lots of loose parts like blocks, pieces of wood, tubing, and string. I'm struck by how quiet it is; despite the joyful play, the atmosphere is calm and focused, and the background to the children's play is birdsong. The children play outside in all weather, equipped with sturdy rain gear (Millie provides this for families who can't afford to buy their own) with a sheltered area for eating snacks and listening to stories. They can even nap outside in a purpose-built wooden pod, lined with cosy blankets and sleeping bags, or spend time in the small classroom building, which has been designed to work with the shape of the garden.

Rather than preparing activities in advance or following a curriculum, Millie and the rest of her team carefully observe the children's interests and experiments, thinking of how these can be supported. A child recently became interested in birthday cakes, so the next day they made sure they had some candles and modelling dough in case she wanted to deepen her play. They embrace the idea that all children want to communicate and can express their ideas skilfully if given the right materials and support to do so. Millie understands the work they do in the garden as deeply political, based on a positive view of children as capable, competent people. She views the children in an unconditionally positive light, and they are never scolded, punished, or told they are naughty; if there is a problem, she works with them to fix it, offering love and reassurance. She and her team view the children as powerful learners and active citizens both within their setting and in the outside world, and they facilitate lots of time in the wider local environment and community including visits to woods, parks, playgrounds, and even local schools. At the start of each year, the children and adults sit together to create a shared agreement around what kind of behaviour they would like to see from each other; even the youngest children are given a say, listened to, and taken seriously.

Based on the understanding that what young children need most is a strong, loving relationship with their caregivers, Millie spends time getting to know each child deeply at the start, through home visits, long settling-in periods, gentle morning drop-offs, and building close relationships with the children's families. Relationships are so important that Millie takes time out of her busy life (she has three daughters and holds a number of leadership roles in the local early years community) to visit the children at home when they experience a big change in their lives, such as the birth of a new sibling or a house move. She explained that this was so that when they next came into the Garden they would feel safe knowing she had witnessed this change. The strong relationships between the adults and the children help support in turn the relationships between the children: on the day I visited, I watched three children aged three and four work for a long time building a — functioning! — water pipe several metres long down a muddy slope, without arguing or annoying each other, listening to each other's ideas and offering encouragement and support when things got tricky.

Her setting has been rated 'outstanding' by OFSTED (the UK childcare and education inspectorate), and there's no doubt that she is providing the children who attend her setting with a quality of care which is tremendously high; I'm sure the Perry Preschool crew would approve. Fully aware of the impact excellent early education can have on disadvantaged children, she recently fund-raised to be able to offer three fully funded places to children from low-income families. But her setting is still small — 12 children — and it's run from her own home; Millie's Garden is, literally, her garden.

Tamsin Grimmer, an early years specialist, describes this sort of care as *loving pedagogy*. 'The main benefit to adopting a loving pedagogy,' she writes, 'is that children will feel loved, and have a sense of belonging, and will want to be part of our setting and spend time in our company. The ethos will give children the message that it's OK to be you here.'[4] Loving pedagogy puts children at the centre of ECEC and is about making children feel secure: caring deeply for them, spending time with them, acting in their best interests, seeing them as individuals, thinking about them and their needs, and offering them warmth and kindness. This may sound utopian — are we really arguing that early years workers not only need to look after children but love them too? — but philosopher S. Matthew Liao has argued that all children have a right to be loved, and to experience loving care, because 'being loved is a condition that is essential for children to have a good life'.[5] Love, he argues, gives children the opportunity to trust in others — and themselves — and is fundamental if children are to thrive. Because young children spend so much of their lives in childcare settings it's vital that they feel valued and cherished, even if their caregiver wouldn't describe their feelings for the child as love.

This love is so important that, as part of a working party made up of early years practitioners, teachers, and members of Bristol's Early Years Team, Mille worked to write the Bristol Baby Rights charter, which sets out best practice when working with babies. This includes the right to a loving, significant relationship; the right to make decisions for themselves, take risks, and be challenged; the right to be responded to as a unique individual; the right for their voice to be respected; the right to unrestricted movement; and the right to be active citizens in their community.[6]

Millie's setting is not the only one that provides exceptional care. All over the world there are examples of brilliant early years spaces, from the Italian preschools of Reggio Emilia to the Nordic outdoor kindergartens and forest schools. Despite their differences (a good sign that they are responsive to the children in their care and local communities), these settings all share key aspects: happy and secure children; warm, loving pedagogy that supports children to develop deep attachments to staff and each other; responsive, child-led care; trust in children's innate capability as learners; access to nature in some way, and natural materials for play; and strong levels of family and community involvement.

Exceptional settings aren't always privately run. Pen Green is a state-run nursery in the heart of England well known for its pioneering work with children. It offers a radical model of co-education, based on engaging parents in their children's learning. One mother whose daughter attended Pen Green told me that she attended weekly sessions with nursery staff and a small group of other parents. 'We would be shown footage of our children's activities that week and the staff would explain what the children had been involved in, what they were showing interest in, and how they were developing. We would then have discussions as a group on what we could do at home to foster this and the staff would also plan nursery activities around these interests — for example one little boy was very into playing post office so the staff organised a trip to the post office, his mum wrote him a letter and posted it to him, things like that. I absolutely loved seeing the footage of my daughter, it was like a secret view into her little world at nursery.'

While it's sometimes viewed from the outside as not 'proper' education, there's no doubt in my mind that the early years sector can be a site of best practice when it comes to creating liberationist spaces for children to play, learn, and explore on their own terms. Although high-quality education doesn't always look the same — it could be in nurseries or in childminder's homes, in small groups or big settings — there are some recurring characteristics and pedagogical approaches. These are the five things I recommend parents look for when searching for a childcare setting for their children:

1. **Loving pedagogy is embedded into ethos and practice.** How does the setting make children feel safe, valued, and loved? Do they take an unconditionally positive view of the children? What happens if children are upset? How would they deal with it if a child didn't want to say goodbye to their parent in the morning at handover time? What is their policy on physical contact — are staff allowed to hug children? What is their approach to settling in — can parents approach it gradually so that their child can build an attachment to their key worker? Do children have key workers? What is staff turnover like?
2. **Inclusive, rights-supporting leadership and policies.** Do they talk to children about their rights? Do staff know about and understand the rights in the CRC? Are children involved in making decisions for the setting? What policies and training do they have in place to tackle racism and sexism, and

build an inclusive culture where all children are seen, valued, and celebrated? How are 'challenging' behaviour and conflicts handled? Do they ever use time-outs or other 'consequences'? Can children eat and drink whenever they want to?

3. **Planning is responsive and child-driven.** Do they have a set plan for activities or are they responsive to children's ideas? Does observation of children's play directly lead into planning? What is their approach to academics like reading, writing, and maths — do they give children formal lessons or support children to develop these things through stories and play?
4. **Children's creativity and capability are respected and supported.** What resources are available for children to explore different art mediums? How is children's creativity protected and encouraged? Are children allowed to get dirty? What provision is there for natural resources like water, mud, and sand? Do they have free access to water outdoors? What opportunities for movement are there?
5. **Access to the outside world, including the environment and local community.** What access to nature is there? Are children able to grow food or flowers, care for animals, or garden? Are there regular trips and outings? Do they have links to any other groups or networks within the community?

All of these questions are helpful — for parents who have good quality, affordable childcare available locally from which to choose! But frustratingly this won't be the case for every family. While I wish every child was able to experience the level of care shown at Millie's Garden or Pen Green, not all children have access to this gold standard of care.

Sold a lie?

While many of the parents and children I've spoken to have been happy with the quality of care they are receiving in early years settings — with some children telling me that they enjoyed their time at nursery or their childminder's home so much that they wished they could go in at the weekend — I've also heard stories where children's experiences have been far removed from the great standard of care the children at Millie's Garden or Pen Green are enjoying.

A recent inquiry into the state of French childcare found that a quarter of early years staff admitted that they worked, or had worked, in a setting they would describe as abusive. The report detailed horrific treatment of very young children, including name calling, harsh punishments including the forced isolation of crying children, leaving children in dirty nappies all day, force-feeding to the point of sickness, and acts of physical violence.[7] One reason the authors gave for this mistreatment was the dreadful working conditions of the staff, who were poorly paid and overworked, often having to look after large numbers of children by themselves because of inadequate cover. The treatment of early years workers undoubtedly plays a role in how children are treated; we see the same patterns of abusive behaviour in other institutional settings where carers are poorly paid, such as elderly care homes and residential homes for disabled people. But at the root of this mistreatment is adultism: both directly, in treating children as not fully human, and indirectly, because caring for children is so poorly valued — and remunerated — by society.

These are not problems unique to France; staff in the early years sector across the UK, Australia, and the US all face similar working conditions, with low pay, high turnover, and a lack of professional development. Even when care isn't abusive it can still be substandard. Back when my daughter was a toddler, a group of nursery children were brought on an outing to the playground where we had spent the morning. Some of the older children were allowed to get out of their pushchairs and play, but the younger children were left sitting strapped in, unable to participate or move their bodies. I watched as one of the adults picked up a girl from her pushchair, put her into the swing, pushed her a couple of times, snapped a photograph — I assume to upload to the girl's learning journal — and then strapped her back into the pram and went back to chatting with her colleague, before repeating the same process with another child. The CRC clearly states that children have a right to play, and I imagine that these children's parents may feel that this right had been enjoyed on the basis of these deceptive photos.

I spoke to Lizzie, an English mother, about her experience of looking for a nursery for her daughter Greta:

> The first nursery we'd signed her up to seemed okay when we visited, but at the settling in session I saw them behave in ways towards the children in their care that shocked me: staff spoke to the children brashly; disrespectfully plucked them, with no prior warning, from activities they were engaged in to take them for nappy changes (and were clearly unreceptive when, on seeing this, I shared that I signed with my daughter at home to help her understand what to expect); and left a distraught child crying with no comfort for an extended period, ultimately removing her to scream in another room when I'd drawn their attention to her obvious distress. They told me that that particular child was new with them — like

> my daughter was soon to be — and struggling to settle in. I asked how long they would consider appropriate to leave a child crying when they were struggling with separation, and they casually recalled that one child 'screamed and screamed' for a whole morning session (which was four hours!). I had to wonder how bad it would be when there was nobody looking. I remember calling my husband when I was walking home with Greta and telling him I wouldn't leave a dog in that place. I hastily cancelled our arrangement and sought an alternative setting.

That we normalise treating children like this — leaving them to cry despite their distress or shrugging off their unhappiness at being away from their caregivers for the first time — is deeply adultist and says a lot about how much we ignore or belittle children's experiences. We know from several studies that children in ECEC settings show heightened levels of cortisol, the stress hormone, when they are at nursery. Far from peaking during the morning drop-off, stress builds up throughout the day, with children in low-quality settings experiencing greater stress.[8] This is rarely discussed in conversations around childcare. When it is acknowledged, reporters and researchers contort themselves to wonder whether perhaps this stress is good for children in some way. I understand the discomfort around questioning whether or not children are thriving in childcare, especially when parents have no option but to go out to work. But surely we owe it to children to be having these conversations?

Although they found a different nursery, Lizzie and Greta's experience of childcare did not improve. 'Greta went through countless keyworkers. They changed at the drop of a hat, and children were not informed of this change. I learned of this practice only when my daughter had mentioned enjoying playing with "Kate" several times, and then became upset that she wasn't in her room anymore. I asked staff if this was a child who had left and only then did I learn that this was "Miss Kate", who had been Greta's keyworker. There was no regard or respect for her experience of that change.' Keyworkers — members of staff who become the child's main point of contact and stability throughout the day — can regularly change due to staff turnover. This can make it hard for children to form the close, loving relationship with them that they need to thrive. When they do form a bond with their keyworkers, like in Greta's case, it can be deeply distressing for them when that person disappears without warning.

Lizzie also struggled with the emphasis the setting placed on 'school readiness'.

> The information I was given about Greta's days there was extremely sparse, sometimes not even including what she had eaten let alone what she'd been doing or had enjoyed. At her last parents' meeting I asked if there was anything I could build on or continue at home, and was told their current focus was encouraging children to 'sit quietly on the carpet', as part of early school readiness. She was two years old! I felt their focus was on training children; meeting pre-determined expectations and benchmarks.

The emphasis some early years settings place on measurable skills and 'school readiness' — rather than creativity, relationships, and learning through play — is one I've come across a lot while talking to families.

Rachel Rosen, a professor at UCL's Institute of Education, writes that the preoccupation with child development is often well intentioned but is 'underpinned by all sorts of ideas about controlling the future: the idea that teaching children to verbally express emotions or sit in a circle will have predictable results such as self-regulation, "school-ready" bodies, and improved school achievement'.[9] This 'conveyor belt' approach to childcare, focused on getting children ready for the next stage of their development, is often in direct opposition to what's in children's best interests developmentally and what children themselves want to be doing with their time — though it would be a mistake to assume children take this quietly. 'Children employ all sorts of embodied responses to such interventions,' Rosen continues, 'for example through screams, silences, hiding, and more.'

This focus on 'school readiness' goes hand-in-hand with an increased focus on measurement and assessment and this can have significant consequences, with a study from UCL's Institute for Education finding that children as young as two years old are grouped by their perceived 'ability'. Researchers found that grouping nursery children by ability does not lead to greater attainment; on the contrary, children in the lower ability groups can get 'stuck' at the bottom of the pile. One of the lead authors of the study remarked that 'Children are aware of which group they are in and it can really damage their self-esteem' and stated his concern that nurseries and schools are becoming 'data obsessed institutions'.[10]

Not all early years educators are in favour of this shift. Many find ways to resist in their daily practice: one educator reported stressing to parents that the developmental checks she was forced to carry out were box-ticking exercises and that they don't reflect the full capability of their child; another said she ignored instructions to group children by ability and let them do their own thing instead. Although this resistance isn't public or collective, it is no less valuable for the children who benefit from those individual educators who are pushing back.[11]

Lizzie wished she could have stayed at home longer with Greta, but due to the family's financial situation she had to return to work part-time. 'After dropping my distraught daughter off at nursery I regularly cried in the car on the way to work at the wrench of unwanted separation. She was miserable. I was miserable. They didn't love her. We finally hatched a workable plan for an alternative childcare arrangement and on my daughter's last day at nursery — where she had been known for two years of her life — there was absolutely no ceremony whatsoever to mark this time or this transition. No card, no photo, no little certificate thrown together in Comic Sans, nothing. I got an invoice though. Putting my daughter in nursery is my only regret as a parent.'

Lizzie was eventually able to take Greta out of nursery. She now home educates, alongside volunteering for the campaign group Mothers at Home Matter, which lobbies for an economic level playing field for stay-at-home parents.[12] She loves spending every day with Greta, but still looks back on the years Greta spent at nursery, wishing she hadn't been forced into a decision that made them both so unhappy.

The case for paid parental leave

What do babies and young children want? Given how much of their lives young children spend in ECEC settings — children who attend full time may spend up to 50 hours a week at nursery

— it's an important question to consider, yet their voices are strangely absent from debates around childcare.

It feels safe to assume that, for children who have a loving and safe relationship with their primary caregiver, they want to be with that person, receiving responsive, warm, and loving care, as often as possible. Decades of research into attachment theory and brain development tell us how important the mother–baby relationship is in the early weeks and months of a baby's life (or their main caregiver if that person is not a mother). New babies and their mothers are often described as being in a quasi-symbiotic state, which is why the first three months after birth are often referred to as the 'fourth trimester'. During this time, what babies need the most is to be close to their main caregivers, to have their needs responded to quickly and warmly, and to feel safe.

If we care about children's wellbeing and rights, then paid maternity leave is one of the most fundamental places to start. Paid maternity leave is associated with a decrease in postpartum maternal depression and improved infant attachment and child development, with an increase in the initiation and duration of breastfeeding. It is also linked to lower rates of infant mortality and of mother and infant re-hospitalisations.[13]

Most countries recognise the need for mothers to take time off from work before and after the birth of their children. Yet the US has no state mandated paid maternity leave at all. Parents can take up to 12 weeks off unpaid and keep their jobs and health insurance, if they work for a company that employs over 50 people, but not everyone is eligible. Although some states — like California, New York, Massachusetts, and Oregon — have their own laws regarding paid leave, only 17 per cent of all employed American workers have access to paid parental leave through their workplace.

Hispanic and Black women receive significantly less paid leave than their white counterparts, with one study stating that 'inequitable access to paid parental leave through both employers and government programs exacerbates racial inequities at birth'.[14]

Family therapist Sepideh Hakimzadeh describes the US's approach to parental leave as 'a dark echo of the days of the enslavement of Black Africans, who were separated from their children to toil for the productivity of the land or raise the white owners' children'.[15] The impact of these policies is stark: nearly a quarter of employed mothers living in the US return to work within ten days of giving birth, because of their inability to pay for their living expenses without any income. Some of these mothers will have given birth via caesarean section and are in significant pain, especially if they are doing physically demanding jobs like cleaning or waitressing. Breastfeeding is also made infinitely more challenging because of the separation of mother and baby, and some workplaces don't have the facilities for nursing mothers to pump milk (which can be made more difficult by being away from the baby; breastfeeding is supported by the 'love hormone' oxytocin, which is released when snuggled up close to the baby and inhibited by stress and tiredness). In extreme cases, some women report they have no option but to leave their children home alone when they go out to work.

The CRC states clearly that families should be afforded assistance by the state, and support in the earliest stages of family life seems particularly important. The consensus among experts is that paid leave should last a minimum of 12 weeks, to reduce harm to both babies and their mothers, and give the family unit the best chance of thriving. Parental leave is not just for mothers, though. One study found that children whose fathers took at least two weeks of paternity leave after they were born reported feeling closer to their dad, with longer periods of paternal leave associated with fathers more frequently caring for their child.[16] A Swedish study found that when men are able to take flexible leave in the first year of their child's life, the mother is less likely to experience physical health complications and poor mental health.[17] Men taking time off is also good for gender equality. German research has found that taking any amount of parental leave increased the amount of childcare dads participated in, but that longer leave of two or more months also increased their participation in housework, leading to more equality in couples' division of labour.[18] Paternity leave has also been shown to increase women's wages, with one study finding that mothers' incomes rose about 7 per cent for each month that a father spent at home.[19] The Fawcett Society have even found that daughters whose fathers spend more time with them are less likely to take up stereotypical careers.[20] There is sometimes a misconception that men wouldn't want to take a break from their work to be with their children, but when men have access to parental leave they tend to use it. Fathers in Sweden — which became the first country in the world to replace gender-specific maternity leave with parental leave in 1974 — average around 30 per cent of all paid parental leave.[21]

Scandinavian countries are leading the way when it comes to inclusive, generous parental leave policies. Parents in Sweden are entitled to 480 days of paid parental leave when a child is born or adopted. If they are a single parent, then the whole 480 days goes to them, whereas in a couple each parent is entitled to half, with 90 days reserved exclusively for each parent in a use-it-or-lose-it set-up. In Norway, parents are entitled to 49 weeks of parental leave at 100 per cent pay, or 59 weeks at 80 per cent (this can be shared between parents), although the amount of pay is capped at around £50,000. In addition to the first 12 months, each of the parents is entitled to one year of unpaid leave for each birth should they want or need to take it. We see similar patterns of long, well-paid parental leave in Bulgaria, Germany, Japan, Estonia, and Iceland.

How to fund parental leave is a political decision — there is no reason other countries could not do the same if they decided to value children's wellbeing more highly. The total lack of support for new parents in countries like the US is a deliberate choice, tied into disregard for children and their caregivers.

A crisis of care

Even when parents are able to take paid leave, the issue of childcare doesn't disappear. Most parents rely on some form of childcare — whether through formal early years settings, or informal care from grandparents and other family members — to enable them to work to put food on the table. Some have argued that childcare needs to be seen as a 'universal basic service' like schools and healthcare. In the UK, the Family and Childcare Trust has found that families face unequal access to early education and childcare.[22] The cost of childcare can be astronomical, with figures from children's charity Coram suggesting that a full-time nursery place for a child under two costs nearly £15,000.[23]

At the time of writing, some two-year-olds and all three- and four-year-olds qualify for 'free' hours of childcare (the number of hours varies depending on family situation), which eases the pressure on parents as their children get older. But these 'free' hours are anything but free. The money childcare settings get paid from the UK government to cover these 'free' places isn't nearly enough to pay for costs, so some nurseries are having to charge high fees for 'extras' like meals, nappies, and additional hours just to make up the shortfall in funding. In affluent areas, parents can afford to pay, but children who need the most support often live in places where parents don't 'top up' as much as needed. This leads to nurseries making a big loss, impacting on the quality of care as they are unable to offer competitive wages. In other words, the most vulnerable children are often getting the worst quality of care.[24] And that's assuming their parents can even get a place: because of issues with funding, in some areas nurseries are simply shutting down, leaving parents with fewer options.

The UK government's recent answer to the problem of access and cost has been to announce an extension to funded childcare, giving working parents of children from nine months to five years 30 hours of funded childcare per week, for 38 weeks of the year, by the end of 2025. But there are several potential issues with this scheme, the most significant of which is the need to recruit and train an estimated 38,000 childcare practitioners to meet the number of new places required. The government's plans don't include extra funding to make up for the shortfall between funded hours and running costs, which inevitably means more settings will have to close, further reducing capacity. And more and more people are leaving the sector due to low pay and poor working conditions, with recent figures suggesting that a fifth of childcare workers are thinking of leaving.[25] What's more, working conditions look set to worsen rather than improve. As part of the package of changes, the government announced a relaxation of adult–child ratios. Each adult will be allowed to care for five two-year-olds, rather than the current limit of four. Early years professionals, experts, and parents alike have spoken out strongly against this, claiming it will make working conditions worse, and create a lower — sometimes dangerous — standard of care. And the changes come with conditions: the other side of increasing 'free' childcare is a pressure on parents who rely on benefits to go back to work earlier and for close to full-time hours now that their childcare is presumed 'covered', never mind that this ignores the difficulty of finding flexible work around caring for children or that some parents would prefer to look after their children themselves. Single mothers will be the most negatively affected by these announcements, with critics arguing it would drive families into debt and push more children into poverty.[26]

There are other issues with the scheme: most parents work more than 38 weeks a year, for example. And despite the claims of much of this care being 'free', the problem is that childcare that is great for children tends to be very expensive for whoever is paying for it, be it parents or taxpayers. There is a gulf between what children need (high-quality, short hours) and what parents need (affordable and long hours) — and what the government is willing to pay for. A clear example of this tension in action comes from Quebec.

In the late nineties, Quebec set up a system of cheap, accessible childcare — available all day, year-round — which helped many mothers go back to work after having their children. So far, so good. But studies have shown that this type of care held few benefits for the children themselves, and in fact caused harm, with increased risk of anxiety, aggression, and hyperactivity. These weren't short-term effects, either: a longitudinal study of the effects of this type of care showed negative social-emotional outcomes that persisted into young adulthood. The most striking finding was a sharp increase in criminal behaviour for those exposed to the day care programme compared to their peers in other areas.[27] These findings are consistent with other research that has found that children who spent long hours in childcare early in life had worse behavioural outcomes than other children, and these lasted well into the teen years.[28]

What we see in the UK is the government taking a Quebec-style approach, increasing funded childcare with the explicit aim of getting more mothers into the workforce to become 'economically active' in a way that looks set to reduce the quality of care. In a balance of needs, children will be the losers. 'If our children are "at the heart of our choice," then the research confirming that children exposed to early, extensive day care are at risk for social-emotional and behavioural challenges must be taken seriously,' writes Jenet Erickson for the Institute of Fiscal Studies. 'What we do know suggests that extensive time spent in non-maternal care in early life has effects that persist across the entire course of development. Though the effects may appear small, they matter in the lives of individual children, and they matter in the collective consequences to communities and society at large.'[29]

Reconciling feminism and children's liberation

In discussions around childcare and women's access to work, children are often positioned as problems to solve; economic burdens who are getting in the way of women's careers and employment (never mind if some parents would prefer to spend more time with their children). Yes, caring for young children can feel hard for many reasons, and figuring out work and money after growing a family can be hugely difficult. But the problem doesn't lie with children. It lies with a political and economic system that sees no value in caregiving apart from its potential to make money. Nowhere in these discussions have I seen young children's experiences of childcare taken into account as part of the policy-making process, although decades of work in childhood studies shows that children can be active participants in research. And we don't always have to turn to formal research: some children communicate their displeasure with their childcare arrangements vocally and regularly. I've spoken to parents who have told me how distressing and painful it is to hand over their crying child, particularly if they have no other choice but to leave them. If an adult was crying every morning before going into work, we would take that as a sign that something was seriously wrong, but we have normalised this happening to children. Rather than looking into ways to ensure the earliest years of children's lives are ones where they feel safe and cherished, the political focus is on incentivising economic growth by separating children from their parents at an ever-younger age.

No parent should have to feel guilty for working, either because they need to or want to. But I don't want to shy away from the seemingly taboo truth that lots of parents — especially mothers — would have liked to stay at home with their children a little longer and felt rushed into returning to the workplace. At a time when we're opening up more about some of the challenges parenting can bring, it can feel like it's unfashionable and uncomfortable to talk about the joy lots of parents feel spending time with their children. Our overarching social and economic systems — capitalism, adultism, patriarchy, and the rest — have conspired together to devalue caring for children and to separate babies and children from their parents, to the point that even voicing the desire to stay at home can feel radical (or regressive, depending on where you stand). Yet in surveys, parents routinely state they would like to work less and spend more time with their children, and research has highlighted what many parents have long known: caring for children can be life-enhancing.[30]

Paid work is important, but it's usually not the most important thing in our lives — though again, capitalist narratives selling us fulfilment through the labour market would have us think otherwise. So often I come across language used to describe mothers who choose to look after their children themselves as though this is a tragedy: 'lost skills', 'economically inactive', 'wasted education'. I can't speak for every parent, nor would I wish to, but despite a great education and an interesting career I have found raising my daughter to be the most rewarding, joyful, and satisfying work of my life. At no point have I felt her to be burden, or a problem to solve (though I have been frustrated by how difficult the society we live in made it for my husband and me to care for her ourselves, despite the huge amount of privilege we hold as a family).

'Many of us are forced away from our babies and young children against our wishes — financial pressures leave us little choice but to find paid work to put food on the table and a roof over our heads,' says Vanessa Olorenshaw, author of *Liberating Motherhood*. 'Our bonds of motherhood are being replaced with binds to the market ... we are witnessing a silencing of mothers who wish to provide loving maternal care to their children.' Patriarchy, misogyny, capitalism, and neoliberalism all combine so that when a mother chooses to care for her children herself, she sacrifices full citizenship and financial security, Olorenshaw argues. And mothers who do work outside of the home often find themselves in low-paid, low-security, low-status jobs — with the 'second shift' of housework and childcare on top when they get home. 'When it comes to mothers, we have to do better for those of us who *want* to work outside the home, as well as those who would *prefer* to care for their children. It's the least feminism can do: value mothers.'[31]

I've found it interesting to note that the feminism of the sixties and seventies — just before ideas associated with neoliberalism became more popular — saw children's liberation as intimately connected with women's liberation. In the feminist classic *The Dialectic of Sex*, Shulamith Firestone writes: 'We must include the oppression of children in any programme for feminist revolution or we will be subject to the same failing of which we so often have accused men: of not having gone deep enough in our analysis, of having missed an important substratum of oppression merely because it didn't directly concern us.'[32] But as some branches of the feminist movement became more intimately linked with capitalism — the feminism of smashing glass ceilings and being a #girlboss — children became separated from the movement, or in some cases seen as holding women back. 'Where feminists once criticised a society that promoted careerism, they now advise women to "lean in",' writes professor of philosophy and politics Nancy Fraser. 'A movement that once prioritised social solidarity now celebrates female entrepreneurs. A perspective that once valorised "care" and interdependence now encourages individual advancement and meritocracy ... As women have poured into labour markets around the globe, state-organised capitalism's ideal of the family wage is being replaced by the newer, more modern norm — apparently sanctioned by feminism — of the two-earner family.' Fraser argues that as feminists, we need to push for the de-centring of waged work and a valuing of unwaged activities, including care work.

Putting care back in childcare

Improving things for children early on in life is critical if we are to support children's liberation. But for that to happen, we need to stop seeing children as a burden, and governments need to stop pitting the needs of children against the needs of their parents. Parents are having to make the choice between paying the bills and choosing childcare that allows their children to truly thrive, and this is not a problem individual parents can fix: it is a political choice, and we should be very angry about it.

In too many countries, children, early years educators, and parents are all treated poorly by a system increasingly focused on profit. The UK government's recent announcement on childcare was deeply disappointing, and the ongoing lack of movement on better maternity leave in the US continues to enact cruelty on new parents and their tiny babies. But for governments looking for some fresh thinking, there are some policies that — alone or combined — could radically change our systems of care for the better, for children and their parents:

1. Provide generous paid parental leave for all parents, ring-fencing some time for non-birthing parents and ensuring solo parents get an equivalent entitlement. The example set by the Nordic countries shows that this is possible — and it works.
2. Properly fund ECEC. 'The cost of "childcare" does not need

lowering,' writes Peter Moss, emeritus professor of early childhood provision at UCL's Institute of Education. 'It needs raising and raising substantially to tackle the scandal of a low-paid, low-qualified and low-status workforce, overwhelmingly women, who are part of a much larger marginalised "care" workforce. The question then is not how to lower "childcare" costs, but how to allocate higher costs between parents and government.'[33] In Sweden, where graduate pre-school teachers account for just over 40 per cent of the ECEC workforce and where early education is considered high quality, fees are capped at a low level (with the maximum payable around £120 per month for the first child).

3. Consider the radical possibilities of what early education could look like. Peter Moss argues that we could redesign early childhood education to centre democracy, experimentation, solidarity, and collaboration as fundamental values. He imagines creating multi-purpose spaces which not only provided a holistic education for young children, but also had space to run projects for families. Each centre would serve a local catchment area and, rather than being run for profit, would make up part of a universal offer alongside other free services such as healthcare and school. 'Where early childhood education has fallen into the market domain and become subject to capitalist relationships, it will be necessary to reclaim it for the public domain and inscribe it with democratic and solidaristic relationships.'[34]
4. Restore and defend child–staff ratios that support children's development and safety. Speaking about the UK government's plans to relax ratios from 1:4 to 1:5, CEO

of the Early Years Alliance Neil Leitch said 'The ignorance and short-sightedness that would lead anyone to suggest relaxing ratios as a solution to the problems our sector faces is frankly mind-boggling. Even a tiny minority of providers who feel they have no choice but to relax ratios could put the safety and wellbeing of young children at those settings at unacceptable risk.'[35]

5. Offer parents an in-home care allowance, where they can either choose to pay someone to look after their child or care for them themselves. Parents living in Finland can take this option; there are also day care settings available for parents who prefer this.
6. Allow parents to take longer periods of unpaid leave while requiring their jobs to be held open for them at the same job title and level of pay. Parents in Germany can have their roles held open for years, meaning that parents aren't penalised if they want to stay home to look after their children during the earliest years of their lives.
7. Bring in a Universal Basic Income, which would make choosing to work less while children are young a financially viable choice for more families, not just middle-class couples. At a time when more children than ever are experiencing the effects of poverty, this could be life-changing.
8. Consider bringing in a four-day week as widely as possible. Results from companies who have trialled it suggest workers are happier, healthier, and still get everything done in four days. The impact this would have on working parents (and their need for childcare) would be huge, and countries around the world — including Spain, Scotland, Japan, and New Zealand — have been considering trialling it.[36]

Most importantly, if we are to have a childcare system that truly works for children and their families, we need to stop seeing childcare as unimportant, low-skilled work — and to recognise children as valuable people and capable learners who have a right to a high standard of care, to thrive, and to feel safe and loved — wherever they are cared for. This should be within our grasp.

*

Even when it is radical and brilliant, childcare is not a magic wand that can solve children's problems — or fix societal ones. As long as we continue tolerating vast inequality, some children will continue to have very difficult lives. And just like childcare policies, this is a deliberate political choice.

CHAPTER SEVEN

Deliberate harm

'It's Dickensian, the kind of life some of these kids are living.' It's early on a grey Wednesday morning, and I'm chatting to Linda as I help her unload food from her van, which will later be handed out to families at one of London's many busy food banks. 'I bet you have memories of going to do the shopping with your mum when you were small, but these children, their memories are going to be of coming here and their parents being handed a bag. Some of them don't have access to laundry facilities or hot water or shower gel to have a wash, some of them don't have safe places to live. And what's awful is I can see it getting worse.'

From the moment the doors open there is a steady stream of people coming through. At the front desk, Linda chats to each person about what food they want, asking them to fill out a tick-box list where they can choose from basic items. The walls of the church hall where this food bank is based are lined with boxes of tinned and packaged food, all of which has been donated and then organised by volunteers. The standard parcel is meant to last for seven days, and includes food like tinned beans and soup, pasta, rice pudding, and tea bags. There are also bags of nappies, a selection of toiletries, period products, and sometimes treats like biscuits and Easter eggs. The system is smooth and efficient; while clients queue up and choose from any fresh or extra food, volunteers rush about behind the scenes making up parcels, whilst others sit labelling donations according to sell-by date and sorting them into categories. Nearby in a makeshift cubicle an advisor helps clients fill out forms for disability allowance and benefit claims, and there is an addiction nurse that works closely with the team.

Most of the clients visiting the food bank that morning are mothers. Jacki has brought her six-year-old daughter Lucy with her. Life has been challenging for them — they've had to move seven times in the last year to escape domestic violence, and Lucy has some recurring problems with her eyesight — but they have a new place to live, and Lucy is finally settling into life at a new school. 'I really like reading,' she tells me as she reaches for a packet of crackers, 'and my teacher is so kind.' Although life now feels calmer, there's little certainty when it comes to the future, and Jacki is deeply worried about the impact all this upheaval and stress is having on Lucy. 'I just want us to be able to settle down, you know? She's a good girl; it's what she deserves.'

Although the space looks well stocked, donations have trailed off significantly in the last couple of years due to Covid-19 and the rising cost of living. This is bad news, as demand has skyrocketed and shows no sign of slowing down. They are seeing more clients with disabilities, as well as more and more people who work but still can't make ends meet; they recently had to start opening on Saturdays so that they can meet the need of clients who work full time. The Trussell Trust, which runs food banks all over the UK just like the one Linda organises, has reported handing out almost three million emergency food parcels between 2022 and 2023, and over a million of these were for children.[1] How did we get to a point where families living in the world's sixth-most affluent country are having to turn to food donations to be able to feed their children?

Deliberate harm

As we have seen over the last six chapters, there is a lot that we can do as individuals to tackle adultism close to home. The impact that parenting and caring relationships have on children — particularly when it comes to building a culture of children's liberation — is not to be underestimated. But to focus solely on the impact of individual parents, caregivers, and educators on children's ability to thrive is to miss something important: the structural harm that is done to children through policy decisions which don't have their wellbeing in mind.

Worldwide, children are more than twice as likely to live in poverty than adults.[2] In a *Catch-22* scenario, children tend to be dependent on their parents' income, while parents find that having children affects their ability to earn and hold on to money. But while we may think of child poverty as something remote — only affecting those in low-income countries or an unlucky few whose parents have made poor decisions — this couldn't be further from reality. In the UK, 27 per cent of children are currently living in poverty.[3] That's eight children in a class of thirty, though this is not evenly distributed; some classrooms will be filled with children living in low-income households, whereas others will contain none. In Australia it's one in six children (16.6 per cent), which is similar to the US (17 per cent).[4]

Some children are at greater risk of poverty than others, both globally and within nations. Race, household size and structure, migration status, and disability all affect children's likelihood of financial insecurity. In the UK, almost half of children living in single-parent families experience poverty; BAME children also face a penalty, with 46 per cent living in poverty compared with 26 per cent of children in white British families.[5] Poverty is far more likely in families where one or more adults are disabled and is especially high where there are both disabled adults and children.[6]

Similar inequality is seen elsewhere. In Australia, most indicators of poverty and related disadvantage show that Indigenous people are between two and three times worse off than non-Indigenous people. About 30 per cent of Indigenous households are in income poverty.[7] In the US, the racial poverty gap is stark: while 11 per cent of white children are living in poverty, this rises to 24 per cent of Latinx children, and 25 per cent of Black children. Rates for Indigenous children are even higher, thought to be around 40 per cent.[8]

The UK, Australia, and the US are classed as high-income economies by the World Bank.[9] They all contain extreme wealth — there are well over 700 billionaires living in the US alone. And yet a 2020 report by UNICEF put all three in the bottom third of high-income countries when it came to childhood, observing that 'many of the wealthiest countries do not manage to convert good economic and social conditions into consistently high child wellbeing outcomes'.[10] All three countries also have high rates of children living in households that experience food insecurity, defined by one or more of the following:

- having smaller meals than usual or skipping meals due to being unable to afford or get access to food;

- being hungry but not eating due to being unable to afford or get access to food;
- not eating for a whole day due to being unable to afford or get access to food.[11]

As UN special rapporteur on extreme poverty and human rights, Philip Alston reported on poverty in the US in 2018. His findings were fiercely critical. 'The United States is a land of stark contrasts,' he wrote. 'It is one of the world's wealthiest societies ... but its immense wealth and expertise stand in shocking contrast with the conditions in which vast numbers of its citizens live.' He noted that about 5.3 million live in conditions of absolute poverty, saying 'its citizens live shorter and sicker lives compared to those living in all other rich democracies, eradicable tropical diseases are increasingly prevalent, and it has ... one of the highest rates of income inequality among Western countries.'[12]

This is something we should be outraged by. In a rich country, no child should be suffering because they are cold or hungry, or their shoes are too small. Yet, too often, headlines about parents struggling to put food on the table are met with the feeling that there's nothing that can be done, that some amount of poverty is to be expected and tolerated, or — worse — that families only have themselves to blame and that people shouldn't be having children if they can't afford to do so. So I want to be clear: child poverty and inequality are neither natural nor inevitable. They reflect political priorities and are impacted by government policy choices, not societal riches.

Alston, who wrote such a damming report on poverty in the US, also published a sobering take on the state of poverty in the UK.[13] His message was stark: the period of austerity ushered in by the Conservative-led government in 2010 had continued 'largely unabated, despite the tragic social consequences'. What were these consequences? The proliferation of food banks, like the one I visited. An increase in homelessness, with tens of thousands of low-income families living in inadequate housing and/or being housed far away from their schools, jobs, and communities. The decimation of the legal aid system, which provided vital access to justice for many. The axing of many social services, libraries being closed in record numbers, and fewer community and youth centres. Increased child poverty. Alston's conclusion was scathing: 'The bottom line is that much of the glue that has held British society together since the Second World War has been deliberately removed and replaced with a harsh and uncaring ethos. A booming economy, high employment and a budget surplus have not reversed austerity, a policy pursued more as an ideological than an economic agenda.'

Alston's recommendations went unheeded by the government; in fact, when he first read their response, he found it so ludicrous that he thought it was a spoof.[14] As Alston makes plain, in both the US and the UK, child poverty is not unavoidable but a product of systemic inequality and deliberate policy decisions. It is a political choice. And nowhere is this clearer than in the example of the UK's two-child benefits limit.

Adultism in action: The two-child limit

On the 25 June 2012, Prime Minister David Cameron stepped onto the podium at Bluewater Shopping Centre in Kent to deliver a blistering attack on the welfare state. Pitting fictional families against each other — a hospital-porter and care-worker who would like to have children but feel they should save up first, versus a couple 'down the road' with four children who haven't worked for a number of years yet get more money than their sensible neighbours — he argued that Britain had become a place where it paid to be unemployed, and that millions of working-age people were 'sitting at home on benefits' while hard-working people struggled to enable this 'culture of entitlement'. He continued: 'We have been encouraging working-age people to have children and not work ... isn't it right that we ask whether those in the welfare system are faced with the same kinds of decisions working people have to wrestle with when they have a child?'[15] No major policies were announced that day, but with his words Cameron was laying the ground for a devastating attack on low-income families — and their children.

The Conservative Party had come to power in 2010 by presenting itself as a party of fiscal responsibility. One of Cameron's key manifesto pledges was to take control of the economy through the 'tough love' of spending cuts — with emphasis on the tough. In 2015 Cameron's finance minister, George Osborne, announced a new policy as part of a package of austerity measures: the two-child benefit limit. Whereas previously families were entitled to claim state benefits for all their children, welfare payments would soon be limited to the first two children in a family.[16] This hit to families was delivered alongside a freeze in working-age benefits and a significant reduction in the overall benefits cap for families.[17] Osborne's budget — which penalised low-income families while sanctioning wealthier families to pass up to a million pounds on to their children free of inheritance tax — was not just about cost saving. It was ideological. To put it plainly: if you can't afford kids, don't have them, and if you do, don't expect us to pay for them.

Except, people do have them. Research has found that the policy led to only a small decline in the birth rate among those households directly affected.[18] Third and fourth children continue to be born into low-income families, it's just that they (and their siblings and parents) are now much worse off than they would have been had the change not come into force in 2017. The limit deprives families of close to £3,000 a year for each child born after their second, or around £56 per week — a lot of money if your family budget is already tight. But as anyone who has considered whether to start a family knows, the decision to have a child is never solely financial. And some parents will have children at a time when their financial situation is fine only to later require assistance — perhaps because they lose their job, become unwell or disabled, or have new caring responsibilities — by which point the children are already here.

Although many parents have continued to raise large families, the number of abortions in England and Wales has increased sharply since 2016, with the largest increase in women aged 30–34. The most recent figures show that a majority of women having abortions were already parents.[19] A 2020 study by the British Pregnancy Advisory Service (BPAS) found that among women who were aware of the two-child limit and likely to be affected, 57 per cent said that the policy was important in their decision-making around whether or not to continue the pregnancy (although it's worth noting that many parents were unaware of the changes until they tried to claim benefits for their child, which might account for the fact that overall the decline in birth rate was small).[20] Just as no one should be forced to continue with a pregnancy they don't want, it is sad to think of people terminating pregnancies that were otherwise wanted because of the two-child limit. This feels especially hard to swallow knowing that the policy was voted in by politicians who claim to be 'pro-life'.[21] It also raises questions around whether government policies that are so clearly tied to decisions to have children should be allowed at all; the fact that a lot of British people accepted the policy while having a dim view of China's one-child policy shows the cognitive dissonance on this subject.

It's no exaggeration to say that the effect of the two-child limit has been catastrophic. A 2022 report into the effects of the policy five years down the line found that it has become the biggest single driver of child poverty; another paper wrote that 'the two-child limit's main outcome is to drive financial hardship and often destitution'.[22] Around 1.4 million children and 400,000 families have been impacted by the limit, with over half of parents affected already working in low-paid jobs and relying on benefit payments to make ends meet, in part due to the staggering cost of childcare.[23]

The two-child limit is a perfect, if infuriating, example of how adultism and class-based prejudice can intersect to punish children simply for being born to parents with less money. The Child Poverty Action Group (CPAG) have estimated that removing the limit would immediately lift a quarter of a million children out of poverty, but as I write this neither of the two main political parties has announced any plans to change the limit, despite a Bill being brought forward to scrap the policy in 2022.[24] Not acting — keeping these children in poverty — is a deliberate political choice.

A culture of blame

Lauren Eve is the kind of teacher every parent hopes their child gets when the next year's classes are announced. Warm, funny, and kind, with bright red hair, she sees good teaching as crucial not just to children's education, but as a form of social justice. She's passionate about children's rights, and prides herself on building a classroom where the children in her care feel known, accepted, and celebrated for who they are, and where their behaviour isn't seen in isolation but is understood in the context of what's happening for them at home.

Lauren has spent her whole career working in primary schools that serve communities with high levels of deprivation and has seen first-hand the role that school can play in supporting children living in low-income families. But when I spoke to her about the impact Covid-19 and the UK's current economic crisis were having on schoolchildren, the picture she painted was unsettling. Due to underfunding, children needing a refuge from insecure or chaotic family lives are no longer finding school as welcoming as they might have done previously: it's physically colder, due to the higher cost of energy, the class sizes are bigger, and the teachers are under more stress, which in turn affects their relationships with the students. The school is no longer able to afford as many teaching assistants, a role that is often vital in supporting children with special educational needs or a disability to learn alongside their friends in the classroom. Lauren is seeing children with additional needs slipping through the cracks. Although some children are coming to school cold and hungry, they are still being taught an academically challenging curriculum that Lauren thinks is unrealistic. 'You might have a child come into school having experienced domestic violence, or living in an overcrowded home with no privacy, and they're being marked on whether or not they're including fronted adverbials in their writing. Some of them can't even spell their own names. We need to have high expectations for children, but the curriculum isn't meeting their needs.'

Lauren feels that her current school lacks a generosity of spirit when it comes to the families in their community, many of whom are having to choose between heating and eating. She has fresh fruit in her classroom for the children to eat, and some of the other teachers buy bagels for breakfast from their own wages. Lauren and her colleagues are not alone in supporting children out of their own pockets: in one poll of 18,000 teachers, almost 80 per cent said they or their school is providing help with uniforms to disadvantaged pupils, with 55 per cent providing free breakfasts, 58 per cent providing extra food during the day, and 31 per cent providing toiletries.[25] This comes at a time when many teachers are struggling to make ends meet themselves.

The last school Lauren worked in was an accredited Rights Respecting School (more on this in the next chapter), and this was evident in how the children were treated. Having built strong links with children's families to understand the challenges they faced, the school decided to offer all pupils free school meals rather than just those who would be eligible. By contrast, her current school doesn't seem to have the will or the capacity to give children the support they need. Things are so bad that, after working in schools for her whole career to date, when we spoke, Lauren had just decided to hand her notice in. One of the things that pushed her to resign was seeing a note on a child's file saying that they should only be given cold lunches until their mother settles their lunch bill. 'Nowhere is there an understanding that the child's mum probably isn't paying because she can't afford to do so. There is a culture of blame, where we see poverty as a personality flaw rather than what it is: state-sanctioned cruelty to children. We need systemic change, and schools can only do so much.'

This culture of blame is important in understanding how we've got to a point where children are coming to school hungry. The language of welfare benefits has been weaponised in political debate and in the media.[26] TV shows like *Benefits Street* helped to shape this narrative. The show, which was on air during 2014–15, documented the lives of residents living in a street where most of the residents were claiming welfare benefits. Described by some as 'poverty porn', the show received hundreds of complaints about its stigmatisation of low-income communities after it showed residents shoplifting, growing cannabis, purchasing drugs, and laughing about committing benefit fraud. (Cast members have since complained about being exploited.)[27] In this imagining, children are reduced to pawns in a game adults are playing to try to scam more money from the taxpayer's purse. The reality is often very different. Low-paid work is a huge problem; families where two adults earn the minimum wage are still falling well short of the income needed to raise a child.[28] Around two-thirds (68 per cent) of working-age adults in poverty live in a household where at least one adult is in work, so the idea that if people want to avoid poverty they can 'just go and get a job' is misleading.[29]

We need to remember that every time there is a decision to 'crack down' on benefit payments, children pay the price. And unlike adults, who could theoretically find better paid work (though the reality may be different), children cannot 'pull themselves' out of poverty. They are reliant on the adults around them. Thankfully, the public attitude to welfare in the UK seems slowly to be softening, perhaps due to the Covid-19 pandemic and the cost-of-living crisis, both of which have laid bare the vulnerabilities in our system as well as exacerbating them.[30]

All children need a soft place to land, and when their homes are damp, overcrowded, or unsafe, other places need to fill that gap. Funding issues combined with more children in need of support have meant that, as in Lauren's experience, many schools are not able to step in as much as children need. In the UK, it's now common to hear headteachers worrying about whether or not they can feed their students, or describing how they are unscrewing 'non-essential' lightbulbs or cancelling school trips to reduce costs.[31] Postcode lotteries are a factor, as state schools in more affluent areas will be able to raise more funds than those in underserved areas. And this lottery isn't limited to the UK: in the US, schools in predominantly white areas receive a staggering $23 billion more than those in non-white districts, further discriminating against children who are already more likely to suffer from racism, poverty, and community violence.[32] Meanwhile, in Australia, government funding for private schools has increased at nearly five times the rate of public school funding over the past ten years, despite predictions of a $74 billion shortfall in money for public schools this decade.[33]

Teachers and support staff are also experiencing difficulties in knowing how to help: many of the services that might have once supported children and their families have been shut down, or are so poorly funded that waiting lists are in the years rather than weeks. In the UK, the Sure Start Children's Centre programme, introduced in 1999 by a Labour government, has had its spending cut by two-thirds since 2010. Over 1,300 children's centres have since closed.[34] This is despite findings that by age 11 greater Sure

Start coverage (one more centre per thousand children aged 0–4) prevents around 5,500 hospitalisations per year.[35]

Equally if not more alarming is the reduction in funding for children's mental health services (CAMHS). While demand has sky-rocketed, funding has stagnated, and more and more children are being turned away despite acute need.[36] Health professionals I've spoken to cite a two-year waitlist for most children seeking help. Agnès Munday, head of training at suicide prevention charity Grassroots, told me that they regularly hear about children who had already attempted suicide being turned away because the services are so stretched, a claim backed up by research from *The House* magazine, which found that almost a quarter of a million children were left without treatment in 2022.[37] Agnès has worked with headteachers who are in tears because they have no way of supporting the children in their care who are self-harming. This is catastrophic, particularly in the wake of Covid-19, which had a brutal effect on children's mental health. This failure to provide necessary services to children is a form of violence. Children are dying because of it.

All these cuts to essential services are actively building a two-tier childhood, with those who have parents who can afford to keep them warm and fed and can pay for necessary support, and those whose parents are struggling to survive. The more the double safety net of welfare and services is worn down, the worse the consequences. And this is having a significant impact on children's lives and futures.

The impact of poverty

Poverty is bad for everyone, but a child experiences it threefold. Firstly, poverty affects their daily lives and experiences here and now, making life harder and more stressful. Secondly, it affects them long term and shapes their futures. Finally, it affects the adults in their lives, whose parenting, caregiving, and teaching abilities may suffer as a result. It's well documented that parental stress can have a negative impact on children; I know that when I feel stressed or worried, I'm much more likely to snap at my daughter or say something I later regret.[38] I can only imagine how much harder it would be to parent calmly and respectfully if I was coping with the long-term stress of struggling to make ends meet, living in a noisy, overcrowded, or dangerous home, juggling low-paid work with inflexible hours with caring responsibilities — or all of the above. I'm not suggesting for a second that parents on a low-income are not capable of raising their children in a manner which respects their rights. But at the same time, tackling adultism in our parenting and within our communities requires a certain amount of energy, time, and introspection, and this is going to be harder when basic needs around housing, food, and safety are not being met.

Expensive, inadequate, insufficient housing is both cause and effect of poverty. Many are trapped in a cycle where they pay more on rent than they would be spending on mortgage payments for the same property, yet they cannot get a mortgage because they don't have a deposit. Social housing, which in theory should be affordable to those who need it, is in short supply, and the quality of available accommodation is often poor. With long waitlists for suitable properties, many find themselves homeless or moved many miles from their schools, jobs, and communities. In her book *Tenants*, Vicky Spratt reports that at the start of 2021 there were 130,000 homeless children living in temporary accommodation in the UK. This might involve a family sharing a single room in a 'hostel', forced to share a bathroom and kitchen with multiple other residents, some of whom will pose a safety risk.[39] Due to the lack of social housing, the number of people in England's private rental sector has doubled over the past 20 years, and because the sector is so unregulated many landlords charge exorbitant amounts for damp, rundown, and uncomfortable housing.

Poor housing can have a very real impact on children's physical health. In 2020, two-year-old Awaab Ishak died from a respiratory condition caused by exposure to mould, despite his father repeatedly raising the issue with the housing association who owned their flat. 'How in the UK in 2020 does a child die as a result of exposure to mould?' asked the coroner reporting on Awaab's death. How indeed. Children have a right to the highest possible standard of health (Article 24) and we know that living in damp or overcrowded conditions is a risk factor for respiratory problems and mental health conditions, yet there is little accountability for housing providers who rent out unsafe properties.[40] Low-quality housing also impacts on children's education, as they are less likely to have somewhere quiet to study, more likely to miss school due to ill health, and more likely to face disruption to their education caused by moving into and between temporary accommodation. Internet access can be a problem, too, with some children resorting to doing homework in branches of McDonald's in order to benefit from the free Wi-Fi.[41] During the Covid-19 crisis, private companies stepped in to offer free internet access to families. Perhaps a similar system could be implemented now.

Getting adequate nutrition is a problem, too. Although food banks are doing their best to plug the gap, there is more demand than they can cope with. Figures from the Food Foundation show that one in four households with children experienced food insecurity in September 2022, affecting around four million children in the UK.[42] Heartbreaking stories have been reported of children pretending to eat from empty lunchboxes at school, and even eating their school erasers because they are so hungry.[43] A recent open letter, signed by clinicians and health experts, has called for a major expansion of free school meals to combat the growing risk of malnutrition and other health conditions affecting children worst hit by the cost-of-living crisis. Footballer and anti-poverty activist Marcus Rashford has similarly called upon the government to expand free school meals and provide meals and activities during school holidays, as well as increasing the value of Healthy Start vouchers given to families with babies and young children.

Extending free schools meals to all children, as well as providing breakfast, would go a long way in tackling the growing malnutrition that some family doctors are reporting.[44] This would be an easy win: research from the Institute of Fiscal Studies has found that providing school breakfasts to disadvantaged children helps pupils to make two months' additional progress over the course of a year, at relatively low cost.[45] Many countries, including India, Brazil, Estonia, and Finland already offer free school meals to every child, and there are welcome developments on this front: the US state of Minnesota recently passed a Bill that means that all students, regardless of income requirements, will get free breakfast and lunch, and the Mayor of London made free meals available to all primary aged children for a year to help families with the pressures of rising costs. When asked about their experiences of breakfast club, children are positive: 'I have something to look forward to in the morning,' said one pupil. 'You won't be hungry for the rest of the day,' said another.[46]

The effects of poverty play out on children's bodies: their teeth, their health, their life-expectancy. Family income even has an impact on brain development, with research finding that infants from low-income families developed lower volumes of grey matter, used for processing information and executing of actions. Differences in brain growth were also found to vary with socioeconomic status, with children from lower-income households having slower trajectories of growth during infancy and early childhood.[47] And the effects of poverty aren't solely physical: living with insufficient money is associated with greater shame, stigma, and chronic stress.

Punished for being poor

Although no one likes to admit it, poverty is a factor in whether children are taken into care when things go wrong, and whether they can stay with family members once removed from home. In her book *Behind Closed Doors*, journalist Polly Curtis writes that 'In a country without the death penalty, separating a child from their parents is arguably the most draconian power the state has to intervene in our lives'. Yet, when Curtis was writing her book, experts estimated that out of the 80,000 children in care in England, around 27,000 could have stayed with their families if they had access to the right support — a heartbreaking statistic, and one which violates children's right to not be separated from their parents unless necessary for their best interests (Article 9).[48]

Deprivation is the single biggest risk factor in a child going into care, with children living in the poorest areas ten times more likely to be taken into care than those living in the wealthiest.[49] Recent research has found that the rise in child poverty from 2015 was associated with over ten thousand additional children entering care.[50]

The overrepresentation of low-income children in the care system is not unique to the UK. In *Torn Apart*, Dorothy Roberts sets out how the vast majority of — predominantly Black — families subjected to child protection investigations in the US have low incomes or are living in poverty. 'Based on state child neglect laws, the investigators interpret conditions of poverty — lack of food, insecure housing, inadequate medical care — as evidence of parental unfitness.' This has horrific consequences for children and their communities, with more than one in ten Black children in America forcibly separated from their parents and placed in foster care by the time they reach 18. Rather than being genuinely protective or caring, she argues, child protection agencies 'respond inadequately and inhumanely to the effects of our society's abysmal failure to care *enough* about children's welfare. Far from promoting the well-being of children, the state weaponises children as a way to threaten families, to scapegoat parents for societal harms to their children, and to buttress the racist, patriarchal, and capitalist status-quo.'[51]

In Australia things are similarly grim. Nearly one in 16 Aboriginal and Torres Strait Islander children is placed in out-of-home care — ten times more than their non-Aboriginal peers.[52] Rather than improving, this number has increased over the last ten years, although in 2020 the National Agreement on Closing the Gap was signed, which includes a target to reduce the rate of over-representation of Aboriginal and Torres Strait Islander children in out-of-home care by 45 per cent.[53] Despite the importance of culture and community to indigenous Australian children, the majority of them in out-of-home care were placed with non-indigenous carers.

What's going on? It's important to realise that this is happening within a landscape where parents cannot easily access support in the community for the three things — or 'toxic trio' — which have long been associated with children going into care: substance abuse, domestic violence, and mental illness. In the UK, well-documented funding cuts across drug and alcohol services, domestic violence services and refuges, and mental health services have made it increasingly hard to get help. If you're a parent on a low income, you're much less likely to be able to self-fund the detox, rehab, therapy, or mental health support needed for substance abuse or mental illness. Although anyone can experience addiction or mental illness, those living in low-income communities are at higher risk.[54] Women in households with low incomes are also three and a half times more likely to experience domestic violence than women in slightly better-off households. The reasons for this include a reduced capacity to flee as well as increased exposure to stressors. Even if children are not being physically harmed themselves, witnessing a parent's abuse is now classed as experiencing domestic violence, and although it seems unfair, parents (usually mothers) are judged by social workers on whether or not they are able to protect their children from this abuse.[55]

I wanted to hear more about these issues from a social worker who is grappling with these things every day, so I spoke to Emily, a children's social worker in the south east of England.

> All of the families I work with are low-income families, and they all struggle with housing in some way, which is a huge problem as there's just so little we can do to help them. I've been in situations where I'm supporting mothers who are fleeing domestic violence but there's no housing available to keep them and their children away from perpetrators, so they end up in temporary accommodation, which is totally unsuitable for families, or in refuges, which can be quite chaotic. And then as a social worker you worry that they can't keep their children safe, or provide adequate levels of care, but if we could provide them with a flat and more money then these problems would at least be de-escalated from a crisis situation. There's a problem with stigma too, and the way low-income families are portrayed in the media. People think they're lazy or undeserving and that it's their fault if they're in a bad situation, and I really think that the funding of services and service provision available to them reflects this. Support for these families needs to start much earlier if they're to have a chance so that they don't get to the point where we have to step in.

Emily is seeing the impact of something Curtis reports on in *Behind Closed Doors*: since austerity began in the UK, funding has shifted from preventative help, which might give families a chance of staying together, to money spent on statutory services like court cases, lawyers, and the care system. Social workers have access to fewer resources to help families get back on their feet and are increasingly doing crisis work rather than providing the deep support that could be the difference between a child being removed from home or not. More funding for early interventions might also help overworked social workers pick up on cases where things are seriously wrong, keeping children safe from terrible harm that might otherwise have been missed. Across the ocean, the US spends billions on policing families and removing children from their parents: that money could be used instead to fund and invest in communities, including investment in early childhood education, mentorship programmes, well-paid jobs, affordable housing, free mental health care, robust public education, arts, and after-school programmes.[56] Taking children into care is not a neutral action; separating children from their parents is deeply traumatic for everyone involved and causes irreparable harm. It isn't a decision to be made lightly — especially when there are other solutions.

Getting money into the pockets of those who need it

Families should be assisted by governments, and children have the right to an adequate standard of living (Article 27). Ensuring that parents can support their families — whether they are in work or not — should be a top priority. As we have seen, having a job does not guarantee that a parent will be able to avoid poverty for themselves and their family, in part due to challenging childcare costs and increased caring responsibilities, but also because of the difficulty in finding well-paid work in the current climate.

One solution would be to provide every person with a living income, a Universal Basic Income (UBI), no matter their employment status, an idea that is gaining traction with many trials and pilots around the world. These grants, delivered like a monthly wage, would provide everyone with enough to live a decent life, with parents as the custodians of grants for their children until a certain age. Payments would be unconditional: they would not depend on the recipient's ability to earn money, or on the income of the people they live with (current benefits are often conditional on the income of the spouse or parents), or on any other criteria such as means-testing.[57]

One example in particular suggests that UBI would have a positive impact on children: in 1996, the Cherokee of North Carolina opened a casino and voted to share some of the profits equally among tribe members, effectively creating a sample group for UBI within the local population. The benefits of this cash injection quickly became clear: the number of Cherokee living below the poverty line declined by half, the frequency of 'behavioural problems' in children reduced by 40 per cent, and children were roughly one-third less likely to develop substance abuse and psychiatric problems in adulthood. Researchers found that the earlier in life children's families received payment, the bigger the impact on them.[58]

UBI may sound extreme to some, and it doesn't address the root causes of inequality and low pay, though I still think it's worth exploring further. But there are other ways of getting money into the pockets of families who need it the most. CPAG estimate that the cost of having a child in primary school is around £19 per day, rising to £39 per day in secondary school, a figure comprised of the cost of uniforms, learning materials, school trips, packed lunch or canteen money, and transport.[59] School uniforms in particular can cause enormous stress for families, with some going into debt or skipping meals just so they could buy expensive (and compulsory) blazers and bags.[60] Countries including France and Scotland have grants for parents on low incomes to help them cover school expenses; these could be increased and made more widely available. Alternately, school uniforms, meals, transport, and learning materials could be given to all children freely at the point of need, especially as most children can't choose whether to attend school or not. If we are going to make children attend, it feels only right that we should give them what they need to do so.

But do we need to go even further and give children their own money? Shulamith Firestone writes that 'the oppression of children is most of all rooted in economic dependence'.[61] Most children, particularly those who are very young, are financially totally dependent on adults. As I have already discussed, children experience higher rates of poverty than adults, and not having access to money deepens this inequality. If we are going to push for UBI, perhaps we need to make it truly universal, including giving children funds of their own. Scotland, Wales, and Northern Ireland all offer an Education Maintenance Allowance of up to £160 a month to young people aged 16–19 to help them stay in education (David Cameron scrapped the scheme in England, triggering strong resistance in the form of widespread youth protests).[62] This helps to pay for transport to and from college, food, clothes, books, study equipment, and trips. Although this is a means-tested payment, it's a great example of how we could get more money directly into the hands of children.

It might sound radical to suggest that children should have their own money, but let's not forget that it wasn't until the late 20th century that women could open a bank account in their own name. Giving more money directly to children would bring lots of complexity — would children then be expected to pay rent, or contribute to bills? Would it increase disparity between children living in high-income families and their less well-off counterparts? Could it open up children to financial abuse? — but I'd be interested to see more discussion of the idea. We could also end the adultist discrepancies in minimum wages that see those aged 23 and over entitled to at least £10.42 per hour while under-18s can legally be paid as little as £5.28.[63] I'm sure that many readers will know the liberating feeling of having a job as a teenager — why should teens be paid less for doing the same work (and why, when we talk about the gender or race pay-gap, does no one seem to care about the children and young adults who are similarly exploited)?

To equalise the playing field once children enter adulthood, we could also consider embracing a scheme like that proposed by Spain's labour minister, Yolanda Díaz. To tackle social inequality, Díaz believes Spain should give every young person in the country €20,000 (£17,000) to be spent on study, training, or setting up a business once they reach the age of 18. This 'universal inheritance' would be funded by raising taxes for top earners, and would give young adults from lower-income families a much needed boost.[64]

Changing the conversation

There is much that needs to change if we are to finally live up to our moral responsibility of ensuring that no child goes hungry, and the issue is more complicated than I can do justice to here. But if I were granted three wishes with which to tackle child poverty, I would probably pick these:

1. A liveable income for all, including free access to medical care;

2. Safe, stable, and affordable housing for all;
3. Generously funded children's services, including mental health services, family centres, and childcare.

Though it would be great if world leaders and deep-pocketed philanthropists read this book (if you know any, please feel free to pass on a copy), my assumption as I write this is that you probably can't personally do very much to make my wishes come true. Some of you might be experiencing poverty yourselves right now. This is why we all need to be voting carefully — scrutinising what political parties have to say about housing, welfare, school funding, and children's mental health services while keeping the most vulnerable children in mind — as well as taking time to lobby political representatives. Our politicians can act, should they wish to, and the more pressure they feel to do so, the better.

Short of tackling the problem at the root, we can support local campaigns and grassroots organisations working to alleviate the effects of damaging policies. Donations of time, goods, and money, if any of this feels possible, will surely be appreciated by those running food, clothing, toy, furniture, and hygiene banks; in the absence of political leadership, many parents rely on these acts of goodwill to keep their families fed and clothed. (One of the saddest statistics I read recently is that in some areas of the UK, Calpol — a children's painkiller — is the most shoplifted product from stores.)[65]

Perhaps the most important thing we can do — which is happily also the cheapest and least time-consuming — is to be intentional about challenging the stigma and misconceptions that surround poverty and state welfare. We need to change the conversation. As you've been reading this chapter, perhaps you have noticed that I've tried to avoid using the word 'poor' when describing children living in low-income families. This is for two reasons. One is that 'low-income' simply describes a fact, whereas the word 'poor' carries many connotations, most of them unkind or stereotypical. The other is that, writing as someone who grew up in a low-income household, I would not describe my childhood as an impoverished one. Although it's true that my parents didn't have much money and I had to do without many of the things my peers enjoyed (I still remember feeling sad because of missing out on school trips we couldn't afford), it was still a rich childhood filled with books from the library, daily trips to the park and seafront, stories, music, and lots of love.

Part of changing the conversation is paying attention to the books and media we share with children, pointing out harmful stereotypes and looking for greater representation and diversity. When my daughter was at the age of reading picture books, it was noticeable how many were set in typically middle-class homes with two parents, a garden, and separate bedrooms — a very different set-up to the one-bedroom flat I shared with my parents and brother when I was her age.

It's never too early to talk to children about things like poverty and why it exists. Even if we have the privilege of being able to 'shelter' the children in our lives from these conversations they will still notice unhoused people on the street or the fact that some of their classmates never have a warm coat in winter. Talk to them about why it's important not to judge people on their clothes or whether they've got the latest gadgets. If you're in a position of not having to worry much about money, be mindful when planning group activities for your child and their friends so that children from low-income families aren't excluded. If you're inviting a friend swimming or to the cinema, is there an expectation that they will pay — and if so, are you confident they can do so? If you're planning a birthday party for your child, is it easily accessible by public transport? Will children need any special sort of equipment, clothing, or experience, to take part?

Sadly, school can be a place where children feel excluded and left out. If your school takes part in lots of non-uniform or fancy-dress days, can you write to the leadership team asking them to reconsider? CPAG found that children sometimes feel embarrassed and left out by the costs of taking part in these days, and by the pressure they feel to have fashionable clothes and shoes. In some cases, teachers reported that pupils from low-income families were missing school on these days. These don't need to be scrapped altogether, but schools should consider how frequent they are and how they can ensure all pupils can take part. Rather than non-uniform days, some schools have 'wear odd-socks' days. Events like school discos could be switched to voluntary payments, with donations taken before the event so children aren't put on the spot when an envelope gets passed around the class. Where these changes have been made, children notice: 'It's pretty anonymous at my school,' said one 12-year-old. 'Nobody needs to know if you haven't donated.'[66]

Teachers also have a role to play in ensuring children from low-income families feel included in class activities and conversations. After the school holidays, especially Christmas, rather than asking children about the presents they received or prompting them to discuss what they did over the break, they could instead offer other activities to settle back in. Some children will not have had a happy time and may feel jealous and embarrassed listening to their peers talk about their holidays.

*

When it comes to changing the conversation, individuals are only part of the picture. Children need an education system that actively disrupts inequality rather than trapping low-income children in cycles of poverty. They need an education system that challenges the rampant individualism and adultism which have contributed so much to child poverty and to the systemic harm children face. And they need an education system that provides all children with a safe and nurturing place to learn — particularly those who experience difficult and stressful home lives — rather than adding to their stress and unhappiness. It's this we'll turn our attention to next.

CHAPTER EIGHT

What we learn from school

I'd like you to imagine three 11-year-old children, who are all in the same class at a school.

Sophie is strong academically and gets top grades without really trying. Because the work tends to be below her level of ability, she's often bored and gets told off for talking and distracting her classmates. Her parents are frustrated that her teachers aren't doing more to push her to develop her abilities, but she likes going to school and seeing her friends.

Abdul is a refugee, who joined the school three months ago after his family fled Afghanistan. Although he likes his teacher, he finds the noise and chaos of school overwhelming, especially at lunchtime. He's still learning English so much of what's being taught doesn't really make sense to him, though he tries his best.

Joe's home life is chaotic. His family have recently been made homeless so he's living in temporary accommodation with his mum and brother, and his dad is in prison. He often comes to class hungry and tired. A lot of the schoolwork feels pointless or too difficult, and he knows he's behind his classmates. He struggles to make friends, often 'acts up' in class, and has just been suspended for three days after kicking another pupil.

Sophie, Joe, and Abdul all have a right to education. It's a right enshrined in international declarations and conventions, and arguably it's a fundamental right. We would find it difficult to fully participate in society, let alone lead dignified and fulfilling lives, without a certain level of education. But is their right being met? And even though they're all sitting in the same classroom, are they all getting the same education?

Rights respecting schools?

Every day teachers stand up in front of children with vastly different needs, abilities, and backgrounds and do their best to teach a challenging curriculum. There is no doubt that for some children, school plays a positive role in their lives; schools can be places where children develop deep friendships, feel a sense of community, and grow in independence away from the family home. Schools also offer certain welfare structures in the absence of other state support, for example by feeding children who might otherwise go hungry, providing free childcare for working parents, and delivering routine vaccinations and wellbeing checks. Many teachers care deeply about their students and are committed to the wellbeing of the children in their care, going above and beyond their paygrade to act all at once as teacher, social worker, nurse, and citizen's advice bureau on any given day.

Some schools have decided to go one step further and affirm their commitment to children's rights by undertaking UNICEF's Rights Respecting Schools Award, which supports schools to embed children's rights across every aspect of school life. In these schools, children are taught about their rights and given the language to describe and advocate for them. Their teachers report feeling more respected in their jobs and enjoying more freedom to teach in their own way.

So far, so good. But UNICEF's figures show that out of roughly 32,000 UK schools, just 5,000 are involved in the Rights Respecting Schools Award, with fewer than a thousand achieving the gold standard and receiving full accreditation.[1] Almost all of these are primary schools, serving children up to age 11; ironically, the older children get, the less we seem to be interested in their rights. If only a small fraction of schools can be said to be rights-respecting, by default does this not mean that the rest are not?

Unfortunately, this is too often the case. Schools can and do function as places where children's voices, needs, and desires are shut down. Under Article 12 of the CRC, children have a right to express their views, feelings, and wishes in all matters affecting them, and to have these views taken seriously. But the majority of schools have no formal mechanisms for pupils' views to be taken into account, far less for them to influence meaningful change. Learning is top down: the teacher tells you what you will learn today, and you must do it. 'One of the philosophically most important distinctions between education and schooling,' writes Harvard Professor of Philosophy Gina Schouten, 'is that schooling as we know it is pervasively coercive ... Schooling coerces children into learning certain things and becoming certain sorts of people. It occupies hundreds of hours of children's lives, whether they want it to or not.'[2] Coercion is baked into the system: when you have one teacher and 30 children in a class, all of whom will have different needs and abilities, how else do you get everyone to show up, follow a specific timetable, and obey adult instructions? Most schools purposefully foster a culture of compliance and obedience where those with less power must obey those with more power — or face the consequences. The system of compulsory education also coerces parents, as it constrains their ability to dictate the terms of their children's education, with many parents given no choice but to send their children into a system whose values and methods they disagree with.

French philosopher Michel Foucault argued that certain techniques — such as ranking school children, controlling their activities through timetables, and insistence on a specific type of physical comportment — are used to produce 'docile' bodies to be 'manipulated by authority, rather than imbued with animal spirits'.[3] Behaviour management techniques including punishments and rewards are an important part of creating docile bodies, as the threat or promise of them works as a constant pressure that acts before the child decides to act a certain way, encouraging them to internalise this obedience to authority. Behaviour management: the clue is in the (deeply adultist) name.

And what of these behaviour management techniques? Article 28 states that school discipline should be administered in a 'manner consistent with the child's human rights and dignity'. Yet many schools around the world still use corporal punishment, which remains legal in 19 US states. (In 1977, the US Supreme Court found that the Eighth Amendment — which prohibits cruel and unusual punishment — did not apply to school students.)[4] Thankfully, most educational institutions no longer beat children. But does this mean that school discipline is consistent with children's dignity? Many schools still use traditional techniques based on shame and coercion: public shaming; loss of break time (despite children's right to play); loss of 'privileges' such as going on school outings or being allowed to play with special games, crafts, or equipment; isolation; detentions; shouting; and suspensions and exclusions. These common behaviour modification techniques are built into an education system that sees children's behaviour as something which can be divorced from their needs or their worries — and they actively reinforce the power imbalance between teacher and student.

Some schools are doubling down on this, enforcing a zero-tolerance approach to behaviour. I visited the Michaela School, dubbed the 'strictest school in Britain', which issues detentions for forgetting to bring a pen, talking in corridors, slouching in lessons, or not looking at the teacher quickly enough. Internal exclusions — where children have to sit apart from peers — can be handed out for wearing the wrong uniform or having a haircut which doesn't meet the guidelines. The children are tested weekly, and in some classes those who don't do well have their names up on the whiteboard for all to see. The rules are so extreme that before joining the school pupils undergo a 'bootcamp' to help them get used to the expectations. Supporters of this kind of school point to the excellent exam results achieved by the children who attend. But isn't school about more than just grades? We would not tolerate this treatment in any other aspect of our lives — why should we force it onto children?

Although not all schools are as strict as this, most mainstream classroom management systems use a mixture of rewards and punishments. At the most extreme end of school punishments are exclusions, which can be either fixed-term or permanent.[5] Exclusion rates are higher for boys, for children eligible for free school meals (FSM), for children with special educational needs, and for children from certain ethnic backgrounds including those from Caribbean and Gypsy or Roma families. Young people who are excluded are more likely to have behavioural difficulties, trouble with peers, and attention difficulties, with lower scores for positive wellbeing, emotional strengths, and support networks. Their behaviour in the classroom may be 'challenging', but these children are facing challenges themselves; to exclude them feels like we are telling them that there's no hope for them.

No More Exclusions is a Black-led, abolitionist coalition movement in the UK that highlights the voices and experiences of children and young people who have endured oppressive education and exclusion. 'We believe that school exclusions form part of a continuum of state violence enacted against communities racialised as Black, brown, Muslim and Gypsy, Roma, Traveller, against disabled people and against working-class communities,' they write. 'School exclusions are a form of drastic disciplinary action that remove children from the classroom and, too often, from education altogether. The most serious of these disciplinary measures turf young people out of their school communities and stigmatise them, just as they are building their identities. Others penalise and often humiliate children and young people for the difficulties they face, magnifying inequalities rather than trying to alleviate them, and treating already marginalised young people as disposable.'[6] They are calling for school exclusions to be abolished, along with the multiple other forms of internal and informal exclusion currently used to discipline pupils within schools including 'isolation booths', where children can spend all day, sometimes for multiple days, alone.

Some schools have voluntarily chosen to end exclusions and take a radically different approach to supporting their students.

Wellspring Academy Trust, which runs 25 schools in the UK, approaches behaviour by drawing on the psychological concept of unconditional positive regard, seeing each child is seen as inherently good and worthy of nurturing and care. The trust has even set up its own training branch where they work with other schools to help them use a model of relational practice and positive behaviour support to repair relationships, build trust, and decrease the signs of stress in children and young people. Since it was set up in 2013, the trust has not excluded a single pupil.[7] In London, the Inclusive and Nurturing Schools programme has been set up to help support children who might otherwise be at risk of being excluded, providing them with support for social, emotional, and mental health difficulties they might be experiencing and helping them feel like they belong. These are positive changes, but there remain issues. Whether or not a pupil is excluded shouldn't come down to the postcode lottery of the types of schools available locally. Treating children with respect and learning alternative methods of supporting the 'challenging' children who need more connection, safety, and support should be embedded into teacher training from the beginning, not left as a voluntary add-on.

Thriving – or surviving?

Even when behaviour policies are gentler, schools are often not set up in a way that supports children to thrive. Despite children's right to the best possible health (Article 24), insufficient opportunities for movement, lack of access to nature, strip lighting instead of natural light, long days, poor-quality food, and not enough sleep all mix to create an unhealthy environment. Rather than encouraging children to rest if they're unwell or exhausted, many schools enact ableist attendance policies that reward children for coming in every day. Worse, some actively penalise children for lower attendance, by stopping them from attending school trips or enjoying the rewards their healthier peers enjoyed. One mother I spoke to told me that her son's school — which cares for profoundly disabled and medically vulnerable children — still hands out attendance awards, despite many of the pupils coping with life-limiting conditions and spending long periods of time in and out of hospital.

Children are also unhappy with how their bodily autonomy is denied and controlled, with access to toilets being a recurring theme in my conversations with parents and children. I spoke to Freddie, age 11, who has been working with his mum to try and change his school's policy; currently, it's up to individual teachers whether they allow children to use the toilet during class, something that has caused him and his friends a lot of stress. Similarly, one mother told me how her young daughter had been told off for taking too long on the toilet, and was now terrified of having to poo at school and increasingly anxious about how much food she was eating. Restriction to toilets can also cause embarrassment and shame for students who are on their period. Children are not passive victims in this, though. Whenever there is excessive adult power we find children's resistance, and in 2023 children at schools across England protested draconian rules restricting toilet use.[8] But should we really be in this situation in the first place?

School rules on eating can be another problem, with many children not allowed to eat or drink when they are hungry or thirsty, having to wait for break times, or not getting enough food throughout the day. Requirements or incentives for children to eat everything on their plate in order to leave the lunch table can also go against children's body autonomy, removing their ability to stop eating once full up. Even when this isn't forced, there can still be subtle coercion: one parent told me about how lunchtime helpers at her child's school had been giving out 'clean plate' stickers to children who ate all their lunch. It didn't sit well with some of the parents, and they grouped together to speak to the school, explaining why they were unhappy with children being rewarded for eating more. Happily, the school changed their approach and now encourage students to 'listen to their tummies' instead.

Children's mental health can also be seriously affected by school. Widespread bullying has a significant impact on how happy children feel, yet few schools have been able to take effective measures to put an end to it. In the US, about 20 per cent of 12–18 year olds report being bullied, and in Australia, 70 per cent of children aged 12–13 had experienced 'bullying-like behaviour' in the last year, with almost half of those who had experienced bullying also bullying themselves.[9] Although we tend to think of this as a natural part of childhood, it is not; rather, it is exacerbated by the nature of institutions such as traditional schools, with set hierarchies, timetables, rules, and entrenched power structures. This is why we also find high levels of bullying in prisons, the army, and other similar institutions. Meanwhile, in the UK a recent review found sexist name-calling and sexual harassment and abuse was rife in schools and colleges, with 79 per cent of girls saying sexual assault was common in their friendship group.[10] Far from schools protecting children's rights, in many cases schools can become spaces where those rights are actively violated. And in the US, the threat of school shootings — and the need for active shooter drills where children learn what to do if someone enters their classroom with a gun — terrifies and traumatises children, teachers, and parents alike.

Racism and education

Children are not the only bullies at school. Studies have shown that Black children are discriminated against by their teachers from the time they are in preschool. Figures from the US show that half of the preschool students who were suspended or expelled in 2021 were Black boys, even though they only represent about a fifth of enrolled children.[11] To try and explain why Black boys were being kicked out of preschool at such high rates, research was carried out by Yale University, which primed participants to expect challenging behaviours while watching a video of preschoolers, balanced by sex and race, engaging in typical activities, as the participants' eye gazes were tracked. Although there was in fact no challenging behaviour on the video shown, the participants — all of whom were early years educators — gazed longer at the Black children, especially the boy.[12] The researchers put this down to implicit bias: the automatic and unconscious stereotypes that drive people to behave and make decisions in certain ways.

The bias does not end in preschool. As recently as the sixties and seventies, Black children in the UK were labelled 'educationally subnormal' and sent to special schools for no reason other than racism (as depicted in Steve McQueen's heartbreaking — and hopeful — film *Education*).[13] Although no school would actively admit to being racist, the statistics tell a different story. Between 2016 and 2021, over 60,000 racist incidents were recorded in UK schools.[14] A 2020 study found that virtually all Black young people had witnessed racist language in education, with over half feeling that racism is the largest hurdle to academic attainment and half saying that teacher perceptions are the biggest barrier to educational success.[15] This racism can have devastating consequences for children. In the US, 'zero tolerance' policies in schools have drastically increased the number of expelled or suspended pupils (with Black children missing five times as much school due to suspension as their white counterparts) and created what is known as the 'school-to-prison-pipeline', which causes a disproportionate number of students of colour to drop out of — or be expelled from — school and enter the criminal justice system.[16]

This is surely exacerbated by the lack of Black teachers and headteachers in education. In *I Heard What You Said*, Jeffrey Boakye writes of his experience of being a Black teacher in the UK: 'There are a number of routes into teaching, and none of them offer focused training on structural racism, unconscious bias, or representation.' For Boakye, being a non-white teacher is an inherently political act within a system that 'force-feeds whiteness and masculinity' to children.[17] This structural racism in schools also plays out in Black children being excluded from school for 'inappropriate' natural hairstyles, like Australian sisters Safhira and Amayah Rowe, who were sent home from school in rural Victoria after refusing to wear their braided hair tied back, and British schoolgirl Ruby Williams, sent home for wearing her hair in an afro.[18]

It would be wrong to paint children as silent victims of racism: children spot racism, name it, and often resist it. In 2021, hundreds of students staged a protest outside a London secondary school over allegations of racism amid changes to the curriculum, its uniform and hairstyle policy, and the placement of a union flag outside the building. Students made several demands, including an end to discriminatory policies and introducing efforts to make students from Black and minority ethnic backgrounds feel more welcome. This paid off: the flag was removed, and the school promised to make further changes in the following months.[19]

Parents can get involved with pushing for change too. I spoke to Nic, a mother to two mixed-race children, and she told me how impressed she was with how her children's school responded to criticisms that came out of the Black Lives Matter movement in 2020. The school have embraced an anti-racism agenda, amending their existing curriculum, strengthening their policies around racist incidents, and seeking guidance from outside agencies to support staff, students, and families. 'As a mixed heritage family, it has been heartening to see the changes they've made, and our kids' pride in their Nigerian heritage has grown. They regularly take Nigerian food to school in their lunch boxes and my husband views this with amazement because he could never have done the same when he was a child.' Some of the changes the school made were relatively simple — using more varied examples of ancient civilisations, learning about Black Romans — showing that a large impact can be made without having to find more money in increasingly tight budgets.

The evaluative gaze

To be at school is to be more or less constantly surveilled, ranked, and graded, from the CCTV cameras that line the corridors of some schools to the regular tests and exams children sit. Education writer and proponent of self-directed education (SDE)

Carol Black has noted the various effects of the 'evaluative gaze' of school:

> Some children eagerly display themselves for it; some try to make themselves invisible to it. They fight, they flee, they freeze; like prey animals they let their bodies go limp and passive before it. Some defy it by laughing in its face, by acting up, clowning around, refusing to attend or engage, refusing to try so you can never say they failed. Some master the art of holding back that last 10%, of giving just enough of themselves to 'succeed,' but holding back enough that the gaze can't define them (they don't yet know that this strategy will define and limit their lives). Some make themselves sick trying to meet or exceed the 'standards' that it sets for them. Some simply vanish into those standards until they don't know who they would have been had the standards not been set.[20]

Being evaluated — formally and informally — is stressful. One former teacher told me that one of her main motivations for leaving the profession and home educating her own children was seeing six- and seven-year-olds who required mental health support for anxiety over their upcoming exams. We assume that exams are vital components of children's education, but they are not. Like so many of the things we do to children, exams are a deliberate choice. The Finnish education system, recognised as one of the best in the world, has no standardised testing apart from an exam students take upon leaving high school to qualify for entry into university. Student progress is monitored through classroom assessment and termly evaluations where they receive a report from their teachers.[21]

But it's not just through exams that we assess children. Children are regularly assessed on their progress in reading, writing, and maths, along with a comment on their behaviour in class. Through testing, marking, and grading, children's intellects — or at least, whatever part of it was being measured — are ranked alongside those of their peers, and later on in school this might even affect which grades they could hope to achieve in certain subjects (in the UK it's common for children in 'lower ability' groups to be put forward for simplified 'foundation' GCSE exams, where the highest grade they can receive is a five rather than a nine).

Even when ability sets are given cute names — cherry class, or pine table — children know which group they are placed in, and how this compares to their peers. Mohammed, 12, told me plainly: 'The top group is where all the smart kids are, and the bottom group is for the most stupid ones. No one wants to be in the bottom group, but if you work really hard you can get moved up.' This 'setting' of children occurs despite research showing that, while the pupils in top sets may do better from being separated, the reverse is true for those in lower sets.[22]

Bringing their work home

Psychologist and advocate of self-directed learning Peter Gray writes that 'children now often spend more time at school and on homework than their parents spend at their full-time jobs, and the work of schooling is often more burdensome and stress-inducing than that of a typical adult job'.[23] I spoke to Gra Conway, whose seven-year-old son attends school in Northern Ireland: 'I think school needs better boundaries with home. The amount of homework he received as a child in the first class [age 4–5] was shocking, and has increased now in second class. It's all "busy work" that does not contribute to his learning or experience of the world and frankly, I feel the school has no right to intrude upon the family's home life in such a way or to monopolise so much of a child's energy with work that they have not chosen.' Fed up with a system that wasn't in his best interests, she pushed back. 'I informed the school that we wouldn't be doing homework. I'm the only parent to opt out but every parent in the class finds homework stressful to both adults and kids, and identifies it as an important factor in deciding how family time is spent during the week, especially when it comes to extracurriculars like sports or visits to relatives.'

Research backs this up: homework is pointless for young children. It has little or no benefit for the academic achievement of children aged 4–11, and may in fact increase inequality between children whose parents can offer them support and a quiet work space and those living in overcrowded, under-resourced homes with parents who are unavailable due to work or other responsibilities.[24] Even encouraging children to read for a certain amount of time each day — something many experts agree is a good thing — can kill the intrinsic motivation to read; there's no better way to make someone resent doing something than forcing them to do it.[25] Although some studies suggest homework may have a moderately positive impact on older children's academic achievement, and may support some disadvantaged students to develop better studying skills and narrow the gap in attainment, this is counterbalanced by the negative impact it has on children's 'free' time — time they need for rest and sleep, for playing music and exercising, for seeing friends and family, for reading for pleasure, and for their own projects and interests — and on their mental health. A Stanford University study found that students who did more homework suffered greater stress and health problems such as sleep deprivation, as well as lacking time for friends, family, and extracurricular activities and hobbies.[26]

No one likes homework — not children, not parents, not teachers who put in yet more work setting, chasing, and marking it — but we rarely question it. Are we so afraid to allow children autonomy when it comes to their so-called free time that we continue to control it with extra work? Children have a right to education, yes, but that doesn't take precedence over their equally important rights to leisure, to play, and to take part in a wide range of 'cultural and artistic activities' (as set out in Article 31 of the CRC). Homework might seem like a relatively small issue compared to things like school funding, curriculum choice, teaching methods, and school discipline. But it is symptomatic of a culture of education where exams are king, and wellbeing comes last on the list.

Failing by their own standards

If we can accept that most mainstream education is fundamentally coercive, and designed without much thought to student wellbeing, it raises a simple question: is it worth it? Is the stress, racism, and bullying experienced by many children a fair trade-off for an education that promises to help them flourish, setting them up with the skills and qualifications they need to have a successful and happy adult life?

To answer this question, I want to begin by looking at the

targets that the education system sets itself: achievement of qualifications. In the UK, figures from 2019 — before the impact of Covid disruptions — show that over a third of primary school leavers were not meeting the expected standard in reading, writing, and maths, despite having been in the education system for seven years (longer for those who attended preschool).[27] And this doesn't get better as children get older. Nearly 20 per cent of all 18-year-olds leave school without basic qualifications; a shockingly high figure for an education system so focused on exams. This figure isn't evenly spread: for children in receipt of free school meals, the number rises to 38 per cent. Children with Special Educational Needs are also overrepresented, as are those living in deprived areas, while refugee children are estimated to be over 17 months behind non-migrant English children by the time they take their GCSE exams.[28] These are children who will almost all have spent 14 years in the school system, and who have had around £100,000 of funding spent on them over the course of their time in education.[29] In Australia things are not great either: in 2019 only 72 per cent of year 12 (final year) students met the requirements for the year, or equivalent qualifications, with this number dropping to around 66 per cent of Indigenous Australians.[30]

Far from tackling inequality, our education systems are reinforcing it. In the UK, while just over 10 per cent of young people in middle-earning families (and fewer than 5 per cent of those in the poorest families) earned at least one top grade at GCSE, over a third of pupils from the richest tenth of families received at least one. The majority of private school students are university graduates by the age of 26, compared with less than a fifth of children from the poorest households.[31] Cambridge education professor Diane Real puts it this way: 'Even within a comprehensive school, when they're all in the same building, the working classes are still getting less education than the middle classes ... Society has got more unfair, and the gap between the rich and poor is a lot greater than it was even 30 years ago.'[32]

Why is it that so many young people are unable to achieve basic qualifications, despite many thousands of hours spent in classrooms? Can we confidently say that their school education has been worth it? In many cases the opposite is true: traditional school practices can actively contribute to children becoming disengaged from education, believing themselves stupid, broken, or bad, and damaging students' intrinsic motivation. Although some children will do well in exams, all children suffer under a school system that is narrow in focus, relies on external motivation and competition, and deepens existing inequality. Peter Gray sums up the problem well: 'We are pushing the limits of children's adaptability. We have pushed children into an abnormal environment, where they are expected to spend ever greater portions of their day under adult direction, sitting at desks, listening to and reading about things that don't interest them, and answering questions that are not their own ... We leave them ever less time and freedom to play, explore, and pursue their own interests.'[33]

The CRC tells us that all children have the right to an education which supports the development of their personality, talents, and mental and physical abilities to their fullest potential. A quick look around shows that our current education system is simply not delivering on its promises. But does education automatically mean traditional schooling?

A different kind of education

'Education has the potential to radically change the course of a child's life for the better. This is true of all sorts of children from all sorts of backgrounds. But it doesn't happen automatically, and it doesn't happen enough.'[34] These words were written by the late Sir Ken Robinson, a renowned education expert whose TED talk 'Do Schools Kill Creativity?' has been watched close to 100 million times. In order for all children to thrive, he argues, we should ditch narrow subject divisions like maths or science and focus instead on helping children to develop eight core competencies: curiosity, creativity, criticism, communication, collaboration, compassion, composure, and citizenship. We need to let go of what he dubs the 'industrial education' model of schooling, which is based on standardisation and conformity, and instead look towards 'regenerative' education, which values every child's strengths, not just those who are academically gifted. This kind of education would:

1. mix age groups, allowing children to be grouped by stage of mastery rather than age, which would support both younger and older students to share, deepen, and reinforce their learning;
2. personalise learning, making the most of technology to enable students to pursue their particular interests and strengths;
3. reflect the importance of play, recognising that play is how we make sense of the world;
4. consider the physical and built environment, noting that students are much more likely to engage if they are comfortable — and that we're living beings who depend on sunshine and fresh air;

5. value children's participation, keeping in mind that education is supposed to be for children and that they should be involved in the process of what happens to them.

An example of regenerative education in action is the Sudbury School model, which believes children learn best in a democratic, supportive environment where they're free to explore their own interests. The original Sudbury school, Sudbury Valley, was founded in Massachusetts in 1968 by a group of educators who believed that traditional schools were failing to meet the needs of many children, and there are currently around 60 schools globally. The schools prioritise trust, respect, and responsibility, value student autonomy over teacher direction, and they're democratic, with every student and staff member having an equal say in decision-making processes. Staff members facilitate learning rather than dictate it, and the goal is to create an environment where students develop a sense of self-direction and agency, while also fostering a strong sense of community and mutual respect. 'Things can happen to anybody, but the kids who go to school here feel deeply that they can influence their lives in any way they want, and that they can influence the world as well by their actions,' reads the website for Sudbury Valley. 'That's a miraculous thing: not to feel that they're being pushed and pulled by the tides, but to feel that they can take charge and do what they want in life.'[35] There is a focus not just on freedom, but also responsibility, and when the community's rules are broken — for example, if someone has been calling someone else names — pupils discuss what's gone wrong with the school's judicial committee, a mixed-age panel that is selected from the community members each week and meets daily.

The Sudbury model is radical, and although it may not suit all children, it's exciting to see that progressive schools can and do work in practice. In the UK, Summerhill School has been running for over 100 years along similar principles of play, self-government (it is also run along democratic principles), and freedom with responsibility. Contrary to what might be assumed, given that the children can choose how they spend their time, the school has a lot of rules to ensure the safety and smooth-running of the community. Voted on by the students and teachers, they include things like 'you must have a working front and back brake on your bike' and 'new children and staff cannot be on committees in their first term'.[36] Official inspections have found the quality of education to be good and its students do just as well academically as those in mainstream schools, proving that children don't need to be controlled or coerced into learning.

Even in a democratic school, you might have to go along with something you really don't like, just because the majority wanted to vote for it. Some schools are going even further by embracing *sociocracy*, a collective decision-making model based on reaching a consensus. Anyone can make a proposal, and then everyone gets to say whether they consent to it or not. If they don't, changes can be made to the original proposal to ensure everyone is happy. The power structure is flattened, which means everyone — from the youngest child to the headteacher — has the same amount of say when it comes to taking decisions.[37] The children who attend these schools can choose how they spend their time, working with an advisor to make a personal learning plan and deciding which lessons and classes they'd like to attend.

Many schools now call themselves 'alternative' or talk about their 'holistic' approach to education. But how can parents know if a school really centres children and embodies a truly progressive approach to learning? In his essay 'Progressive Education', education writer Alfie Kohn sets out the values of a truly progressive school:

- attending to the whole child (school isn't just focused on academics, and there is a broad curriculum);
- a deep sense of community (practices that encourage competition are avoided);
- collaboration (there is a focus on working together to solve problems and children's behaviour is not looked at in isolation);
- social justice (students are supported to act in ways that improve the lives of others);
- intrinsic motivation (educators seek practices that support students' interest in learning);
- deep understanding (teaching is often interdisciplinary, organised around projects, problems, and questions, rather than separated into subject silos; students are invited to think deeply about ideas and issues);
- active learning (students help to design the curriculum, ask their own questions, evaluate their learning, and actively participate in every stage of learning);
- taking children seriously (the curriculum is based on the interests of the specific children in each group, so each class — even within the same school and year group — will be different). [38]

Unfortunately, it can be hard to find progressive settings. The sorts of schools mentioned above are still relatively uncommon. When available, they can be expensive as they are rarely funded by the state. But not everyone believes that children need school full stop. Instead, a growing number of families — including many ex-teachers — are choosing a different path altogether, opting out of school and choosing to educate their children themselves at home.

Home-schooling & self-directed education

Our daughter is nine, and she's never been to school. Her days and weeks are organised to meet her needs and interests. Our mornings are peaceful: she sleeps until she's no longer tired, dresses in comfortable clothes that reflect her style (and the UK's changeable weather!), and has the time to eat breakfast slowly — usually with a thick novel in her hand. We are lucky that British law doesn't require home educators to follow the National Curriculum; all that is required is that we deliver a full-time education suitable to a child's age, ability, aptitude, and any special educational needs they may have. Most days we do some structured learning together, based on her current interests and the skills and goals she's working on; on any given day this might look like working through our maths curriculum, drawing while listening to a history podcast, working on a science experiment, embarking on an ambitious craft project, practicing Latin, or watching a documentary. Because she can learn at her own pace she never has to feel 'behind'; conversely, she's not held back by her age when she's interested in something. Because she gets one-to-one support from us, structured learning doesn't take up the whole day, leaving plenty of time for reading, playing, and pursuing her own interests. In summer we often pack our books and towels and spend the day at the local lido or head to the seaside; during winter we might hang out with friends at home or make the most of London's museums and galleries. If she is unwell, she can take as long as she needs to rest and get better, and if she wakes up wanting to go on an adventure we can usually say yes. Learning is a part of her life rather than something that requires her to put on a uniform, and she can throw herself into her interests safe in the knowledge that she won't be tested on them.

While my husband and I discuss our daughter's goals with her regularly and remind her what she needs to do to meet them, we don't force her to do anything she doesn't want to do. Research supports this consent-based approach: children really do learn best when they feel motivated and are able to act autonomously.[39] Although there are some things we feel it's important for her to learn, everything gets discussed, and it's ultimately her choice (as is being home-educated; if she decides she wants to try school then we'd support her). She doesn't sit any exams, but that doesn't mean that we don't think about her progress: we consider this by looking at her work, discussing ideas, talking to her about what she's learnt, and observing her play and self-direct art projects. These often reflect the subjects we've been covering together, a sign of deep learning and sustained interest.

I'm often asked about how we meet our daughter's need for socialisation, or whether home educating means she's only spending time with a limited group of people. This is something I worried about, particularly when she was younger. Thankfully my fears were mostly unfounded. Our daughter has a busy social life where she spends time with other children (in mixed age groups, unlike most schools) and with other caring adults. Across the week she takes piano, swimming, climbing, and ice-skating lessons, sees friends through regular playdates, and attends a big weekly meet-up for home educated children in local woods. As for whether or not our daughter is losing out on spending time in a diverse group of children, I've found our local home education community to be vibrant and inclusive, with a very high number of neurodivergent and disabled children. She spends time with friends of different nationalities, skin colours, and religions. Although there is a stereotype that home education is only for rich, white people, my experience couldn't be more different. Many home educating families I know are managing on low incomes and some have made enormous sacrifices — living with extended family, working multiple flexible jobs, moving to a smaller home — in order to keep their children out of school.

For some children for whom school simply isn't working, home education isn't so much a choice as it is a lifeline. I've spoken to many different parents of neurodivergent children, many of whom are Autistic or have ADHD, who have used almost identical language to describe the feeling of taking their unhappy child out of school: 'I finally got my child back.' I've met families where children who have experienced racism at school have blossomed at home, and spoken to children who are finally free from bullying after years of unhappiness.

A lot of parents I meet see home education as a deeply radical act, a daily practice that affirms their belief in children's inherent motivation to learn and rejects dominant power structures in society. This educational style, where children decide what and when they want to learn and how they spend their days, is commonly known as 'unschooling' or life learning. It's a pedagogy that rejects school as the primary place for children to learn, and recognises that children are intrinsically motivated to learn about the things which interest them.[40] Parents are still highly involved, but see their role as supporting their children to meet their own goals, by sourcing materials, facilitating activities, or helping their child to learn a new skill.

Fran Liberatore, who we met in chapter five, unschools her two children. 'Children don't need schools. And adults don't either — we just don't realise it because we don't know there could be another way! What we need is places of care and learning and community. It doesn't have to look anything like school, or be called a school. For me, a school is a very specific thing with a very specific hierarchy — regardless of whether it's a conventional or progressive school, they all look very similar structurally. We don't necessarily need schools. We can create various systems and structures of care that look a million different ways.'

Self-directed education (SDE) settings are becoming more popular now, catering to home-educating families who don't want their children to attend school but still want them to experience the deep connection and community that comes with spending several days a week with the same group of people. I visited one of these SDE settings in Bristol, south-west England. Bean Learning welcomes children between the ages of nine and 14 who are home educated, providing a safe and nurturing place for them to visit three days a week. The adults running the setting are passionate about children's rights and running a space that centres on emotional wellbeing, connection, and consent-based decision-making, and the children I spoke to told me they loved attending. Each day looks different depending on their goals, though they agree on certain activities such as swimming in advance. The young people who attend are given a lot of freedom, but when I visited it didn't feel chaotic or without purpose: everyone was engaged in something, from practicing an instrument to cooking lunch for the whole group. The facilitators are able to help if anyone wants to learn a particular skill — one adult is currently running a weekly maths class following popular demand — but they are very much led by the children's needs and interests.

Is home education the holy grail: a way of delivering a strong education while respecting children's other rights at the same time? Not necessarily. Not all parents want to or can home educate their children, and not all children want to leave school; as we've seen, there are negatives to mainstream schooling, but many positives too. I don't think I would have wanted to leave school, even though I often found the rules baffling and frustrating, because I liked seeing my friends too much. Even for parents who do want to home educate, it's not legal in every country. And when it is legal, home education is still a huge financial and practical commitment. Some parents, including my husband and me, get around this by both working flexibly; some organise co-ops or childcare swaps; and some send their children to part-time, alternative education settings like Bean Learning, which usually charge a low fee and are often run by home educating parents themselves. This will not be a solution for everyone, though.

There's another problem with assuming home education could be the magic ticket to solving the problem of rights-based education. While my husband and I don't always get it right, we're trying our best to offer our daughter a progressive education free from adultism. But that's not the case for all home educators. Some combine traditional top-down teaching and set curriculums with authoritarian parenting practices, and in some cases — as has been documented in some orthodox religious communities — home education can be used as an excuse for not giving children much of an education at all.[41] It's also been used, particularly in the US, by conservative Christian families who don't want their children exposed to ideas such as evolution and critical race theory, or information about sexuality and gender.[42] There are harrowing stories of children being abused under the guise of home-schooling, and some of these families openly talk about beating their children as a form of discipline. To put it bluntly, while home education can be a way to support children's rights away from adult oppression, this is only going to be the case if parents have embraced a liberatory pedagogy that supports children's autonomy and recognises them as leaders of their own learning.

Sticking up for children

While there are serious issues with mainstream education, it's an important part of millions of children's lives and isn't going anywhere at present. Whether we call them schools or not, places where children can spend time and be supported to learn are necessary in our current society. It is easy to criticise the system, particularly as someone outside of it, but I've had countless conversations with families whose children have been supported beautifully by dedicated teachers and headteachers who have gone out of their way to build inclusive, warm, loving school communities. Many of these educators are actively pushing back and resisting within a system that makes it very difficult for them to do their jobs well, making the best of inadequate funding and finding ways to cope with the enormous pressure they face from regulators. Sometimes just one kind teacher is enough to make a real difference to a child's life. And of course, parents play a vital role, too. I have worked with a lot of parents whose children are in mainstream education who can't — or don't want to — move their children to an alternative school or home educate but who have wanted advice on how to support their child within the school system.

Prevention is better than cure, so for parents whose children aren't yet in school I would always recommend doing as much research as you can before you choose a setting. Rather than looking at grades and attainment, I'd be interested to look at the school's behaviour policies — do they use shaming methods of punishment or make children lose out on playtime or other enjoyable activities? Do they explicitly talk about children's rights, and if the option is available, are they a Rights Respecting school?

Second, whether your child is already at school or not, you can support them to develop self-advocacy skills. Talk to them regularly about their rights, and make sure they know that they should always expect to be treated well by other adults and children. From a young age, you can help your child learn to clearly describe their needs, and to tell you if something is happening that they aren't happy with. This also means listening to them and taking them seriously when they show or tell you something is upsetting them, rather than dismissing it. If they know you will always believe them when they tell you something, it keeps the communication doors wide open, and you will be in a better position to help them if something has gone wrong.

Third, understanding the unequal power structure of schools and their impact can help us to have empathy and to ally ourselves with children when they need support, rather than taking the side of the school. What every child needs is to be able to come home to a loving, trusted adult who has their back, even if they have gotten into trouble or not achieved the grades you were hoping they would get. Showing children that they are unconditionally loved, and that their worth has nothing to do with exam results or whether they've been given detentions, can mean a lot, as can sympathising with them when they are frustrated by unfair school rules.

Fourth, parents can use their power as adults to push back on adultism within the school system. Several teachers told me they like it when parents email or call with their concerns before requesting a face-to-face meeting, so that they have time to process their thoughts and focus on solutions. Apart from extreme circumstances, they recommend always talking to your child's class or form teacher first if possible, rather than leapfrogging them and going straight to the head, which can cause conflict and escalate issues unnecessarily. Most teachers actively want to help and make things better: I've heard from parents who have successfully advocated for their child to attend school flexibly, who have opted out of testing and homework, who have gotten their child moved to a different class when they were unhappy, and who have worked with teachers to remove behaviour charts from the classroom. It can be done.

Fifth, sometimes pushing for change works better if it comes from a group, particularly when it comes to school-wide issues around curriculum, behaviour policies, or their approach towards children. Can you get together with other parents to show the school that there is collective appetite for change? For example, if your child's school hasn't sought out Rights Respecting accreditation, could you try and convince them to go down this path?

Sixth, as well as advocating for your child, if you're in a position to get involved with the school leadership or in supporting the school more generally this can be a great way to improve things for all pupils. Can you join the PTA or the board of governors? Is there a way you can fundraise for better supplies, or otherwise donate time and resources? Remember that a lot of schools are struggling with funding cuts, low staffing numbers, and the rising cost of food, utilities, and resources. It can help to approach the school with empathy, even if there are policies or actions you disagree with.

Finally, if things are really bad — if your child is miserable, and nothing is making it better — don't be afraid of looking for a new school that better suits your child or taking your child out of school if that's a possibility. Even if you can't home educate long-term, giving your child a break for a few months until you find a school that's a better fit could be a game changer. There are many part-time settings that cater to home educating families, allowing parents to work and children to spend time with peers and caring adults. Education shouldn't be something to be endured.

The school children want

Just because we collectively rely on schools to make society work it doesn't mean that we need to settle for how things are. Children now face a very different future to the one we looked towards in our youth. The jobs they will do will be different, the technology they use will be different, and the challenges they face will be different. Can we still justify an education that encourages competition for the top grades over conflict-resolution and group problem-solving (if indeed, we ever could)? Do we really still believe in raising children in institutions that demand their obedience and conformity, or do we want to support them to be critical thinkers, ready to push back when they come across injustice?

Radically changing the education system would be the quickest way to dismantle adultism and advance children's liberation. While involving them in school decision-making structures is a good start, we could go further and involve children as co-designers of a new education system, built for them and centred around their ideas, needs, and priorities. In chapter three, I wrote about a *Guardian* newspaper competition — 'The School I'd Like' — in which young people in the UK between the ages of five and 18 were asked to imagine their ideal school. Repeated twice, in 2001 and 2011, they received thousands of responses that offer us a clear indication of what children are looking for from their schools. This was written up in an excellent book-length study by Catherine Burke and Ian Grosvenor, titled *The School I'd Like: revisited*.[43] Although all of the children's responses were different, some key themes emerged, which were summarised in the following 'Children's Manifesto':

> The School We'd Like is:
>
> A beautiful school
> A comfortable school
> A safe school
> A listening school
> A flexible school
> A relevant school
> A respectful school
> A school without walls
> A school for everybody.

Let's look at some of the children's ideas in a bit more detail:

The school children want is a beautiful, comfortable school. How schools look and feel matter a lot. 'I want lots of colours,' writes Liam, four, and he's not alone. Many of the responses talk about colours — warm reds, cool blues, bright paints — and voice their frustration that their schools are run down, dirty, and worn. A school for children might ditch the strip lighting and overstimulating classroom displays in favour of soft lighting and comfortable, beautiful spaces where children could move, work, and rest. This may seem unimportant, but look up photos of classrooms in Steiner Waldorf, Montessori, or Reggio schools and you'll immediately notice how calm and welcoming they feel. 'I hate waking up every weekday knowing that this day, that is so valuable to me, will be spent in a giant magnolia prison,' writes Angela, 15. 'I want colours. I want beauty in my surroundings, but most of all I want to be filled with inspiration by a place that I can call my home from home.' Many of the children wrote about the need for better, cleaner toilets with doors that locked and full cubicles to ensure privacy; improved soundproofing so that noise from other classrooms didn't disturb them; bigger classrooms; and an eco-friendly design, with solar panels and wind turbines, and a recycling area. It would be comfortable, so that school would be 'just like being at home,' says Gavin, 13. Lots of entries talked about wanting a modern school, with access to new technologies and futuristic design including glass domes and walls.

The school children want is a school with great playgrounds and more outdoor space. 'I want a playhouse in the playground and a hopscotch. I would like to see the flowers grow,' writes Sebiah, six. 'I don't like to be lonely. It would be nice if there was a pond and some frogs inside the pond and some tadpoles.' Lots of children wrote about their desire for wildlife gardens with lots of trees, bird boxes, and animals. They also wanted better play equipment with slides, swings, rope bridges, climbing frames, and the space for different sports and activities. 'The school I dream of has a wildlife garden, a wood, as well as a fantastic adventure playground with a wooden pirate ship big enough to climb on,' says Alix, seven.

The school children want is a school with good food — and time to eat it. Lots of children wanted better food, which was cheaper, healthier, and included a wide range of options to cater for vegetarian and religious children. 'Teachers and pupils should all eat together and have exactly the same food,' writes Nat, 11. 'This would probably lead to an improvement in school meals.' 'I would like to have more time to eat my dinner,' writes Rachel, nine. 'I sometimes don't finish it and I seem to get thinner.' 'There would be a big cafeteria overlooking the river and lots of choices of healthy food,' writes Hannah, eight. Schools could become climate-friendly community centres where people of all ages could come together to grow and collect food, and to nurture habitats for wildlife. 'I think we should have a small farm so we can learn to plant and grow our food and look after animals.'

The school children want is a school with a broad, exciting curriculum, where every child can thrive and where class sizes are smaller. 'In my school pupils would have freedom to choose lessons they wanted to do,' writes Jonathan, 17, 'where one is not expected to forsake being a human being to teach or be taught.' Children wrote about their desire to have a wider range of subjects and activities to choose from, particularly around art, science, and nature, and for schools to embrace holistic, project-based learning where they could learn about the world around them, including by going on more trips. Many talked about students being able to choose their own subjects. They also spoke out against age-based standards: 'I don't like the way children are expected to do this by seven and that by 11, plus if you have not achieved all those things by 16 then you are told you won't get a decent job!' argues Kate. Some want to scrap homework, and many spoke about the need for more time and space to rest and relax.

The school children want is a school with great teachers. 'My perfect teachers would have a very big smile,' writes Ellis, seven. The children wrote about the importance of having reliable, passionate, fun, approachable, fair teachers they can trust. Some wrote about the unequal power dynamics between teachers and pupils, and about how teachers can be 'terrifying'. 'Rightly or wrongly, the power relationships between pupils and teachers are unequal at most schools,' writes Lorna, 14. 'I think that teachers frequently abuse their authority.' 'I don't understand why teachers ask so many questions,' mused Hero, also 14. 'It seems to me that it is the learner who should ask the questions.' Some suggested feedback should work both ways, with pupils able to give their teachers reports.

The school children want is a school where every child can be themselves, free from bullying and control. 'My ideal school would be where everyone can be equal,' writes Philip, 12. 'There would be no bullying, no racism and no division by intelligence, abilities, or sex.' Many children wrote about the importance of inclusion, particularly with regards to disability and race. Some children noted that the atmosphere was often set by staff. 'Bullying is wrong but people don't realise that actually teachers bully children more than you may think!' argues Rowan, 12. 'My dream school would be one where children are treated with respect,' writes Megan, 13. 'Children and teachers would think of each other as equals.'

It's important to recognise that within the children's responses, some children weren't convinced school could change. 'My ideal school would be not coming,' wrote Robert, age 12. The biggest hurdle to a school that would work for all children would not be funding (if we leave to one side the requests for swimming pools or glass domes) or training, but rather changing our collective way of thinking about education. If we could trust that children are born curious, capable learners who don't need to be coerced into learning and developing skills, it would shift everything. 'In my ideal school, the whole philosophy that dominates schools now will be dropped,' writes Miriam, age 15. 'We will no longer be treated as herds of an identical animal waiting to be civilised before we are let loose on the world. It will be recognised that it is our world too.'

*

When thinking about education, it can help to trace the word back to its roots. 'Education' comes from the Latin *educare*, broadly meaning 'to lead out'. This suggests a gradual leading out from infancy and the home towards independent life within society, with all of the knowledge and understanding that entails. At its very best, as bell hooks writes, learning can be a practice of freedom.[44] Education can broaden our horizons, challenge our views, give us new skills and tools, and help us to be kinder and more empathetic — and it has nothing inherently to do with schooling.

It can be hard to imagine children successfully leading their own learning if we've never seen it happen before and have been told all our lives that education only happens in a classroom with a teacher. The schools, settings, and home educating families around the world embracing something radically different provide an active challenge to a lot of adultist beliefs about children — and provide some possible pathways towards a kinder, fairer, liberatory education system that works for all children.

CHAPTER NINE

A future built for children

My mother was born in 1966, when the concentration of carbon dioxide in the Earth's atmosphere was 319 parts per million (ppm).[1] Just a few months after her birth, an article was published in the *Mining Congress Journal*, titled bluntly 'Air Pollution and the Coal Industry'. It was penned by James Garvey, then president of a fossil fuel company. 'There is evidence that the amount of carbon dioxide in the Earth's atmosphere is increasing rapidly as a result of the combustion of fossil fuels,' he wrote. 'If the future rate of increase continues as it is at the present, it has been predicted that ... vast changes in the climates of the Earth will result. Such changes in temperature will cause melting of the polar icecaps, which, in turn, would result in the inundation of many coastal cities, including New York and London.'[2] This was not the first warning that CO2 emissions could put our planet in grave danger: as early as 1856 a scientist named Eunice Foote concluded that increased proportions of CO2 in the atmosphere would lead to rising temperatures.[3] In the year Foote published her paper, global CO2 emissions totalled around 0.277 gigatonnes (a gigatonne is a billion tonnes). When my mum was taking her first breath, 110 years later, they had risen to 11.87 gigatonnes.[4]

By the time I was born in 1988 (carbon in the atmosphere: 348 ppm; yearly CO2 emissions: 22.1 gigatonnes), the link between global heating and carbon emissions was no longer new. I wasn't even four weeks old when climate scientist James Hansen testified to the United States Congress that climate change was not only already happening but that it was a consequence of greenhouse gases directly linked to human pollution.[5] Essayist Nathaniel Rich has described the eighties as the decade where the world could have solved the climate crisis: we understood global warming and its impacts, and there was a high level of political will, evident in the forming of international instruments such as the UN Framework Convention on Climate Change (UNFCCC).[6] Instead, our reliance on fossil fuels — and our carbon emissions — increased. Earth continued to get hotter.

My daughter was born in 2015 (401 ppm; 35.5 gigatonnes). When she was a couple of months old, a heatwave hit the UK and we experienced the highest July temperature ever recorded (a record that has since been broken multiple times). Roads melted, transport systems were in chaos, and I vividly remember the panic of trying to keep my tiny baby cool in our poorly insulated London home. Later that year, a historic moment occurred: the Paris Agreement was signed, a legally binding international treaty that by the year 2100 aims to limit global warming to well below 2°C, preferably to 1.5°C, compared to pre-industrial levels. Although the agreement isn't perfect — many have argued that it doesn't go far enough and there is not enough accountability included — when it was signed, I felt cautiously optimistic. Was the climate emergency finally being taken seriously, just in time to prevent things from getting worse for my daughter's generation?

Fast forward to today, and the Climate Action Tracker predicts that current policies in place around the world are projected to result in about 2.7°C warming by 2100. We've already hit 1°C, and according to the Intergovernmental Panel on Climate Change (IPCC) we're due to hit 1.5°C by 2040. Despite some good news, like the plummeting cost of renewable energy and the decline in coal use, we are not on track to reach the Paris goals. If nations follow through with their stated plans to slash emissions, scientists think we could potentially limit total warming to around 2–2.4°C — but they also agree that this is too risky, and could trigger multiple catastrophic tipping points.[7] Even small increases can have devastating impacts: half a degree could be the difference between a world with coral reefs and Arctic summer sea ice and a world without them.[8] 'Once in a lifetime' weather events now happen on a yearly basis. It seems we still have a long way to go.

Don't look away

Naomi Klein, Professor of Climate Justice at the University of British Columbia, writes that most of us practise a specific kind of climate denial. It is a denial that accepts that we're living through a man-made climate emergency, but which looks away from the severity and urgency of what is happening.[9] Despite evidence and scientific reports to the contrary, we still think of the climate crisis as something that will happen in the future, or as something which we can insulate ourselves, and our children, from the worst of. Capitalism, the endless pursuit of economic growth, and blind faith that technological solutions will save us at the eleventh hour have all contributed to the belief that industrial societies are somehow 'exempt' from nature's constraints.[10]

So I want to be clear, and I want you to look: we are in a climate emergency that is creating a children's rights crisis on an unprecedented scale. Because the climate crisis affects everyone — child or adult — to some degree, it can be difficult to think of it as a problem that is of special relevance to children's liberation. But it is children, especially those who are already vulnerable, who suffer first and suffer most. According to UNICEF, every year environmental factors take the lives of 1.7 million children under five, and the growing number of extreme weather events around the world is putting more and more lives in danger. Lower respiratory tract infections, diarrhoea, and malaria are currently responsible for over half of childhood deaths globally. All three of these will likely worsen as the impacts of climate change increase.[11]

Not all children will be affected by the climate crisis in the same way, or to the same degree. Those hardest hit are children living in countries with limited resources for adapting to the effects of the climate crisis. In 2022 Pakistan was battered first by stifling heatwaves and drought, with temperatures reaching as high as 51 °C, and then by devastating floods that plunged a third of the country underwater. Around half of those affected — 16 million — were children, with over three million in need of lifesaving support. These numbers sound incomprehensible, I know; the scale of suffering is so immense that it's hard to fathom. But each of these children have people who love them, a future ahead of them, and a right to survival. 'I wince when I hear people say these are natural disasters,' said Sherry Rehman, Pakistan's climate minister at the time. 'These are man-made disasters.'[12] The climate emergency is not an environmental crisis, but one created by a global economy that allows the benefits of increased consumption to be enjoyed in one place — mostly by those who are already rich — and the costs to be borne in another.

Hurricanes, cyclones, and wildfires are increasing in both number and severity. By 2040, it's predicted that 600 million children — one in four worldwide — will live in areas with extremely limited water resources.[13] Deaths from malnutrition are also expected to increase with climate change because of rising food insecurity linked to floods and droughts. In a worst-case scenario of accelerating emissions, areas currently home to a third of the world's population will be as hot as the hottest parts of the Sahara within 50 years.[14] Children are particularly vulnerable to extreme temperatures, as they have a reduced capacity to regulate their body temperature and protect themselves. They also tend to spend more time outdoors than adults in many parts of the world. Researchers have estimated that global heating may have already doubled heat-related child deaths in Africa — and that taking appropriate climate action could prevent thousands of child deaths a year.[15] Another study has found that a billion people will either be displaced or forced to endure insufferable heat for every additional 1°C rise in the global temperature.[16] Displacement in turn increases children's risks of being separated from their parents through orphaning, abduction, and trafficking, as well as being subject to poor treatment from countries they are displaced to. We only have to look at how many European states have treated asylum seekers in the past decade to see that being a refugee is a dangerous, often dehumanising, process.[17]

Our lack of care in how we treat our environment won't just be felt in the future or in 'other' places. It is having an effect where we live right now — and it is already proving deadly.

Ten million a year

As a young child, Ella Adoo-Kissi-Debrah loved swimming, gymnastics, reading, and playing music. Like many six-year-olds she enjoyed creating performances with her friends, and she dreamed of being an air ambulance doctor when she grew up. But a few months before she turned seven, Ella developed a chest infection, which quickly turned into disabling asthma. Over the next two years of her life, her lungs collapsed five times. She would be admitted to hospital as an emergency patient over 30 times, sometimes coughing so much that she blacked out from lack of oxygen. In 2013, aged nine, Ella died of an asthma attack.

Years after her death, thanks to her mother's tireless campaigning, an inquest ruled that Ella had been killed by air pollution. Her home was just 25 metres from the busy South Circular Road in London, which she would walk along to get to school. Air pollution was found to have spiked around the same time as her lungs collapsed and in the days before she died. Ella's mother has spoken out saying she didn't know that the air her daughter was breathing was unsafe, and the coroner agreed, saying there was a 'lack of information given to Ella's mother that possibly contributed to her death'. Had she known, she would have done everything within her power to move house immediately — anything to protect her beloved daughter. But despite the pollution levels in the area reaching illegal levels, no one warned local families.

Ella became the first person in the UK to have air pollution listed as the cause of death on their death certificate, but not every death from air pollution becomes a news story. Climate journalist David Wallace-Wells writes: 'In February 2020, the world began to panic about the novel coronavirus, which killed

2,714 people that month. This made the news. In the same month, around 800,000 people died from the effects of air pollution. That didn't. Novelty counts for a lot.'[18] Ten million deaths a year is about 20 times as many as the current annual deaths from war, murder, and terrorism combined; it equates to roughly 20,000 people dying a day. It is hard to picture death from air pollution in the same way as we can imagine dying from the impact of a hurricane or landslide, but its effects are just as real. Wallace-Wells continues: 'The calculus for air pollution is the same as for smoking: take the problem away, and the number of premature deaths will fall by many millions.' A study carried out in the US backs this up with its findings that air pollution triggered irregular heartbeats and could contribute to sudden cardiac death in healthy teenagers.[19]

In 2020, Black and Brown teenagers living in London created Choked Up, a campaign responding to Ella's death. Furious that the people most at risk of the health impacts of air pollution were people of colour and working-class communities, they wanted the UK government to recognise that air pollution is a social justice issue as well as an environmental one — and they wanted to help communities understand the serious dangers associated with the toxic air they were forced to breathe. They worked to 'hack' street signs around pollution hotspots, putting up signs in the same style as street signs. These pictured an adult and child standing in a cloud of smoke and read 'Pollution Zone: Breathing Kills'. Accompanying text explained that people of colour are more likely to live in an area with illegal levels of air pollution. The campaign had a big impact locally, and it was covered by national media outlets. Their work helped to make air pollution a key issue in the 2021 London Mayoral elections, and members of Choked Up were invited to speak at several COP26 events, which allowed them to share their learnings with other clean air organisations.[20]

No liberation without life

Children have a right to life, and to the best possible health (Articles 6 and 24). The CRC states that governments must do all they can to ensure that children survive and develop to their full potential, and yet global heating, pollution, and environmental degradation puts these basic rights at risk. The collective failure to adequately tackle the climate emergency — and the air pollution that goes hand-in-hand with it — is already killing millions of children.

Global heating is also having an impact on children's mental health. There is a clear relationship between increased temperatures and number of suicides, and of severe distress following extreme weather events.[21] Even children who are not directly affected by global heating can suffer distress because of it. As children have little power to limit its harm, they are especially vulnerable to climate anxiety. A landmark study that surveyed thousands of children and young people across the globe found that over half reported feeling sad, anxious, angry, powerless, helpless, and guilty about the climate crisis. These feelings negatively affected their daily lives, and many had dark thoughts about the future, worrying that humanity is doomed or that they will not be able to live normal lives or have families of their own.[22]

Children are doubly impacted by climate anxiety when their parents, caregivers, or teachers are struggling with their own climate-related mental health. To feel anxiety over the future of our planet is normal; the statistics are bleak. But this is one area where we can support children. My daughter recently told us that she was feeling sad and worried about the climate crisis, so after listening to her fears and getting clear on what exactly it was she was feeling upset about, I sat down with her and we made a list of all of the things we could do to help the environment, both big and small, and put it up on the wall. Some of these things we can do easily — writing to our MP together, planting more seeds — and some will take a little more planning, like organising a fundraising sale to raise money for a green charity. But she felt much better knowing that she wasn't powerless and that she could make a tangible difference. Rather than individual action such as recycling or switching products, collective action — community outreach, peer education, participation in advocacy groups — has been found to be the most effective action in improving climate mental health. A Yale study of young people suggests that engaging in collective action can buffer the effects of climate-related anxiety and prevent it from leading to feelings of sadness and hopelessness that would be consistent with depression.[23]

Tackling adultism and embracing children's liberation requires us to stand in solidarity with all children. Professor Mary Chesney writes: 'Those committed to caring for the health and wellbeing of children can no longer sit on the sidelines and ignore the urgent, existential threats environmental degradation, pollution, and climate change pose to the world's children.'[24] Children's liberation cannot happen without climate justice; if we care about one, we cannot ignore the other. The good news is that all of us can do something very simple, very easy, and totally free to help move us in the right direction: we can talk about the climate crisis.

25 per cent

Damon Centola, a social scientist at the University of Pennsylvania, studies how social change happens. In 2018, he published a study in *Science* showing that it only takes 25 per cent of a group to believe something to create a 'tipping point' and change the majority viewpoint.[25] This means that a committed minority can change which behaviours are seen as socially acceptable, potentially leading to outcomes such as reduced energy consumption and more acceptance of the changes we will need to make if we are to drastically reduce our emissions and phase out fossil fuels. Just by talking to our friends, family, coworkers, and neighbours about the climate crisis we can help move closer to that 25 per cent. Although sharing a social media post about the climate crisis or chatting to a neighbour about extreme weather patterns might not seem like it counts as activism, this study suggests that its exactly actions like these which get us to a point where enough of the population wants to see political change — and will vote accordingly. We might be closer to that 25 per cent than we think; the only thing to do to be certain we get there is to keep telling the truth about the crisis we're in.

Vanessa, a mother of three, told me how she finally plucked up the courage to start talking about the climate crisis:

> I spent over a year feeling anxious, despairing, and crying at random times, once the full reality of the climate crisis had sunk in for me. After chatting with friends my 'solution' became to block it all out, unfollow people talking about it, practise mindfulness and find joy wherever I could. It semi-worked for a little while but of course I couldn't block it out

> — and didn't want to. When I tried to, I just felt guilty. I didn't want to be a part of denying my three children, and children everywhere, a healthy, safe, and happy future. I saw a post which changed it all for me. It simply said, 'at the very least, in years to come I want to be able to look at my children in the eyes and be able to tell them that I tried'. That did it for me. I started sharing climate content online and in conversations. Shakily to start with but now with a steely determination. I feel less anxious and guilt-ridden and spend far more time feeling motivated, encouraged, and present with my kids.

The children's fire

It's not surprising that children around the world are feeling more betrayed than reassured. They are watching as politicians fail to take their concerns seriously, and they know what this will mean for their own lives and those of others. Rather than embracing the long-term thinking and international coordination that is needed to get a handle on the climate emergency, states are falling back on short-termist nationalism.[26] Politicians may care about the environment personally, and political parties may make claims about lowering emissions in their manifestos, but both depend upon getting reelected by voters in the next electoral cycle. This prevents them from adequately considering both the needs of children alive today — and the need to safeguard the future for those yet to be born.

Oxford philosopher and avid proponent of long-termism Will MacAskill puts this question to us: 'If you knew you would live in the future', he asks, 'what would you hope we do in the present?

How much carbon dioxide would you want us to emit into the atmosphere? How much attention would you want us to give to the impact of today's actions on the long term?'[27] Children need us to act — to ignore this is a moral failure that places a heavy burden on those not yet born. We — especially those of us living in industrialised nations — are the pivotal generation.[28] If we are to become good ancestors and cultivate long-term thinking and intergenerational justice, we need to think seriously about the inheritance we want to leave the world.[29]

There is a story about the elders of a tribe in North America, who ordered that a fire be kindled in the centre of their council circle. This fire — the Children's Fire — would serve to remind the council that they should take no decision which would harm the children. All Chiefs took a pledge to the Children's Fire: a pledge to the welfare of children yet to be born, a commitment to the responsibility carried by each generation to safeguard the next.[30] In 2016, Wales became the first country to have a future generations commissioner, following The Well-being of Future Generations Act that passed the year before. The Commissioner's role is to promote the sustainable development principle, which states that public bodies should meet the needs of current generations without compromising the needs of future generations. This involves helping public bodies to think long term and help them change their behaviours, not just around climate change but also around future jobs and skills, health, and infrastructure.[31] This seems like a straightforward way to embed long-term thinking into short-term governments. I would love to see a lead or department for future generations — a Children's Fire — embedded into every public institution as a way of ensuring that those with the least say still have a voice, backed up with a legal framework.

Why don't we act?

Amma is seven years old, and she wants you to know that she wishes adults would take the climate crisis seriously. For her most recent birthday, she asked to plant a tree; she is passionate about tackling deforestation and the environmental degradation it can bring and spoke to me at length about the benefits tree-planting have on the environment. Amma wants adults to know that it's their job to make a difference to the planet. 'Everything is being destroyed. The world is changing fast and is coming to a disaster with global warming, and grown-ups aren't doing enough. Children and grown-ups should both be fighting against climate change.'

Amma lives in the UK, where she is shielded from the worst impacts of the climate crisis. Yet as I speak to her, I find myself wishing that she didn't have to think about ice caps melting, coral bleaching, or rising CO2 levels. She openly admits to feeling sad about what's going on, though she finds that taking action helps her to feel better. This isn't a crisis of her making, yet she is doing what is in her control to alleviate it. The fight for climate justice is being led by children and young adults, and they are pleading with us to join them. That should be reason enough for us to act.

What prevents us from doing so? Cambridge Professor David Runciman writes that climate change is like a bad case of writer's block: we know what we have to do, the stakes feel high, and it's hard to get started. 'When something is long overdue, it's hard to get going because the moment is never right. Once the threat materialises there won't be enough time to do anything about it; if there is still enough time then the threat must be distant. The threats and incentives are never productively aligned.'[32] This resonates with me a lot. I often feel overwhelmed and too busy to get involved with climate activism, and I have moments of wondering if anything I do can really make a change. Why take shorter showers when water company leaks waste over a trillion litres a year in England and Wales alone?[33] What is one person giving up flying on commercial airlines when the super-rich keep private jets to hand for 15-minute flights?[34] When the richest one per cent of the world's population is responsible for more than twice as much carbon pollution as the poorest half of humanity, is it really worth trying to get our own carbon emissions down? When climate breakdown is not caused by one 'baddie', but rather threaded through all our systems and structures, trying to tackle it feels a bit like whack-a-mole. It's easy to feel hopeless.

Hopelessness isn't a neutral feeling, though. Christiana Figueres and Tom Rivett-Carnac, both of whom were instrumental in achieving the 2015 Paris Accords, write that 'we can no longer afford the indulgence of feeling powerless ... This is an everyone-everywhere mission in which we must all individually and collectively assume responsibility.'[35] To give up on hope, sticking our heads in the sand or deciding to accept our fate is a self-fulfilling prophecy that guarantees that things will get worse. Not only is fatalism irresponsible, but it is a privilege afforded only to those of us who are not already suffering directly as a result of global heating. Fatalism doesn't work for those who are at the frontline of the climate emergency, and it doesn't work for children who will bear the consequences of the climate emissions we are contributing to now.

If my daughter was diagnosed with a life-threatening health condition, I would do everything in my power to get her the help she needed, even if there was only a tiny chance that a cure could be found. There's no way I would think 'oh well, this is too hard, and anyway it's probably too late'! Nor would I leave it to someone else to fight for her. Yet the climate crisis puts all children at grave risk. We need to tap into the love and care that we feel for the children in our lives — our children, grandchildren, nieces, godchildren, students, and neighbours — and then we need to fight for them.

Who shapes the narrative?

If we cannot afford fatalism, what is the answer? This is where it gets difficult: individual actions simply aren't enough in the face of deep-rooted problems, but to do nothing is to seal our collective fate. A myopic focus on individual consumer and lifestyle choices as the way to solve climate and environmental collapse feels like it gives corporations a free pass while putting undue pressure on individuals. And corporations themselves have been active in shaping this narrative. Climatologist Michael Mann explains how fossil fuel companies are no longer denying that global heating is happening, but are now focusing their efforts on deflecting attention away from the need for real policy change, sowing climate doom that breeds inaction, and shifting the focus back to individuals.[36] The personal carbon footprint calculator was created in 2004 by oil titan British Petroleum (BP) as part of an advertising push designed to manipulate people into looking away from oil companies and at their own lifestyles instead.[37]

The industry even has its claws in what and how children learn about man-made climate change. *Scientific American* has reported on how members of the fossil-fuel industry have participated in each stage of the Texas science standards adoption process, working to influence what children learn in the industry's favour, and in some cases shaping the language used around energy and climate.[38] What I hadn't previously realised is that because Texas is one of the largest textbook purchasers in the US, publishers pay attention to the Texas standards when they create materials. These textbooks, drafted with one eye on conservative campaigners, then get sold to schools across the nation, shaping the education of millions of children.[39]

So many consumer brands now employ 'greenwashing' — clever marketing that makes their products and business practices look more sustainable than they are — that it can be hard to know the impact of what we're spending our money on, even when we think we're making good choices. The uncomfortable truth is that even drastically reducing our personal carbon footprints still won't bring about the change we need, because every aspect of our lives is still so reliant on fossil fuels, especially in high-income countries. We are constrained by the options available to us. In 2008, MIT researchers tried to calculate the carbon footprint of different people including a Buddhist monk and an unhoused person. They found that there was a 'floor' below which environmental impacts for people living in the US did not drop of around 120 gigajoules of energy usage (more than twice the global average), even for the most modest of lifestyles.[40] Income and lifestyle choices had a clear impact on energy usage and carbon footprint, but only up to a certain point. The rest was structural.

We need big, audacious policy changes befitting the scale of the problem. Governments need to be more aggressive in pursuing net-zero, starting by abolishing the fossil fuel industry and funding investment in renewable energy. High-income countries need to step up and pay the trillions needed yearly for low-income countries to mitigate and adapt to the climate crisis (the US alone caused an estimated $1.9 trillion worth of damage to the rest of the world through emissions between 1990 and 2014).[41] There should be a way of criminalising the mega-rich individuals, international corporations, and politicians and lawmakers who continue to wreck our global home with impunity. In March 2023, the IPCC published the final part of its sixth assessment report. Its message was stark: act now, or it will be too late. The UN secretary general, António Guterres, was clear: 'Our world needs climate action on all fronts: everything, everywhere, all at once.' But despite the urgency of the message, it contained hope too: if we act now — if rich countries can reach net zero greenhouse gas emissions by 2040 — then we can still secure a liveable and sustainable future for all. Every tonne of carbon we save, every bit of warming avoided, gives our children and all future generations a better chance of surviving and thriving.[42]

The systemic change we need is not here yet. We must keep fighting for it, but in the meantime, we can make changes in our own lives that allow us to live according to our values. Both collective and individual actions are needed, and both add up.

We create the future

Lifestyle changes are necessary if we are to collectively change our patterns of (over)consumption, and our ideas around what a good or aspirational life should look like. As writer Rebecca Solnit puts it, 'we do influence others through our visible choices. Ideas spread, values spread, habits spread; we are social animals and both good and bad behaviors are contagious.'[43] Your action or my action alone might not do much, but if we all act then we can shape the future.

I know that knowing where to begin can feel overwhelming, so below are some suggestions for actions or changes, both individually and collective. Some are focused on smaller changes, and others on shaking up the system (don't worry, none include giving up shampoo). I want to be upfront: many of these suggestions assume a certain level of privilege when it comes to your finances, time, and access to things like public transport and plentiful food options, so please ignore suggestions that aren't realistic for you. It also feels important to say here that many countries around the world are clamping down on protest and activism. Not everyone is able to take part in direct action or risk arrest safely. Institutional racism and prejudice mean that we are not all treated the same way by the police, or judged the same way by juries. But we all have something to offer: movements need artists, lawyers, cooks, writers, litter pickers, lobbyists, sign makers, architects, scientists, politicians, teachers, designers, fundraisers — and generous donors! — press officers, online campaigners, and childcare providers. There is a role for all of us in building a better, more beautiful future together.

Dream big

In the words of writer and academic Bayo Akomolafe, 'the time is very urgent – we must slow down'.[44] Dreaming about what the future could look like is a necessary part of building it. Global heating poses a grave threat, but it also prompts us to think creatively about what the world could and should look like.

When I imagine a near future where we take care of ourselves and the Earth we live on, one of the things I picture is children playing in community gardens on street corners, picking fruit growing on trees where parking spaces or neat lawns once were, and learning to cook with local produce. When I found myself jotting down my own vision, I realised that we could take a small step towards it. My daughter and I have now planted fruit bushes in our small front garden, where before there was only grass. When the fruit ripens, we'll invite the children in our street to pick as much as they want. It's a tiny thing, but it brings us closer to the future we want to be living in, and these actions help her to feel empowered rather than overwhelmed about the climate crisis.

Join together with others

If there's one thing all climate experts and activists seem to agree on, it's that we're better when we work together. A collective crisis requires collective action, and there is something for everyone: big international climate action groups, groups aimed at families or parents, local climate groups, and issue-based campaigns and pressure groups. Many now meet online, making them more accessible. And collective action does work. There are countless examples of activists forcing policy change, successfully encouraging institutions to divest from fossil fuels, blocking new oil fields, and attracting coverage and support in the mainstream media. Research has suggested that it generally only takes 3.5 per cent of a population to be involved in civil resistance for meaningful change to happen, as long as a larger proportion of the general population support the movement (this 3.5 per cent refers to activism, as opposed to the 25 per cent of opinion holders I discussed previously).[45]

I should probably confess at this point that I don't usually like joining groups. But researching this chapter convinced me to put aside my discomfort and join climate action group Parents for Future. I am so glad I did. I've been inspired and energised by the other parents in the group, and it's pushed me to make more time for climate action. Rachelle, a fellow member, told me how she used to feel overwhelmed by the idea of activism.

> It felt like it was such a big problem, surely my actions wouldn't make a difference. But then I saw the things that were happening in the Global South, and I started to do more research. One of the things that pushed me into action was learning that the Philippines, the country of my heritage, was at risk. I wanted to protect my heritage and my culture, my history, and my family. I couldn't stand by and let things happen, I needed to take action. So I joined Parents for Future!

The climate movement needs us to work together, and we are so much stronger when we do. And being part of a group with others who share our hopes, dreams, and concerns can help us keep going when things feel difficult or hopeless. Part of what has gotten us into this mess is rampant individualism: we have forgotten that we belong to each other. Collectivism and community is the only way to build a liveable future.

Get political

The climate emergency requires political action. Governments have made public commitments around emissions reductions, and we need to hold them to account with these while campaigning to put an end to new fossil fuel projects and investing in renewables, green technology, and jobs.

As individuals, there is a lot we can do. We can vote with the climate crisis front and centre, regularly write to and meet with our political representatives, attend protests, donate to and help out on the campaigns of genuinely green politicians, and even stand for political office ourselves. We can take governments to court, as several groups of children and young people have successfully done (see below for some examples).[46] We can also push back on the populism and xenophobia that make international political cooperation so much harder, and recognise that climate justice, economic justice, and social justice go hand-in-hand. If we are to truly tackle the former, then we need to be willing to confront the role colonialism and capitalism have played in creating the conditions we are in, and push for reparations for lower-income countries who have been harmed by the profligate carbon spending of the rich. I don't have the space to go into the arguments for climate reparations here, but *Reconsidering Reparations* by Olúfẹ́mi O. Táíwò is a good place to start if you want to find out more.

Support children's right to political participation

Children have the right to express their views privately and publicly, and to have their views considered and taken seriously (Articles 12 and 13). 'Because children don't have the same legal and political standing as adults, they often do not have a platform to have their voices heard, or accountability mechanisms to ensure they are acted upon, and are often not being heard,' UNICEF argues. 'Limiting their opportunity to have a say on the ambition of climate action at local, national and international levels inhibits their rights.'[47]

Although children are often used symbolically in environmental politics as the 'next generation', their involvement is not only symbolic. Children are at the forefront of environmental movements, standing up for their own rights and futures, and they deserve to hold the politicians who are gambling with their futures accountable. In 2021, Germany's supreme constitutional court ruled that the government's climate protection measures were insufficient to protect future generations, following a complaint brought by young environmental activists and supported by green NGOs. In 2018, the Supreme Court of Justice of Colombia issued the government an order to reduce deforestation in the Amazon region following legal action filed by 25 children and youth.[48] In 2023, a judge in the US state of Montana ruled in favour of 16 children and young adults — the youngest of whom was just five — who had accused state officials violating their right to a healthy environment with pro-fossil fuel policies.[49]

Put your money where your mouth is

Where we put our money matters. First, the 'quick fixes': if you can, consider switching your bank account to an ethical bank (the website bank.green can tell you which banks in your country are environmentally friendly, and which invest heavily in fossil fuels). If you have a pension fund, find out where that money is invested, and request that it is shifted away from fossil fuels; the same goes for investments. At the time of writing, there is an energy crisis that has led to many smaller green energy providers collapsing, but, if possible, switch your energy provider to one which focuses on renewables.

In the longer term, it's important to change our consumption patterns. Collectively, we need to be consuming less — recycling just doesn't cut it, and much of what we think we're recycling ends up in landfill anyway. Social media can have us believing that it's normal to constantly update our homes and decor, wear new clothes, travel around the world, own big cars, and upgrade our phones each time a new model comes out. Instead, maybe it's time to start glamorising sharing tools with friends, mending clothes, growing food communally, and chatting to neighbours on the bus! Something that comes up a lot in my conversations with parents is the waste which is generated through children's birthday parties through excessive gifts, single-use decorations, and party-bags. If your child is having a party, you could ask politely for no gifts (or ask for pre-loved presents), use natural decorations like flowers or hand-made ones like paper chains, and give children a lollipop, temporary tattoo, or some wildflower seeds to scatter instead of a party-bag full of plastic that will immediately get broken, lost, or discarded. If you're worried about family members buying too many toys for your child, you could instead suggest experiences, money towards sports classes, a subscription to a nature magazine, or craft materials that you know will get used up.

Make three lifestyle changes

First, change how you travel. Transport accounts for around a fifth of global CO2 emissions. Reducing the number of flights you take — especially domestic flights — can make a difference. We've made a decision as a family to take the bulk of our holidays in the UK, and it's been brilliant exploring not-too-distant places we'd never been to before (plus travelling is much less stressful this way). I'm not ruling out flying again at some point — there are places we'd love to visit with our daughter that are too far to reach otherwise — but we see flying very much as an exception rather than something we do regularly.

Closer to home, make sure the next car you buy is low on

emissions, or better still take the train, bus, or cycle if this is possible. One of our friends recently sold their car and has embraced getting the whole family on bikes. With the money from the car sale, they were able to buy a comfortable bike trailer for their children to sit in on longer journeys. These personal changes have to go hand-in-hand with campaigning for better and cheaper public transport, safer cycle routes, measures to tackle air pollution, and for an end to artificially cheap air ticket prices, which drive up demand and reduce incentives for greener flights.

Second, change what's on your plate. I recently asked a friend who works for a climate consultancy about what individuals could do to tackle global heating. Her answer: eat less meat and dairy. Researchers have found that greenhouse gas emissions from animal-based foods are twice those of plant-based foods.[50] Not only does animal industry cause vast amounts of CO2 and methane to be released into the atmosphere, but it leads to land degradation, disease, and causes huge amounts of suffering to sentient beings. You don't have to go fully vegan to make a difference; eating less meat and fewer animal products can still have a big impact on your 'carbon footprint'.[51]

When our daughter was six she decided to become vegetarian, and she asked us to join her. My husband and I agreed that we would become a meat-free family — another example of how children can make change happen! Although I initially wondered about things like iron levels and protein, reading more about family nutrition reassured me that children can get everything they need from a vegetarian diet and a couple of supplements.

Going vegetarian can have positive moral and emotional implications for children. Philosophers Sue Donaldson and Will Kymlicka argue that children are naturally deeply attuned to animals. 'Children live, breathe, and dream animals. Their earliest dreams are of animals, and the first words learned by infants, apart from mama and dada, are the names of animals.' Yet, they argue, children are habituated into eating and developing pleasure from meat before they can understand what it is. 'The process is so normalised,' they write, 'that as a society we have barely yet asked what might be the costs to children of this assault.'[52] We were always honest with our daughter about what 'meat' was, but when it really clicked for her she was visibly upset and still now feels a lot of guilt for having eaten animals as a young child. I don't have many parenting regrets, but giving her animals to eat before she could give informed consent to it is one of them.

Third, change how you get dressed. The fashion industry currently contributes around 10 per cent of global carbon emissions and pollutes rivers and streams.[53] Buying clothes from genuinely ethical brands costs more, because the cost of the garment reflects the improved pay and working practices across the supply chain, and this is great if you can afford it. However, nothing is as sustainable as buying second-hand — or not buying anything new at all.[54]

Tell children the truth

Children have a right to reliable information from a variety of sources (Article 17), and this extends to information about the climate and the environment. But how we speak to children about the climate emergency matters. Just like adults, young people — especially those prone to worry — may feel overwhelmed, stressed, or depressed by the scale of the climate emergency. They may also have fewer tools at their disposal to work through these feelings.

Climate anxiety is not only a big cause of stress for young people, but it can also prevent positive action.[55] While I don't think we should lie to children about what is happening, it's important to be mindful when it comes to the kind of language we use and follow the lead of the children in front of us when it comes to how much information — and how many of our fears — to share. Some children will want to know as many details as possible; others will want only the basics. It's important to not overload children with frightening statistics, images, or pictures, particularly if they are too young to really comprehend these.

Recognise that we are part of nature

It is impossible to truly love and care for something we do not know or have a personal relationship with. Environmentalist David Sobel writes that 'what's important is that children have an opportunity to bond with the natural world, to learn to love it, before being asked to heal its wounds'.[56] Children who are given the chance to connect with the natural world — to know the trees, plants, birds, animals, insects, and fungi in their local area, to be able to touch and name and smell these things and see how they fit into the life of the neighbourhood — will be willing to make sacrifices and to fight to protect what they know and love in the future. The best thing about this kind of connection with nature is that it's likely to decrease any anxiety or stress they might be feeling; spending time in nature has been shown to bring tremendous physical and mental health benefits.

It's easy to forget sometimes that nature is not something separate to us; instead, we are part of it. As philosopher Timothy Morton puts it, 'You are breathing air, your bacterial microbiome is humming away, evolution is silently unfolding in the background. Somewhere, a bird is singing and clouds pass overhead. You don't have to *be* ecological. Because you *are* ecological.'[57]

Let go of perfectionism

You don't have to be perfect to take action. I know there are people who put off joining a climate group or writing to their MP because they worry that they have to be doing it all — going vegan, protesting regularly, cutting out flights — lest someone calls them a hypocrite or makes them feel bad for not doing enough. But the crisis is urgent. Children need all of us to join them in the climate struggle and to do what we can, imperfectly.

Making some changes to how we live our lives is vastly better than making none at all. Over the time I've been writing this chapter I've bought both second-hand clothes and new ones, I've put cheese in my sandwiches and poured plant-based milk in my coffee, and I've written to my MP and I've missed protests. In short, I've committed to doing what I can and also to pushing myself. My aim is to stretch myself a little further with my actions each month, which feels more sustainable than going 'all in' immediately only to burn out, something I've seen happen time and again in activist circles.

*

When Zen master Thich Nhat Hanh was asked what we should do to save our world, he replied, 'What we most need to do is to hear within us the sound of the Earth crying.' We must also hear the sound of children who are begging us not to look away. If we care about children — those we share our lives with, those living around the world, and those who have yet to be born — we simply cannot ignore them any longer. Children bear the least responsibility for global heating, and are suffering the most. As adults, particularly those of us living resource heavy, carbon-rich lifestyles, we have a moral responsibility to do what we can.

As I write this, the carbon dioxide in the Earth's atmosphere is 423 ppm, and it's getting hotter.

CHAPTER TEN

Votes for children

In 2021, an English activist named Jude Walker set off to walk over 200 miles as part of his call for a carbon tax. En route from Hebden Bridge in West Yorkshire to Parliament in Westminster he met with and lobbied several MPs, including the leader of the Labour Party. Jude had launched an online petition on carbon taxation to coincide with his walk, which reached over 100,000 signatures and triggered a parliamentary debate, and he was interviewed on a number of national outlets.

This was not Jude's first political action. He's been attending protests and demonstrations for most of his life and had already staged a climate protest in his local area in 2020. Chatting to Jude over Zoom, where he joined me from his brightly painted living room, it fast became clear that politics is a huge part of his life. It's what he chats about with friends, and the main topic of conversation around the dinner table at home. He spends his spare time researching ways to halt the climate crisis; like many of us, Jude wishes politicians would take the environmental crisis more seriously and he feels deeply concerned about the slow speed of political action. He believes that in order to get the change we need, the UK needs electoral reform, and he would like to see the country embrace voting systems which offer proportional representation rather than the 'first past the post' system currently used for general elections. Reform would mean more power going to parties like the Green Party, whose proportion of seats under first past the post has always been vastly smaller than their share of votes.[1] With more Green politicians in power, Jude believes we would get more concrete action on tackling the climate crisis.

As we spoke, it was clear that Jude is confident when it comes to engaging with politics and politicians. He has researched his views, can articulate them clearly, and follows what's happening in the news. But despite this, he has never voted. This isn't down to apathy or disillusionment, but simply because Jude is 12.

Failed by democracy

Speaking on an episode of the (now sadly defunct) *Talking Politics* podcast in 2018, Cambridge University Politics Professor David Runciman claimed that young people have been triply discriminated against by Western representative democracy.[2] Firstly, this is because young people cannot usually vote for someone their age, so they are not represented in parliaments. Secondly, the political parties young people vote for keep losing elections (at least in the UK), so the issues they care about are not being adequately addressed.[3] Finally, despite this, young people are still expected to care about, campaign for, and improve things for future generations, particularly when it comes to the environment, as we saw in the last chapter.

An ageing population combined with a minimum voting age of 18 means that votes are increasingly weighted towards older voters, who can vote up until the day they die. These are voters 'who aren't going to live into the future and can just care about the present,' Runciman says. This can be seen as a gradual shift towards gerontocracy, or the rule of the oldest. Writing in the *Financial Times*, Simon Kuper concurs: 'Old people's parties — which will mostly grow out of the centre-right — can look ahead with confidence. Today's developed countries are the oldest societies in history. There are always new old people... [and their] politics move rightward with age. Future politicians can ditch the futurism.'[4]

There are, Runciman continues, two things we can do about this. First, we should reject the notion that only young people should care about the future and press upon older voters their responsibility to safeguard the world for future generations. Second, we should lower the voting age to address this imbalance and give children the right to vote — specifically, he suggests, by lowering the voting age to six. This idea might sound shocking at first. Six? Not 16? But Runciman is serious. He argues that reducing the voting age by just a couple of years wouldn't go far enough towards redressing the balance when we have people at the other end of life voting into their nineties and hundreds, regardless of whether they are still capable of understanding what they are voting for.[5]

Children may not have the same political priorities or interests as adults, but that is exactly the point. Shouldn't a true democracy provide a voice for the needs and desires of all its citizens? 'Preferences are preferences, interests are interests,' writes Runciman, 'and the fact that they emanate from children does not invalidate them. All preferences should count. It would be better for everyone if they did.'[6] We have a situation where every policy decision ever made that affects children — their rights, their education, their safety — has been voted in by adults.

Why does this matter, as long as the adults making the laws have children's best interests in mind? To put it simply, they evidently don't. Childhood poverty, food insecurity, and inequality is at an all-time high in many countries. Far too many children are being failed by the education systems that are supposed to serve them, and the climate emergency, which will impact children the most, is already with us. Giving children the vote wouldn't solve all the problems they face overnight, but it would give them more political power, legitimising their concerns and forcing elected officials to take them seriously. It would push politicians to take the views, needs, and lived experiences of young people into account, and to canvass around issues that they care about.

When the podcast aired, Runciman's proposal was met with a mixed reaction, with critics claiming that it would be akin to handing extra votes to parents. Speaking in an interview with *The Guardian* newspaper, Runciman defended his position: 'That was the argument that was made against votes for women, that it was effectively just giving two votes to husbands ... I don't think we should be entirely sure that children would do what their parents said.'[7]

Changing the voting age so radically might sound like pie-in-the-sky thinking (or irresponsible nonsense, depending on one's views of children) because we tend to think of our current democratic systems as relatively set in stone. But when we look back, we see that democracy has always been a living, shifting thing, and that who gets to vote — and who is left out — has been a site of contestation since democracy began.

Who gets to vote?

The word democracy comes from the Greek *dēmos,* meaning people, and *kratia,* meaning power or rule, and it is interesting to trace how 'people' has been defined throughout the history of suffrage. Who has been included and who has not? It is only fairly recently that all adults have been given the franchise. In ancient Athens, where democracy is said to have begun, the only people eligible to vote were adult male Athenian citizens who had completed their military training. Women, slaves and former slaves, children, and foreign residents were all ineligible. Since then, voting rights around the world have variously been linked to age, gender, property ownership, wealth, paying tax, and education.

The arguments made against women's suffrage — that they had smaller brains and wouldn't be able to understand the complex issues at stake or the political processes, that it would be handing an extra vote to their husbands as they would vote as they were told, that their interests could be represented fairly through their husband's votes, and that they wouldn't be interested in political life as they have other concerns — are mirrored by the arguments made for not extending the vote to children. We hear critics argue that children won't be able to understand the political process, that it would mean effectively giving an extra vote to parents, that their parents can vote on their behalf, that their brains are insufficiently developed, and that they wouldn't want to vote anyway.

John Wall is professor of philosophy, religion, and childhood studies at Rutgers University, and thinks all children should have the vote. He writes: 'Denying children the right to vote is like denying them the right to free speech. It is simply not the kind of right that ought to be limited by age … they lack voting rights not because of something deficient in children; they lack voting rights because of something deficient in democracies.' It is not good, he claims, for anyone to live in such an unrepresentative system, or for us to tolerate such enormous imbalances of power. Although we may feel intuitively that children should not be allowed to vote, this same 'intuitive sense' was used in the past to deny other populations their rights. 'It is equally unjust', he continues, 'to deny suffrage to children as it was to deny it to the poor, minorities, and women'. He points out that every other group in history to gain suffrage has, both immediately and in the long term, ended up much better off, as politicians have come under pressure to respond to their otherwise ignored concerns. Giving children the vote, he argues, would mean putting children's issues on the agenda.[8]

Little harm could come of lowering the voting age but there would be multiple moral and practical benefits, not least contributing to the democratic system by increasing turnout and giving more people a say. It's also generally accepted by experts that lowering the voting age would be good for democracy and encouraging young people to vote, helping children to learn the habit of voting and to be more politically engaged throughout their lives. 18 is a particularly bad age for starting to vote as it's when many young people move away from home for the first time, either to attend university or further education, go travelling, or to start a job.[9]

How low should we go?

Democracies evolve, and over the decades we have seen a gradual reduction in voting age. But if we agree that 18 is too high for the minimum voting age, just how low should we go?

It's a difficult question to answer, because apart from age there — rightly — tend to be no other conditions attached to having the right to vote. We do not require voters to know how to read, or to pass a test, or to understand how international trade or environmental regulations work. If there is any unofficial requirement made of voters, it is that we should vote with our consciences according to our beliefs, something that young children are able to do just as well as adults. It's hard to see where the line should be drawn.

Generally, campaigners for voting reform have called for the cut-off point to be lowered to 16, bringing the voting age in line with other laws and policies around military service, marriage, and the age of sexual consent. But these arguments miss the point, both about what democracy is supposed to be about — treating every person's vote as equal — and about why we have age limits for certain things. The age of sexual consent and the minimum age for entering the army are both in place to protect children and young people from being exploited, harmed, or killed. But voting does not pose a personal risk to children, so it cannot be grouped together with these other age limits.

The voting age in both Austria and Brazil is 16, and 16-year-olds can vote in German regional elections as well as some Norwegian and Maltese elections. 16- and 17-year-olds were allowed to vote in the 2014 Scottish independence referendum and in subsequent Scottish Parliament elections, with Wales following suit and allowing votes from 16 for the Welsh Assembly. In 2022, New Zealand's Supreme Court ruled that the country's current voting age of 18 is discriminatory and breaches young people's human rights, with calls from the Make It 16 campaign to lower the voting age to 16, although no change has been made at the time of writing.[10] But is this low enough? If we agree that not allowing older teens to vote is age discrimination, why not 15 or 14? What about six, as advocated by Runciman and others?

At age six most children have begun formal schooling and know how to read at least simple words; the start of school could begin with the knowledge that you were going to learn to read, count, and vote. But we don't require literacy from adult voters, so why should we expect it from children? Many still alive today will remember the racist Jim Crow laws that linked voting to literacy tests in many of the southern US states, resulting in many Black people (and some poorer white people) being prevented from voting. Literacy isn't even needed in order to be able to vote successfully. In India, ballots with pictures on have been used to support illiterate voters. Many adults worldwide struggle with literacy, so making election materials more accessible would also help them to vote.

What about knowledge? It is true that most young children won't know or understand the finer points of government policies, but this is not a requirement for voting adults. If we can't use literacy or knowledge as a criterion, then maybe we should look to other skills. By age seven, most children have developed cognitive skills that allow them to understand others' mental states including their beliefs, desires, and knowledge, and the ability to comprehend that these may differ from their own.[11] This is the age at which many children begin to be interested in questions of fairness, justice, and right from wrong, and by age seven or eight, children have been shown to favour egalitarian distribution of resources.[12] Again though, we do not require proof of these faculties in adults. And if we don't require these things from adults, but do require them from children, then it starts looking an awful lot like adultism.

So we could go lower still. In democratic and sociocratic schools, where all children are equally included in decision-making, children as young as four and five have shown to be capable of successfully taking part in these processes, thinking about their own preferences and how these would affect others in their communities. There is no reason to think that children would not be able to use those same skills to vote in national or local elections.[13]

The problem with having an age limit for voting is that it will always end up being somewhat arbitrary. In *Give Children the Vote*, John Wall does away with the need for any age limit by making the case for truly universal suffrage from birth. Under his system, everyone would be provided with a proxy vote at birth, which would be exercised by their parent or guardian until they chose to claim their own vote. No one would be barred from voting on their own behalf should they wish to do so, and children would be able to claim their voting right whenever they liked.[14] The only condition for voting would be the desire to vote, which in itself demonstrates democratic competence. 'It is discriminatory and a double standard to bar children from the right to hold governments accountable to their interests at the ballot,' he writes.

Young children may need parental support to vote, but as Lyman Stone writes in *The New York Times*: 'If older people with dementia can be escorted into the voting booth by a family member who will assist their decision, as they can be under the Voting Rights Act, it's difficult to explain why small children with an incomplete understanding of the process couldn't be assisted by those who are raising them in the same way. The results of that election will affect a child's life for far longer than an elderly person's.'[15]

The competence question

Even if we don't legally require adult voters to be competent, as adults we tend to think that we are more competent than children, simply because of our age and greater life experience. We assume that adults are competent until proved otherwise but do the exact opposite when it comes to children; we don't trust children to make good decisions. But children are often far more capable of grappling with challenging issues than we give them credit for — we're just not very good at seeing it. Wall writes that women used to be in a *Catch-22* situation where they were thought of as less politically competent than men because they hadn't yet been given the chance to exercise voting competence. In much the same may, maybe we will only really believe in children's ability to meaningfully engage in the voting process if we give them the opportunity to do so.

Josh, age 11, told me that 'Adults don't think we have the capacity to think for ourselves ... They think that things like racism, sexism, war, the pandemic, the cost-of-living crisis — they think things like that are inappropriate for us to know about. But when it's real life, you have to know what's going on.' He feels strongly that children have the right to be well informed and enjoys learning about what's happening in the world around him; I have no doubt that if he was able to vote, he would do so as carefully as any adult.

Philosophy teacher Andy West agrees that children are more than capable of tackling big issues; we just need to give them space to do so, and to take their thoughts seriously. 'In my classes, I offer children the space to have a complex response to something, and to figure out what they believe. Even aged four or five a child comes into a classroom full of ideas, values, and inner conflicts ... they are not empty vessels to be filled with knowledge.'[16] The children in his classes are able to thoughtfully discuss complex political and ethical ideas like retribution, fairness, conscience, willpower, and justice.

Not all children are given the opportunity to take part in philosophy classes. But in my experience as a parent, these 'big' conversations come up naturally, time and time again. When we pause to recognise it, we can see that children are just as capable of curiosity and complex, moral thought as adults; children think about political subjects all the time in their daily lives and tend to be radical and creative thinkers.

Most of the children I have spoken to have had clear and deeply held views on the need to tackle environmental degradation and the climate crisis, reduce poverty, increase animal wellbeing, and end violence against children, all things which would make the world a better place for everyone. I asked Viv, aged eight, what she would change if she was prime minister, and her answer was instant: 'I would make it so that children weren't punished, that it was fairer for them.' It turned out that she had recently witnessed a child being treated in a harsh and threatening way by their caregiver in a playground; she had found this frightening and upsetting, and didn't think adults should be allowed to treat children in this way.

As the founder of Philosophy for Children movement, Matthew Lipman, writes, 'As it turns out, the vocabulary of very young children contains many of the very terms utilized by philosophers, which suggests that the two groups may have interests in common, particularly in language.'[17] Young children have to make ethical decisions every day, from what it means to be a good friend to how to fairly share resources. They come across challenging moral issues in the books they read and the stories they listen to.[18] Adults consistently underestimate how capable even the youngest children can be when it comes to working through complex ideas, even when we are surrounded by evidence to the contrary. This feeds into a generally held belief that childhood is not the time for politics and that children cannot be trusted to make decisions for themselves, let along make choices which could affect the whole nation.

Who gets to be political?

One of the main reasons we don't give children the vote is because we don't see children as proper citizens. Citizenship can be understood as a contested concept that has included and excluded different populations throughout history, as we have already seen.[19] Although most children are granted automatic legal citizenship from birth, entitling them to certain protections, they have been excluded from political participation through their characterisation as 'citizens in the making' or 'human becomings'.[20] Because we tend to view children through a deficit lens, where they are assumed to be incomplete until they reach adulthood, we overlook their political nature — and their capability.[21] Children's involvement in the politics of everyday life — their resistance, negotiation, and skill at pushing for change — is ignored and their political agency is erased, even though their lives are profoundly political.[22]

The history of working children's movements shows us how political children can be. We may instinctively recoil at the idea of children working, because it feels hard to square with many of our beliefs around what childhood should look like. But around the world children do work for wages, and to look at their organisations is to get a snapshot of children actively involved in political struggle, working together to secure better conditions for themselves and their peers.

The Peruvian Movement of Working Children, founded in 1976, involves thousands of children between the ages of eight and 17. 'Most of the children work in the informal economy, helping out in small family businesses and agriculture, and nearly all of them are also in school,' writes Professor Jessica Taft. 'They come together in local, national, and regional groups to discuss how to support each other, improve working children's lives, and create a more just and equitable world for all children.' Taft says that she has seen some 12-year-olds facilitate meetings better than some 35-year-olds. 'We need to decouple experience and age. Sometimes the youngest kids get listened to the most.'[23]

Although these groups often involve adult support, they are led by the children fighting for better working conditions and recognition. The groups vary by location but share some characteristics: they base their claims on the rights set out in the CRC, while arguing for the right to work to be included; they believe that not only do they have rights, but they are capable of working to realise these rights; they want respect for the work they do, both in terms of paid work and organising work; they call for an equal relationship between adults and children; they want to be consulted on all decisions concerning them at local, national, and international levels; and they understand their organisations as a means to gain more influence in society as well as to bring about a better life.[24]

I think anyone would be hard pressed to see these young people at work — both politically and in their jobs — and argue that they were simply 'playing' at politics, incapable of making rational decisions or understanding political processes. 'They are proof,' Professor Manfred Liebel writes, 'that children can take their interests and rights into their own hands even under difficult conditions.' This is not the only example of children taking their rights into their own hands, even when the consequences for resisting and organising are severe. In September 2022, young adults and children — mostly young women and girls — took to the streets of Iran to protest the oppression and inequality they face under the rule of the Islamic Republic, triggered in this instance by the killing of 22-year-old Mahsa Amini who was beaten to death by the morality police for not wearing her hijab correctly. Amnesty International has reported that Iran's security forces have killed at least 44 children — 14 per cent of overall deaths — and injured, jailed, and tortured many more in a bid to crush the spirit of resistance among the country's youth.[25]

Children are involved in political resistance around the world, from the youth-led groups pushing for gun reform in the US to the children taking climate criminals to court. The field of childhood studies has tried hard in recent decades to change the view of childhood as a time of apolitical incompetence, and there is a growing body of work that highlights how children can and do act in ways which are political. But this shift towards slowly seeing children as capable of political action and understanding has not yet entered the mainstream or translated into changes in policy or practice. Because we still mostly view children as lacking political agency, we don't tend to recognise the role children have played in pushing for major social change.[26] But to ignore this, and to deny their political rights, is to continue to uphold adultist beliefs and practices.

Power to the children!

When children's political agency *is* recognised by adults, it is still mainly through the involvement in processes and practices led and defined by adults, such as adult-led youth parliaments or student councils, projects that are arguably less about children exercising their democratic rights and more about education.[27] But this is not always the case.

Children all over India have taken their lives into their own hands, founding their own parliaments in order to stand up for their rights. The documentary *Power to the Children* follows some of these parliaments, showing the impact they are having on the lives of the children involved and on their communities. In the film, the members of a children's parliament are shown discussing some local village children that seem to have dropped out of school, and how they can best be supported. The 12-year-old minister for public affairs thinks they should get advice from a child helpline; another member wants to dig into the root of why these children are no longer attending school. If the reason is lack of money, he suggests, perhaps the parliament can raise funds in order to help them continue their schooling. They agree that their prime minister, law minister, and education minister will go and speak to the missing children's parents to see what is going on. Later, we see the 12-year-old law minister writing to the village head asking him to intervene to fix some of the village street lights that aren't working.

15-year-old Shaktivel has been a member of children's parliament for the village of Patti since he was ten, and at the time of filming he had recently been elected as cultural minister. His father comes home drunk every day, which is causing real problems for him and his family. 'We can't predict when he will begin to fight,' he tells his colleagues, 'He becomes aggressive ... he beats me really badly. Only when he is drunk does he behave badly.' His experience is common in the village. 14-year-old Jayanthi's father keeps beating her mother, and preventing her from studying; things are so bad that Jayanthi and her mother have both attempted suicide. 12-year-old Keethana says that she comes home from school, washes dishes, cooks dinner, and studies, but her father comes home drunk and complains that she doesn't do any work and beats her. She is sometimes thrown out of the house. 'This alcohol is the problem in my family,' she sobs quietly. 'We should prohibit alcohol. That's what I wish for.' The parliament is working to try and ban alcohol sales in the village, and they stage a play for the adults to watch to raise awareness of the impact that alcohol is having on them.

Throughout the documentary, we see the children juggling daily work such as washing clothes and dishes alongside their political work and their formal education. These children are caring for each other and their communities, interested in the world around them, optimistic that they can push for change, and driven to make it happen. We see them in sharp contrast to the adults who come across as detached, resigned, and even apathetic.

These parliaments bear little resemblance to the children's parliaments that children in the so-called global North might join in with as extra-curricular enrichment activities set up to encourage youth participation. In these activities, 'parliamentary participation engages children with a system that is dedicated to governing them ... it binds children to systemic norms, morals, and knowledges.'[28] In India, we see something very different: children fighting and working together to bring about genuine changes that will improve their lives both now and in the future. These children are led by their own morals and are committed to changing the system rather than just playing at it.

It is important to note that some children and young people will always be listened to and taken more seriously than others; some will get to be more political than others. Which children are seen and competent and capable — and worth listening to — matters.[29] Children from underserved communities are often treated differently to their affluent peers, particularly those racialised as white.[30] This is also clear when we look at young children. In comparison to teenagers and older young people, whose political activities and competence are generally more accepted, we tend to see young children as incapable of acting in ways that are political.[31] Yet when we widen our definitions of what political action and agency might look like, we can see that children of all ages are enthusiastic agents in their own lives.[32] As we have already explored in previous chapters, we can even read children's 'bad behaviour' as a form of resistance, which itself is a form of political action. When we ask ourselves whether children and young people should be given the right to vote, it's worth remembering that political interest and competence doesn't have to look a certain way to be valid. If we believe in universal suffrage, we should make it truly universal.

'You write down what you want and the president has to do it'

As a teenager I was outraged that I couldn't vote. My friends and I read newspapers, listened to the news on the radio — as well as Monday night punk hour, which felt equally political — and had strong views on social change. We discussed politics over the beers we begged older friends to buy us and went to protests as well as gigs and parties. During the UK 2005 general election I was studying for my A-level in politics and government, and I remember how unfair if felt that I was spending hours every week studying, dissecting, and arguing about our political system — while also working part time and paying taxes to the treasury — but still couldn't vote. This is a view shared by the British Youth Council 'Votes At 16' campaign, which calls for all political parties to incorporate full voting rights to 16- and 17-year-olds in national elections and referendums.[33]

We know that at least some people under the age of 18 would like to vote. But what about very young children, the sort of age Runciman and Wall are writing about? I was speaking about this with Maria, who lives in the US, and she shared with me part of a conversation she had had with her daughter Isabella, who was three at the time. The conversation surprised her so much that she noted it down:

Isabella: *I want to vote.*

Maria: *Really? Why?*

I: *You write down what you want and the president has to do it.*

M: *What do you want to write down?*

I: *Fix things.*

My own daughter has always accompanied us to the ballot box and has also been asking to vote since she was three. She regularly writes to our local MP, and has sent drawings and 'notes of encouragement' to her own preferred political party. During the 2019 UK General Election she wrote to the Green Party asking them for posters to put in our window; when they arrived, she proudly stuck them up. She was four at the time, and people walking past our home will have seen a clear demand from her to vote for them. When elections happen — national or local — we discuss them as a family, and my husband and I take her preferences into account in our own voting. She regularly tells us how unfair she finds it that children cannot vote; in her words, 'I have ideas and I'm a person too.' Josh, mentioned earlier, also feels strongly about voting. 'Kids are going to be living in the world for the longest time,' he told me, 'so not allowing us to vote is adultist.'

Clearly this will not be the case for every child. My daughter lives in a home where both of her parents are politically engaged and have the privilege of time and resources to discuss these topics with her. We try to talk about politics in a way that resonates with her, and we mostly keep her updated on key events in the news. We take time to share some of the arguments for and against different political parties and encourage her to think about issues from different perspectives. We buy her books on politics, and she is subscribed to a weekly news magazine aimed at children. But the fact that some children will not naturally show as much interest — or have access to adults who can help them understand the basics — isn't a good excuse to bar them from voting; after all, not every adult is engaged or interested in politics.

Lawmakers underestimate how keen children would be to vote. Research shows that when they can vote, young people generally choose to do so. The Scottish Independence Referendum in 2014 saw 75 per cent of 16- and 17-year-olds voting, with 97 per cent saying they planned to vote in future elections.[34] This figure was much higher than 18–24-year-olds (54 per cent), showing that giving young people the chance to vote earlier — while still being in school and more likely to live at home — is likely to increase voter participation. However, statistics from Wales, where voting take-up by young people is lower, shows that it's not enough to simply enfranchise children; this must go hand-in-hand with accessible information about voting, candidates, and political parties, ideally at school as well as at home.[35]

If we take time to listen to their opinions and ideas, children have many thoughts about how the world could work and become fairer. Like adults, not all children will be able to grasp the finer details of policies and their consequences. But even young children could, with a trusted adult's support and guidance, compare how an MP has voted on the issues that they care about. If a five-year-old can remember 35 different dinosaur names and their physical characteristics, they can remember a handful of political parties and their main messages and values. And young people have proven over and over again that they are as capable of political conviction and action as anyone else. They are already bringing about political change despite being locked out of the system.

The shock that people feel around the notion of inclusive suffrage doesn't seem to be linked to any substantive argument.

Instead, it is another symptom of adultism, where adults feel deep distrust around children's capacity to engage meaningfully in 'grown-up' or complicated issues. But if we can move past the fears many of us hold around trusting children, we could see that involving them in our democratic processes would not just be fairer to children but would benefit the whole of society for generations to come. It would ensure politicians focused on the policies younger voters cared about — the climate emergency, social justice, education, jobs, affordable housing — and communicated these in ways that made political debate and discourse comprehendible to all citizens. This would also benefit adults who experience barriers to voting because of language, disability, or level of education.

Meaningful votes

If we were to bring in real universal suffrage, we would need to ensure that participation was truly meaningful. After all, is a democracy truly democratic if voters don't understand what they are voting for? I don't think it's contradictory to call for voters to be better informed while simultaneously arguing for young children to be given the vote. Better informed parents would be able to teach their children about the bare bones of their country's democracy around the kitchen table; schoolteachers would feel confident answering political questions in an age-appropriate way. By engaging children in the democratic process from birth, the whole populace would be better informed, more engaged, and more tolerant of each other's beliefs.

For all people to be able to participate meaningfully in the political process, we would need to ensure that each person received good quality, age-appropriate education and information around politics and democratic processes. This could take place in many different ways, but the most obvious route would be through the formal schooling system. Jude, who walked the Carbon Tax Walk, told me that some of his schoolmates think politics is boring. 'I think that if they had some education on how politics is connected to everything at school, then maybe they would become more interested,' he mused.

There is one argument against extending suffrage to children that I haven't touched upon yet, which is that children have the right to a worry-free childhood, away from serious or 'grown-up' issues. Political philosopher Hannah Arendt argued that children should be kept apart from politics, and that children's involvement in the political sphere was a sign that something had gone very wrong, with children forced to take on adult roles because adults were denying their own responsibility for taking care of the world.[36] I share this concern to some extent; there can sometimes be a tendency amongst adults to think that the next generation will come and fix things for us, so we don't need to worry too much about doing it ourselves. I also agree that we should be careful about how we speak to children about distressing subjects, especially when they are very young. But this line of reasoning ignores the assumptions and privileges at play in the idea that children should be protected from difficult issues and ideas, not least that this ignores those children who are already living through the impact of these issues themselves. Children are already political, whether they can vote or not.

Surely it is possible for children to be politically engaged in an age-appropriate way. As adults, we could work with children to design materials — books, videos, pictures, songs, podcasts, games

— that explain complex ideas in a way which is simple to grasp. I can easily imagine discussions being held in classrooms around, say, whether it is right to build a big road that would help people get to work and school faster but which would destroy an old forest, or whether everyone should be paid the same amount of money for doing different jobs.

Giving all children the opportunity to attend regular philosophy classes would be a good step in this direction; even better, philosophy and politics could be embedded across a broad and engaging curriculum. As children got older, they could access more detailed and complex materials, providing an opportunity to learn about different subjects with real life application at the same time as being involved in the democratic process. As well as giving children and young people a way to meaningfully engage with voting, this would support them to grow into engaged and informed citizens.

This shouldn't be controversial, as it already forms part of the CRC. Article 17, which focuses on access to the media, states that every child has the right to reliable information from a variety of sources, and that governments should encourage the media to provide information which children can understand. This democratic shift could also pave the way for children's voices being heard and listened to more broadly. Children could write newspaper columns, author books, and have their art displayed in galleries. When we start viewing children as people, a lot becomes possible.

As parents, we can lay the groundwork for power sharing in our homes. I know that for me, it can sometimes feel easier to think about big ideas such as giving children the vote than to consider how I might be able to make changes in our family life to ensure our daughter's voice is heard and listened to. If I believe that children should have a say in who runs the country, then how does this translate to how our home is run? We've already looked at the idea of sociocracy in an educational context. But the principles behind sociocracy — taking a consent-based approach to making decisions that ensures that every voice is heard and ensuring that everyone can at least tolerate the agreed-upon outcomes — lend themselves just as well to family life as they do to schools. Although it might feel unnatural at first, having a weekly family circle could be a way of embedding collaborative decision-making processes into the home, with children bringing their own ideas and objections to the table. Family holidays, budget decisions, meal ideas, bedtime negotiations; all of these could be worked through together.

So many of us live in homes where, whether we are aware of it or not, decision-making power is concentrated at the top. Spreading this power out so that everyone has an equal say would not only honour children's right to be listened to and taken seriously but would develop active citizenship and negotiation skills as they grow. As adults, we can also speak up for children's right to vote, making the most of the fact that our voices are more likely to be listened to. We can support campaigns pushing to lower the voting age, amplify children's voices, and pay attention to their ideas and take them seriously. We can write to our representatives about universal suffrage, talk about the idea on social media, and start conversations. If we have children, when it comes to election time, we can consider making family voting decisions and sharing our votes with our children. Liberation, after all, starts at home.

A politics for children

Perhaps the argument that we should give children the vote still seems eccentric to you. But if feminism is 'the radical notion that women are people', then the same can be said of children's liberation: if we believe that children are indeed people — fellow citizens with much to offer — then extending them voting rights doesn't seem quite so odd.[37]

As well as giving children the vote, we could make other changes to increase our chances of having a political system that works for children and young people: offering political training to young people; creating forums where children and young people could provide advice to elected officials to ensure that their perspective is heard within the democratic process; guaranteeing that a certain number of young people are shortlisted for candidacy within political parties (or that they are included and highly placed within list-based electoral systems); and creating stronger rules ensuring that the impacts of policy decisions on young people are calculated, including having ministers, departments, or commissioners solely focused on children and future generations, as previously discussed.[38]

If I could change the law tomorrow to give all children the vote, I would. But despite believing without hesitation in universal suffrage, I don't think it would solve everything. No matter who votes, there exist deep flaws within our existing political and economic systems, and we will have to start by tackling these. Politicians are not engaging with the long-term thinking we so urgently need, and with an electoral landscape that seems to be veering increasingly towards populist, right-wing discourse — with attacks on refugees, trans people, and climate protestors all taking up place on the front pages of popular newspapers and during parliamentary debates — I feel increasingly despondent about the likelihood of radical change coming from traditional politics. I would be interested to see a shift towards more use of citizen's assemblies, and the development of new decision-making structures focused on building consensus and working collaboratively, rather than systems rooted in confrontation and division.

We could also look towards new forms of knowledge-gathering and decision-making that honour the capacities and knowledge of even the youngest children. This might mean going to the places where young children are — homes, nurseries, playgrounds, and schools — and listening to them, observing them, and seeking their input on the things that matter to them. 'Children have the capacities for communication, trust, and engagement,' write philosophers Sue Donaldson and Will Kymlicka, 'and these make possible new modes of participation through interdependent agency and supported decision-making.'[39]

*

The fight for children's liberation will not be won in parliaments or in the ballot box, although systemic change is crucial if we are to improve children's lives. For there to be enough political momentum to push through the changes children want and need — ending child poverty, cleaning up the environment, reforming the childcare and education systems, protecting children from violence, and supporting votes for children — showing those in power that we want change is not enough. We need to build change in our own lives, working with children and adults alike to build homes, schools, and communities based on solidarity, mutual support, and love, where children's voices are heard, respected, and acted upon and where all children — regardless of who they are or where they come from — are cherished and respected right from the start.

CONCLUSION

Widening circles of care

Changing the way we think about children and noticing the adultism that surrounds us isn't easy. We have become adjusted to adultism through the way we were parented, educated, and socialised. It is so normalised that when children resist adult control and oppression — when they tell us we're being unfair, when they refuse to attend school, when they argue, when they fidget and break rules and shout too much, when they disobey — we label them as in need of correction, training, or punishment. Rather than being grateful to children for shining a light on unequal power dynamics and oppressive practices, we seek to stamp out their resistance in the name of development, good manners, and discipline.

In a speech given in September 1967 to the American Psychological Association, Reverend Dr Martin Luther King Jr took the word 'maladjusted' — a word that psychiatrists and psychologists were increasingly using to diagnose people who didn't fit in with societal norms — and turned it on its head, calling on his audience to embrace what he termed 'creative maladjustment':

> There are some things in our nation and in the world to which I'm proud to be maladjusted, and which I call upon all men of good will to remain maladjusted until the good society is realised. I must honestly say that I never intend to adjust myself to segregation and discrimination. I never intend to become adjusted to religious bigotry. I never intend to adjust myself to economic conditions which take necessities from the many to give luxuries to the few. I never intend to adjust myself to the madness of militarism and the self-defeating effects of physical violence ... Through such maladjustment I believe that we can emerge from the bleak and desolate midnight of man's inhumanity to man into the bright and glittering daybreak of freedom and justice. I haven't lost faith in the future.[1]

Dr King was speaking at the height of the civil rights movement, which pushed to abolish legalised racial segregation and disenfranchisement throughout the United States. But his idea of creative maladjustment is one that feels intensely relevant when thinking about children's liberation. In a society that asks us to adjust to adultism — to child poverty, exploitation, violence against children, environmental destruction, and the use of punishment and humiliation to force children into bending to adult power — we should embrace being maladjusted. This maladjustment is a gift, a positive adaptation that helps us notice what is broken in our society and gives us the courage to fix things.

Systems and institutions can change. Recent decades have seen improvements for children in the countries that have banned smacking, the schools that protect children's rights, the researchers who work alongside children to co-create knowledge, and the caregivers who have decided to break cycles of coercive parenting practices. But too many children still cannot trust our political systems or institutions to keep them healthy or happy, and the pace of change is not quick enough. In some places children's rights are actively being wound back, eroded through regressive laws and appeals to keeping kids 'safe' while restricting their choices and autonomy.

Relying on systemic change will not get us towards children's liberation if it is constrained by a fundamentally exploitative economic and political system steeped in adultist beliefs. There have been decades of activism, research, and a solid bank of studies showing that the way we treat children is simply not working. But collectively, we are still not quite getting the message. And while we cannot give up or stop agitating for things to improve, I no longer believe that the urgent radical change children need will come from within existing systems of power. Instead, we need to move towards a collective ethic of solidarity and care.

Widening circles of care

'I live my life in widening circles that reach out across the world,' wrote the poet Rainer Maria Rilke. Ever since I started writing this book, I have found myself coming back to these words. We need to widen our circles of care. I see these widening circles as building on the deep love and care we feel for ourselves and our own children, expanding outwards to think about how we can stand in solidarity with all children, including those in future generations to come. Like a pebble dropped into a pond, these circles ripple out: when we treat ourselves with compassion, it's easier to treat our own children with care and respect; when we start by treating our children as equals, they are more likely to treat others similarly.

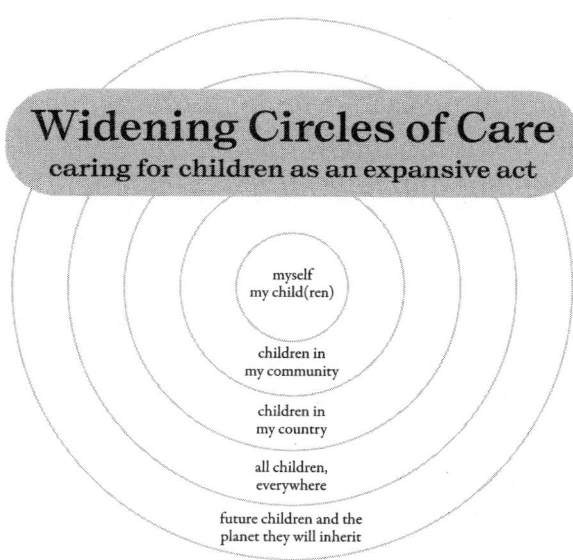

First circle: *caring about our own children and ourselves.* We work towards a home culture that actively disrupts adultist beliefs and practices, and provides space for children's liberation to take root. Part of this is caring for ourselves, and the child we once were, recognising the harm done to us through adultism and affirming that the cycle ends with us.

Second circle: caring about the children in our local communities. We start thinking about how we can make things better for children in our local communities, and we build networks with others to change things for the better. We get involved in planting community gardens; organise play streets; clean up public spaces; support our neighbours; donate to food banks; volunteer at the local school; get to know our political representatives. We step in if we see children being mistreated, despite this feeling uncomfortable or awkward, because they need to know that how they are being treated is wrong.

Third circle: caring about the children in the country where we live. We understand that our economic and political systems are actively harming children, and we find ways to push back. We inform ourselves about children's issues on a national level and vote with children's rights and services in mind; write to our local politicians; get involved in national campaigns; write to newspapers; fundraise; and protest.

Fourth circle: Caring for all children, everywhere. Caring about children means fighting against all forms of oppression where we find it. We might donate to organisations doing good work in other countries; think about the impact of the products we buy, boycotting companies that rely on child slavery and researching the use of child labour in the fashion, agricultural, and mining industries; and, if we live in a rich country, lobby our governments to redistribute resources to support countries which have been (or continue to be) exploited and colonised. We recognise that children's liberation is inextricable from other forms of social justice and that these cannot be separated out.

Fifth circle: caring about future children and the planet they will inherit. If it feels difficult to think about children who are not yet born, we can think about future children we will know and love — grandchildren, great-grandchildren, the future children of dear friends. We change our patterns of consumption; talk openly with others about the climate crisis; lobby politicians; and continue to embody our own values and priorities even when things are feeling hopeless, because we know that future children will not be able to make up for the destruction we are collectively causing now. It is up to us.

These circles are not phases or steps to move through; we don't stop caring about our children or local community because we're taking part in climate activism. Instead, each circle reinforces the others, with the ripples from the first supporting and deepening our work on the last.

I like the idea that there is no such thing as other people's children; that we must recognise our duty of care towards children and that we should strive to be in solidarity and community with them. As adults, we collectively have the voice and means to challenge adultism and contribute to children's liberation — not just for our children, but for all children.

Towards children's liberation

When I started planning this book way back in 2018, I was certain that I knew what I was going to say: we should change how we treat children because doing so will change the world for the better. It seemed inconceivable to me that writers exploring questions of social justice weren't shouting from the rooftops about how we treat children. The problem seemed so obvious: just stop raising children to normalise oppressive power dynamics and the world will be a better place within one generation — two, maximum! But the more I wrote, the more I moved away from this way of thinking. I still believe that ridding ourselves of adultism would transform all of our lives for the better. But it's dangerous to see treating children well as a means to an end, even if the goal is a worthy one. This way of thinking still sees children as 'future people'. Thinking about the sort of society we want to live in brings us back to how we treat children here and now. I don't need research to tell me that I want to live in a world where we act compassionately, kindly, and respectfully towards children, where we value their contributions and honour their wisdom and vision, and where we safeguard the natural world they are a part of. I now think that rather than asking how children can make the world better, we should instead be seeking to build a world that is worthy of the children we care for so much.

An argument I often hear against treating children well is that they won't be prepared for 'real life'. Life is hard, so the education and parenting they receive should prepare them for that; how else will they be able to tolerate unjust working conditions or the harsh realities of living in a deeply unequal society? My answer to this is simple: I don't believe that children should be taught to expect bad treatment — in any aspect of their lives. Instead, I dream about a society where everyone is treated fairly: where we do not tolerate bosses exploiting their workers, or landlords hoarding property and pushing families into poverty, or men who use violence to break the women they are supposed to love, or politicians who allow our planet to be destroyed. I want my daughter to expect to be treated decently. I want the same for all children.

That fairer world is within our grasp. I could not have written this book without a deep sense of hope. Despite some of the grim statistics and stories I've shared with you, that sense of hope has not left me. Children's liberation isn't something 'out there', a utopia that lives only in the pages of radical theorists. It is present in the moments when we take time to listen to what children are telling us, when parents take a deep breath and apologise, when teachers challenge their school's behaviour policies, when politicians allocate more money to low-income families, when grandmothers chain themselves to buildings to fight so that their grandchildren have a liveable planet to grow old on. It is a daily practice of resistance, hope, and love.

As philosopher Martha Nussbaum puts it, 'In the end, ethical thought has to become practical, or it is idle.'[2] This book has been about developing that ethical thought and becoming attuned to the problem of adultism. Now it is time for action.

Summary of the UN Convention on the Rights of the Child (CRC)

The **Preamble** (the text at the beginning of the document) sets out that:

- Families should be afforded the necessary protection and assistance so that they can take care of children and other family members;
- Children should grow up in a family environment, in an atmosphere of happiness, love, and understanding;
- Children should be brought up in the spirit of peace, dignity, tolerance, freedom, equality and solidarity; and that
- Children need special safeguards and care, including appropriate legal protection, before as well as after birth.

There are fifty-four **Articles** that set out children's rights and how governments should support children to enjoy these rights:

Article 1 *(definition of the child)*: The rights set out in the CRC apply to everyone under the age of 18.

Article 2 *(non-discrimination)*: The rights set out in the CRC apply to every child without discrimination, regardless of ethnicity, sex, religion, language, abilities, or any other status.

Article 3 *(best interests of the child)*: The best interests of the child must take priority in all decisions and actions that affect children.

Article 4 *(implementation of the CRC)*: Governments must do all they can to make sure every child can enjoy their rights by creating systems and passing laws that promote and protect children's rights.

Article 5 *(parental guidance and the child's capacity)*: Governments must respect the rights and responsibilities of parents and carers to provide guidance to their child as they grow up, so that they fully enjoy their rights. This must recognise the child's growing capacity to make their own choices.

Article 6 *(survival and development)*: Every child has the right to life. Governments must do all they can to ensure that children survive and develop to their full potential.

Article 7 *(birth registration)*: Every child has the right to be registered at birth, to have a name and nationality, and, as far as possible, to know and be cared for by their parents.

Article 8 *(identity)*: Every child has the right to their identity. Governments must respect and protect that right, and prevent the child's name, nationality, or family relationships from being changed unlawfully.

Article 9 *(separation from parents)*: Children must not be separated from their parents against their will unless it is in their best interests. Children whose parents have separated have the right to stay in contact with both parents, unless this could harm them.

Article 10 *(family reunification)*: Governments must respond quickly and sympathetically if a child or their parents apply to live together in the same country. Children whose parents live apart in different countries have the right to visit and keep in direct contact with both of them.

Article 11 *(abduction)*: Governments must take steps to stop children being taken out of their own country illegally by their parents or other relatives, or being prevented from returning home.

Article 12 *(respect for children's views)*: Every child has the right to express their views on matters affecting them, and to have their views considered and taken seriously. This right applies at all times, for example during immigration proceedings, housing decisions, or the child's day-to-day home life.

Article 13 *(freedom of expression)*: Every child has the right to find out and distribute information, and to express their thoughts and ideas through varied forms of expression.

Article 14 *(freedom of thought, belief, and religion)*: Every child has the right to think and believe what they choose, and to practise their religion, as long as they are not stopping other people from enjoying their rights. The state must respect the rights of parents to provide direction to their child that is appropriate to their development.

Article 15 *(freedom of association)*: Every child has the right to meet with other people and to join groups and organisations, as long as this does not stop other people from enjoying their rights.

Article 16 *(right to privacy)*: Every child has the right to privacy, including their family and home life, and should be protected from unlawful attacks that harm their reputation.

Article 17 *(access to the media)*: Every child has the right to reliable information from a variety of sources. Governments should encourage mass media information that children can understand and that supports their wellbeing and development. Children should be protected from media that could harm them.

Article 18 *(parental and state responsibilities)*: Both parents share responsibility for bringing up their child and should always consider what is best for the child. The state must support parents by creating support services for children, and giving parents the help they need.

Article 19 *(protection from violence, abuse, and neglect)*: The state must do all it can to protect children from all forms of violence, abuse, neglect, exploitation, and bad treatment by their parents or anyone else who looks after them.

Article 20 *(alternative care)*: If a child cannot be looked after by their parents, the state must provide alternative care that is continuous and respects the child's culture, language, and religion.

Article 21 *(adoption)*: Governments must ensure adoptions are safe, lawful, and in the child's best interests. Children should only be adopted outside of their country if a suitable family cannot be found in their own country.

Article 22 *(refugee children)*: If a child is seeking or has refugee status, the state must provide them with appropriate protection and assistance to help them enjoy all the rights set out in the UNCRC. Governments must help children who are separated from their parents to be reunited with them.

Article 23 *(disabled children)*: Disabled children have the right to live a full and dignified life, and as far as possible to play an active part in their community. Governments must support disabled children and their families.

Article 24 *(health and healthcare)*: Every child has the right to the best possible health. Governments must provide good quality healthcare, clean water, nutritious food, a clean environment, and health education. Richer countries must help poorer countries achieve this.

Article 25 *(review of treatment in care)*: If a child has been placed away from home for the purpose of care or protection, they have the right to a regular review of their treatment, the way they are cared for, and their situation.

Article 26 *(social security)*: Every child has the right to benefit from social security. Governments must provide social security to families in need of assistance, and consider the circumstances of children and their family in addressing their need for assistance.

Article 27 *(adequate standard of living)*: Every child has the right to a decent standard of living that meets their physical and social needs and supports their development. Governments must help families who cannot afford to provide this, particularly with a child's nutrition, clothing, and housing.

Article 28 *(education)*: Every child has the right to an education. Primary education must be free, and different forms of secondary education must be available to every child. School discipline must respect children's dignity and rights. Richer countries must help poorer countries achieve this.

Article 29 *(aims of education)*: Education must develop every child's personality, talents, and mental and physical abilities to the full. It must encourage the child's respect for their own rights and those of others, for their parents, their own and other cultures, and the environment.

Article 30 *(minority and indigenous groups)*: A child from a minority group has the right to enjoy their own culture, use their own language, and practise their own religion.

Article 31 *(leisure, play, and culture)*: Every child has the right to relax, play, and take part in a wide range of cultural and artistic activities.

Article 32 *(child labour)*: Governments must protect children from economic exploitation and work that is dangerous or might harm their health, development, or education. Governments must set a minimum working age and ensure that working conditions are safe and appropriate.

Article 33 *(drug abuse)*: Children must be protected from using, producing, or distributing illegal drugs.

Article 34 *(sexual exploitation)*: Children must be protected from all forms of sexual abuse and exploitation.

Article 35 *(abduction, sale, and trafficking)*: Governments must protect children from being abducted, sold, or trafficked to another country for the purpose of exploitation.

Article 36 *(other forms of exploitation)*: Governments must protect children from all other forms of exploitation.

Article 37 *(cruel treatment and detention)*: Children must not be tortured, sentenced to the death penalty, or suffer other cruel or degrading treatment or punishment. Children should be arrested, detained, or imprisoned only as a last resort and for the shortest time possible. They must be treated with respect and care, and be able to keep in contact with their family. No child should be given a sentence of life imprisonment, or put in prison with adults.

Article 38 *(armed conflicts)*: Governments must protect children under the age of 15 from taking part in war or joining armed forces. Special protection and care should be given to children affected by war and armed conflicts.

Article 39 *(recovery from trauma)*: Children who have experienced neglect, abuse, exploitation, torture, or who are victims of war, must receive special support to help them recover their health, dignity, self-respect, and social life, and to reintegrate.

Article 40 *(juvenile justice)*: Every child accused or guilty of breaking the law must be treated with dignity. They should be presumed innocent until proven guilty, and have the right to legal assistance and a fair trial that takes account of their age. Governments must set a minimum age for criminal responsibility.

Article 41 *(national standards)*: If a country's laws and standards go further than the CRC in promoting children's rights, then the country must keep these laws.

Article 42 *(knowledge of rights)*: Governments must actively work to make sure children and adults know about the principles and provisions of the CRC.

Articles 43–54 are about how adults and governments must work together to make sure all children can enjoy all their rights.

You can read the full text of the CRC online.

Recommended further reading

Although I've tried to keep *It's Not Fair* as accessible and practical as possible, I've read a lot of theory while writing it! Some of the academic texts I've returned to time and again include Anca Gheaus, Gideon Calder, and Jurgen de Wispelaere's *The Routledge Handbook of the Philosophy of Childhood and Children* (Routledge, 2018); Jens Qvortrup's *The Palgrave Handbook of Children's Studies* (Palgrave Macmillan, 2009); Wouter Vanderhole et al.'s *Routledge International Handbook of Children's Rights Studies* (Routledge, 2015); and David F. Lancy's *The Anthropology of Childhood* (Cambridge, 2015).

Chapter One: How we see children

Two texts were key in helping me make sense of the way children are positioned as 'future people': Jens Qvortrup's *Childhood Matters: social theory, practice and politics* (Aldershot, 1994) and Emma Uprichard's article 'Children as "Being and Becomings": children, childhood and temporality' in *Children and Society* (Vol. 22, 2008). David Archard's *Children* (Routledge, 2015) sets out how the way we see children has changed over time. I drew on Toby Rollo's work to understand how conceptions of childhood have been used to support colonialism and white supremacy, particularly his articles 'Feral Children: settler colonialism, progress, and the figure of the child' in *Settler Colonial Studies* (Vol. 8, 2018) and 'The Color of Childhood: the role of the child/human binary in the production of Anti-Black racism' in the *Journal of Black Studies* (Vol. 49, 2018).

Chapter Two: Adultism

Manfred Liebel's article 'Adultism and Age-Based Discrimination Against Children' in D. Kutsar and H. Warming's *Children and Non-Discrimination Interdisciplinary Textbook* (CREAN, 2014) has been central in my understanding of adultism, as has John Wall's writing, including his book *Ethics in Light of Childhood* (Georgetown University Press, 2010), and Harry Shier's work, particularly his paper 'What Does "Equality" Mean For Children in Relation to Adults?', which can be found on his website (https://www.harryshier.net). The Childism Institute (childism.org) has been a useful resource for thinking about how we challenge adultism. John Holt's *Escape from Childhood: the needs and rights of children* (E.P. Dutton, 1974) was pivotal in growing the children's liberation movement of the 1970s, and I owe much to Holt's body of work. Miranda Fricker's *Epistemic Injustice* (Oxford University Press, 2007) showed me the importance of having accurate, shared language to label and challenge injustice. On children's liberation and youth autonomy, I wholeheartedly recommend *No! Against Adult Supremacy*, an anthology of excellent zines (Stinney Distro, 2023), and *Trust Kids! Stories on Youth Autonomy and Confronting Adult Supremacy,* a collection of short pieces edited by carla joy bergman (AK Press, 2023).

Chapter Three: Understanding children's rights

When writing this chapter, I returned to Priscilla Alderson's *Young Children's Rights* (Jessica Kingsley, 2008) and Phil Jones and Sue Welch's *Rethinking Children's Rights* (Bloomsbury, 2018) often. Harry Shier's article 'Pathways to Participation Revisited' in B. Percy-Smith and N. Thomas's *A Handbook of Children and Young People's Participation* (Routledge, 2010) helped me understand what meaningful participation can look like, as did Laura Lundy's groundbreaking work on the #CovidUnder19 project. Afua Twum-Danso's paper 'A Cultural Bridge, Not an Imposition: legitimising children's rights in the eyes of local communities' in the *Journal of the History of Childhood and Youth* (Vol. 1, 2008) puts forward a way of bridging the divide between universality and relativity when it comes to children's rights. Manfred Liebel's *Children's Rights from Below: cross-cultural perspectives* (Palgrave Macmillan, 2012) shows how children's rights need to be understood in the context of their lives, not just as theory.

Chapter Four: Body politics

Central to my understanding of children's bodies as sites of political struggle was Kathrin Hörschelmann and Rachel Colls' *Contested Bodies of Childhood and Youth* (Palgrave Macmillan, 2009). Eliza Hull's edited collection of essays *We've Got This* (Scribe, 2023) showcases some of the experiences of disabled parents and their children, and Kerry Murphy's *A Guide to SEND in the Early Years* (Featherstone, 2022) sets out how poorly neurodivergent children's needs are catered for in the education sector. Virginia Sole-Smith's *Fat Talk* (Ithaka, 2023) solidified for me the harms that diet culture causes children, and I was grateful for Laura Thomas's newsletter *Can I Have Another Snack?*. Shon

Faye's *The Transgender Issue* (Allen Lane, 2021) helped me understand the struggles faced by trans youth.

Chapter Five: Parenting as a radical act

Alice Miller's *For Your Own Good* (Virago, 1987), Robin Grille's *Parenting for a Peaceful World* (The Children's Project, 2008), and Theresa Graham Brett's *Parenting for Social Change* (Social Change Press, 2011) all shaped my understanding of the parent-child relationship as a deeply political one, and adrienne maree brown's (2020) *We Will Not Cancel Us (*AK Press, 2020) helped me to understand punishment as part of wider punitive culture. Alfie Kohn's *Unconditional Parenting* (Atria, 2009), Joan Durrant's *A Guide to Building Healthy Parent-Child Relationships: a positive rights-based approach* (Save The Children, 2011), and Philippa Perry's *The Book You Wish Your Parents Had Read* (Penguin, 2019) all help parents in laying the foundations for a more equal and collaborative relationship with their children. Dan Siegel and Mary Hartzell's *Parenting from the Inside Out* (Scribe, 2014) and Emma Svanberg's *Parenting for Humans* (Penguin, 2023) provide helpful exercises for those who want to reflect on their past experiences and how this impacts on their parenting today.

Chapter Six: Loving pedagogy

The *Analysis* episode 'The Early Years Miracle?' (BBC Radio 4, 2020) was crucial in shaping how I approached this chapter. Tamsin Grimmer's *Developing a Loving Pedagogy in the Early Years: how love fits with professional practice* (Routledge, 2021) was helpful in thinking about the role of love in childcare, as was Matthew S. Liao's *The Right to be Loved* (Oxford University Press, 2015). The *Contesting Early Childhood* series (Routledge,

2005–2023) transformed the way I thought about early years education and care, particularly the volumes edited by Peter Moss. Rachel Rosen and Katherine Twamley's edited volume *Feminism and The Politics of Childhood: friends or foes?* (UCL Press, 2018) enriched my thinking about care, motherhood, and balancing children's needs with their mothers', as did Vanessa Olorenshaw's *Liberating Motherhood: birthing the purplestocking movement* (Womancraft, 2016).

Chapter Seven: Deliberate harm

On the UK's housing crisis, I turned to Vikki Spratt's *Tenants: the people on the frontline of Britain's housing emergency* (Profile, 2022). I found Polly Curtis' *Behind Closed Doors: why we break up families - and how to mend them* (Virago, 2022) invaluable in understanding the UK's child social care system. Dorothy Roberts' *Torn Apart: how the child welfare system destroys Black families - and how abolition can build a safer world* (Basic, 2022) helped me get to grips with the US equivalent, and the immense harm it causes children and their families. *Chavs* by Owen Jones (Verso, 2020) sets out clearly how the working class have been demonised in the media and by politicians.

Chapter Eight: What we learn from school

Michel Foucault's *Discipline and Punish* (Penguin, 1991) first made me think about how children are shaped and controlled by the education system. On the radical and liberatory potential of education, I am grateful for bell hook's *Teaching to Transgress* (Routledge, 1994) and Paolo Freire's *Pedagogy of the Oppressed* (Penguin, 2013). Peter Grey's *Free to Learn* (Basic, 2013), Alfie Kohn's writing, particularly *Feel-Bad Education and Other*

Contrarian Essays on Children and Schooling (Beacon, 2011), Naomi Fisher's *A Different Way to Learn* (Jessica Kingsley, 2023), and Carol Black's essay 'Children, Learning, and the "Evaluative Gaze" of School' (https://carolblack.org/the-gaze) helped me to think about alternatives to mainstream education, as did Ken Robinson's TED talks. On unschooling, Akilah. S. Richards' *Raising Free People: unschooling as liberation and healing work* (PM, 2020) is excellent. Catherine Burke and Ian Grosvenor's *The School I'd Like: revisited (*Routledge, 2015) gives deep insight into how children view school. Two documentaries shaped this chapter: Maya Newell's *In My Blood It Runs* (2019) highlights the injustice Indigenous children face within the Australian education and judicial systems, and Charlie Shread and Marianne Osorio's *School Circles* (2018) shows sociocratic education in action.

Chapter Nine: A future built for children

On air pollution, David Wallace-Wells's article 'Ten Million a Year' in the *London Review of Books* (Vol. 43, 2021) helped me understand the scale of the problem. On the climate crisis, I drew on Naomi Klein's *This Changes Everything* (Penguin, 2015), David Wallace-Wells's *The Uninhabitable Earth* (Penguin, 2019), Andreas Malm's *How To Blow Up A Pipeline* (Verso 2021), and Mikaela Loach's *It's Not That Radical: climate action to transform our world* (DK, 2023). Aja Barber's *Consumed* (Brazen, 2022) shows the links between colonialism, consumerism, and the climate crisis. In thinking about what we owe future generations, I turned to Roman Krznari's *The Good Ancestor* (Penguin, 2020) and Rupert Read's *Parents for a Future* (UAE Press, 2021). David Sobel's *Beyond Ecophobia* (Orion, 1999) highlights the need for children to form a relationship with the natural world.

Rob Hopkins' *From What Is to What If* (Chelsea Green, 2021) highlights the power of dreaming of a better future.

Chapter Ten: Votes for children

David Runciman's podcast episode *Democracy for Young People* (Talking Politics, 2018) was crucial in shaping this chapter, as was all of John Wall's work, especially *Give Children the Vote* (Bloomsbury, 2021). Kirsi Kallio's work helped me better understand the complex relationship between children and politics, notably her three articles with Jouni Hakli 'Are There Politics in Childhood' in *Space and Polity* (Vol. 15, 2011), 'Tracing Children's Politics' in *Political Geography* (Vol. 30, 2011), and 'Theorizing Children's Political Agency' in *Establishing Geographies of Children and Young People* (Tracy Skelton and Stuart C. Aitken (eds.), Springer, 2018), as well as her article 'The Body as a Battlefield: Approaching Children's Politics' in *Human Geography* (Vol. 90, 2008). Also illuminating is *Political Activism Across the Life Course,* edited by Sevasti-Melissa Nolas, Christos Varvantakis, and Vinnarasan Aruldoss (Routledge, 2017). Anna Kirsteng's documentary *Power to the Children* (2018) provides a powerful example of how capable children can be when they have political power.

Acknowledgements

So many incredible people have been involved in shaping and producing this book.

My agent, Carrie Plitt: thank you for championing this book, for shaping it into something coherent when it was just a jumble of ideas, and for all of your guidance and expertise over the years. A huge thanks also to the rest of the team at Felicity Bryan Associates: Michele Topham, Cathi Holden, Aoife Inman, Juliet Garcia, Ria Chatrath, and Katerina Lygaki. Thanks also to the team at Andrew Nurnberg Associates for helping my words reach new audiences.

My editor, Simon Wright: thank you for everything. Working with you has been one of the highlights of my professional life. Your energy and enthusiasm for the book made writing it a joy, and it is infinitely better because of you. Many thanks also to Laura Ali: your meticulous attention to detail during the copy edit made such a difference, and I'm infinitely grateful for your keen eye. A massive thank you also to the rest of the Scribe team: Nicola Garrison, Adam Howard, Molly Slight, Patricia Chido, and Richard Humphreys. Thank you for all your hard work in bringing the book to life, and for being such a pleasure to work with.

Special thanks are due to Sarah Braybrooke, who first believed in this book's potential: thank you for saying yes, and for all of your support with my writing to date.

Two people gave me crucial feedback in the early stages of planning and drafting. Penny Wincer: thank you for all your insightful comments during our conversations about the book in Cornwall, and for your ongoing support. Rebecca Schiller: thank you for sitting with me for hours, surrounded by index cards and biscuits, as we tried to figure out a structure that made sense.

Nicola Washington: thank you for helping me talk about my work and ideas online, and for your advice and encouragement.

At UCL, thank you to Professor John Vorhaus for your lecture series on rights and education, which helped me think deeper about many of the topics in this book through a philosopher's lens, and which inspired the beginning of chapter eight. Thank you also to Dr Deniz Arzuk for offering such excellent reading suggestions, and to the whole of the UCL MASCCR team.

Thank you to everyone, adults and children, who agreed to speak with me for this book, including the children at the Michaela school and everyone at the Bexley Foodbank. Special thanks to Jude Walker, Kerry Murphy, Andy West, Fran Liberatore, Catherine Kenny, Adele Jarrett-Kerr, Lauren Mittell, Nicola Haggett, and Cathy McCulloch. I also want to thank everyone who has taken time to respond to my various polls, surveys, and questions on Instagram, and who has sent me their experiences and thoughts. Thank you too to all of my clients. I'm grateful for every message and conversation.

Two visits in particular shaped my understanding of what a world built for children could look like. Millie Colwey: thank you for letting me spend a day in your garden, and for your ongoing friendship. You are doing world-changing work. Thank you also to all of the wonderful children who played with me in the mud. Sarah Rigeon, Jo Wood, and all the young people at Bean Learning: thank you for welcoming me and talking to me about how you spend your days. It was so beautiful to see rights-based education in action.

Thank you also to our local home education community: it's a pleasure to live life without school alongside you.

My friends have been so tolerant of me disappearing for two years to write. Thank you to Jess, Matilda, Celia, Pippa, Dan, George, Katy, Davy, Helen, Freyja, Ju, Elinor, Owen, Matty B, Kathy, Tom, Seb, Kate, and Matt. An extra big thank you to Camille. Thanks especially to Jamey, Fran L, Catherine, Claire, and Julia, who all took the time to read early chapters of the book and offer insightful feedback.

My parents Agnès and James, my brother Eden, my sister Dylan, my grandmother Liliane, my parents-in-law Jill and Dan, and my sister-in-law Dina: you have all been so patient with me as I repeatedly missed birthdays and celebrations because I was writing. I owe so much to you all. Thank you for your unwavering support and love.

My nephews Reuben, Ezra, and Jonah, my niece Mollie, and my youngest sister Noemi: thank you for constantly reminding me how funny, capable, interesting, kind, brilliant, and thoughtful children are.

My husband, Sam: thank you for reading my terrible first drafts, and for always believing in my work. Thank you for not complaining when I spent every weekend for two years writing, even when your own work piled up. Thank you for all the cups of tea, the conversations, and the endless patience. Thank you, above all, for being such a wonderful partner to parent alongside. I'm sorry writing books takes such a long time (and I'm even sorrier that I will probably try to write more). I love you.

My daughter, Frida: thank you for teaching me so much about adultism and what it means to be on the side of children, for forgiving easily and generously, and for never being afraid to speak out when things are unfair. Thank you for making me laugh and keeping my spirits up, even on the days when writing felt impossibly hard. You are an explosion of wonder and delight, and you astonish me daily. There aren't enough books in the world to tell you how much I love you.

Notes

Introduction

1 For example, Emma Dabiri, *What White People Can Do Next* (Penguin, 2021).
2 Definition of the language of radicalisation taken from: https://esmeefairbairn.org.uk/latest-news/what-were-doing-about-diversity-equity-and-inclusion/

Chapter One: How we see children

1 Jane C. Hu, 'The Myth of the 25-Year-Old Brain', *Slate* (2022), https://slate.com/technology/2022/11/brain-development-25-year-old-mature-myth.html.
2 Mariam Arain et al., 'Maturation of the Adolescent Brain' in *Neuropsychiatric Disease and Treatment* 9 (2022), pp. 449–61.
3 Sultana Norozi and Torill Moen, 'Childhood as a Social Contruction' in *Journal of Educational and Social Research*, Vol. 6 (2) (2013).
4 Cindi Katz, 'Childhood as Spectacle: relays of anxiety and the reconfiguration of the child' in *Cultural Geographies* 15 (1) (2013), p. 5–17.
5 Rachel Rosen and Jan Newberry, 'Love, Labour, and Temporality: reconceptualising social reproduction with women and children in the frame', in Rachel Rosen and Katherine Twamley [eds.], *Feminism and The Politics of Childhood: friends or foes?*, UCL Press (2018), p. 126.
6 Carlo Rovelli, *The Order of Time* (Penguin, 2019), p. 92.
7 Toby Rollo, 'Child as Other/Stranger' in Daniel Thomas Cook, *The SAGE Encyclopedia of Children and Childhood Studies*, (SAGE, 2020).
8 Guy Roberts-Holmes and Peter Moss, *Neoliberalism and Early Childhood Education: markets, imaginaries and governance* (Routledge, 2021).
9 Jean-Jacques Rousseau, *Emile; or On Education* (Penguin, 1991), p. 52.

10 Jens Qvortrup, *Childhood Matters: social theory, practice and politics* (Aldershot).
11 L. R. Knost, *Jesus, the Gentle Parent: gentle Christian parenting* (Little Hearts Books, 2013).
12 Akilah Richards, 'Raising Free People', TED (2019), https://www.ted.com/talks/akilah_richards_raising_free_people.
13 John Holt, *How Children Learn* (Da Capo Press, 1995), p. 2.
14 See for example, Abigail Tucker, 'Are Babies Born Good?', *Smithsonian Magazine* (2013), https://www.smithsonianmag.com/science-nature/are-babies-born-good-165443013/.
15 Charlotte Mason, *Home Education* (Living Books Press, 2017).
16 Nelly Ali, 'The Vulnerability and Resilience of Street Children' in *Global Studies of Childhood* 1 (3) (2011), pp. 260–64.
17 Alison Cooke and Amy Halberstadt, 'Adultification, Anger Bias, and Adults' Different Perceptions of Black and White Children' in *Cognition and Emotion* 35 (7) (2021), pp. 1416–22.
18 Rebecca Epstein, Jamilia J. Blake, and Thalia Gonzalez, 'Girlhood Interrupted: the Erasure of Black girls' childhood' (Georgetown Law, 2017), https://genderjusticeandopportunity.georgetown.edu/wp-content/uploads/2020/06/girlhood-interrupted.pdf.
19 Phillip Atiba Goff et al., 'The Essence of Innocence: consequences of dehumanizing Black children', *Journal of Personality and Social Psychology* 106 (4) (2014), pp. 526–45.
20 Katherine Brown Rosier, 'Children as Problems, Problems of Children' in Jens Qvortrup et al. (eds.), *The Palgrave Handbook of Childhood Studies* (Palgrave Macmillan, 2009), p. 266.
21 If the accommodation provides food, this payment is reduced to just £9.10 per person per week (£2,366 a year for a family of five). The food served in these so-called 'hotels' can frequently be rotten and prepared in cockroach- and mouse-infested kitchens, not at all fit for human consumption. Diane Taylor, 'Asylum seekers crammed into rat-infested rooms', *The Guardian* (2019), https://www.theguardian.com/world/2019/aug/20/asylum-seekers-crammed-into-cockroach-infested-accommodation-home-office; 'Asylum seekers: scabies and abuse at Stockport hotel, council claims', *BBC News* (2022), https://www.bbc.co.uk/news/uk-england-manchester-63598305; Alan Travis, 'Value of asylum housing contracts doubles after criticism of conditions', *The Guardian* (2017), https://www.theguardian.com/uk-news/2017/nov/23/value-of-asylum-housing-contracts-doubles-after-criticism-of-conditions.
22 Diane Taylor, 'Children in England's asylum hotels suffering from malnutrition', *The Guardian* (2023), https://www.theguardian.com/uk-news/2023/jun/17/

children-in-englands-asylum-hotels-suffering-from-malnutrition.

23 Mark Townsend, 'Revealed: scores of child asylum seekers kidnapped from Home Office hotel', *The Guardian* (2023), https://www.theguardian.com/uk-news/2023/jan/21/revealed-scores-of-child-asylum-seekers-kidnapped-from-home-office-hotel.

24 A report by the independent chief inspector of borders and immigration (ICIBI) found that 'the housing of these extremely vulnerable children in hotels represents a significant challenge to the Home Office, in both ethical and operational terms ... the practices and procedures developed by the Home Office did not represent a child-centred approach that fully acknowledged and provided for the safeguarding and wellbeing needs of the young people in the department's care.' ICIBI, 'Inspection Report Published: an inspection of the use of hotels for housing unaccompanied asylum-seeking children March–May 2022', *GOV.UK* (2022), https://www.gov.uk/government/news/inspection-report-published-an-inspection-of-the-use-of-hotels-for-housing-unaccompanied-asylum-seeking-children-march-may-2022.

25 Arj Singh, 'Home Office has painted over Mickey Mouse murals at asylum centre for lone children', *I News* (2023), https://inews.co.uk/news/politics/home-office-painted-mickey-mouse-murals-children-asylum-centre-2461147.

26 See for example, 'Children and young people who are refugees', Anti-Bullying Alliance, https://anti-bullyingalliance.org.uk/tools-information/all-about-bullying/at-risk-groups/children-and-young-people-who-are-refugees and 'the educational outcomes of refugee and asylum-seeking children in England', Education Policy Institute (2021), https://epi.org.uk/publications-and-research/the-educational-outcomes-of-refugee-and-asylum-seeking-children-in-england/.

27 Toby Rollo, 'The Color of Childhood: the role of the child/human binary in the production of anti-Black racism' in *Journal of Black Studies* 49 (4) (2018), pp. 307–29.

28 Toby Rollo, 'Feral Children: settler colonialism, progress, and the figure of the child' in *Settler Colonial Studies* 8 (1) (2018), pp. 60–79; see also Ian Austen, 'How Thousands of Indigenous Children Vanished in Canada', *The New York Times* (2022), https://www.nytimes.com/2021/06/07/world/canada/mass-graves-residential-schools.html.

29 Kenneth Robey et al., 'Implicit Infantilizing Attitudes About Disability' in *Journal of Developmental and Physical Disabilities* 18 (2006), pp. 441–53.

30 Leyla Safta-Zecheria, 'The Infantilization of Intellectual Disability and Political Inclusion: a pedagogical approach', *Journal of Educational Sciences* 38 (2) (2018), pp. 104–12.

31 Emma Uprichard, 'Children as "Being and Becomings": children, childhood and temporality' in *Children and Society* 22 (4), pp. 303–13.
32 Peter Moss et al. (eds.), *Loris Malaguzzi and the Schools of Reggio Emilia: a selection of his writings and speeches, 1945-1993* (Routledge, 2016).

Chapter Two: Adultism

1 Miranda Fricker, *Epistemic Injustice: power and the ethics of knowing* (Oxford University Press, 2007).
2 Jack Flasher, 'Adultism', *Adolescence* 13 (51) (1978), p. 517.
3 Harry Shier, 'What Does "Equality" Mean For Children in Relation to Adults?', Official background paper for the UN global thematic consultation on 'The Heart of the Post-2015 Development Agenda and the Future We Want for All' (2012), https://www.harryshier.net/docs/Shier-What_Does_Equality_Mean_for_Children.pdf.
4 See for example Jamelle Bouie, 'What the Republican Push for "Parents' Rights" Is Really About', *The New York Times* (2023), https://www.nytimes.com/2023/03/28/opinion/parents-rights-republicans-florida.html; Sarah Jones 'Children Are Not Property: the idea that underlies the right-wing campaign for "parents' rights"', *New York Magazine* (2023), https://nymag.com/intelligencer/2023/04/children-are-not-property.html.
5 Manfred Liebel, 'Adultism and Age-Based Discrimination Against Children' in D. Kutsar, and H. Warming (eds.), *Children and Non-Discrimination: interdisciplinary textbook* (CREAN, 2018), pp. 120–42.
6 Jelena Vranješević, 'Convention on the Rights of the Child and Adultism: how to deconstruct a myth?', *Šolsko polje* 31 (3–4) (2020), pp. 45–61.
7 Aoife Daly, *Children, Autonomy and the Courts: beyond the right to be heard*, (Brill Nijhoff, 2018).
8 Mosquito, the anti-loitering alarm, https://mosquitoloiteringsolutions.com/why-mosquito/sound-deterrent-for-under-25s/.
9 Katherine Brown Rosier, 'Children as Problems, Problems of Children' in Jens Qvortrup et al. (eds.), *The Palgrave Handbook of Childhood Studies* (Palgrave Macmillan, 2009).
10 Colby Tootoosis, *The Cunning of the Adult Supremacist* (2020), https://www.colbytootoosis.com/writings/adult-supremacy.
11 Tanu Biswas et al., 'Childism and Philosophy: a conceptual co-exploration' in *Policy Futures in Education* (2023), pp. 1–19.
12 Childism Institute, https://www.childism.org/.
13 See for example, Mathilde Lévêque '« Childism » et « Enfantisme », réflexions sur une notion, une pratique, un engagement', *Magasin des Enfants* (2022), https://magasindesenfants.hypotheses.org/10268.
14 Alison Bailey, 'Privilege: expanding on Marilyn Frye's "Oppression"',

Journal of Social Philosophy 29 (3) (1998), pp. 104–19.

15 Bob Pease, 'The Other Side of Social Exclusion', *University of Tasmania* (2015), https://www.childcomm.tas.gov.au/wp-content/uploads/2015/08/Understanding-Adultism-and-Adult-Privilege-Seminar.ppt.

16 Full list available here: Rights for Children, PBWorks (2012), http://rightsforchildren.pbworks.com/w/page/53433613/adult%20privilege%20checklist.

17 Rebecca Adami and Katy Dineen, 'Discourses of Childism: how Covid-19 has unveiled prejudice, discrimination and social injustice against children in the everyday' in *The International Journal of Children's Rights* 29 (2021), pp. 353–70.

18 Witnessing domestic violence is now increasingly recognised as a form of domestic violence itself because of the damage it can cause children, see for example, Areti Tsavoussis et al., 'Child-witnessed domestic violence and its adverse effects on brain development: a call for societal self-examination and awareness' in *Frontiers in Public Health* 2 (2014).

19 'Free School Meals: mother's "sadness" at "mean" food parcel, *BBC News* (2014), https://www.bbc.co.uk/news/uk-55641740.

20 See for example, Lavinia Loperfido, 'The Hidden Impact of COVID-19 on Child Poverty', *Save the Children* (2020), https://resourcecentre.savethechildren.net/pdf/the_hidden_impact_of_covid-19_on_child_poverty.pdf/; Zhané Edwards et al., 'Poverty in the pandemic: an update on the impact of coronavirus on low-income families and children', *Child Poverty Action Group/Church of England* (2020), https://cpag.org.uk/sites/default/files/files/policypost/Poverty-in-the-pandemic_update.pdf; Russell Taylor, 'Covid-19: impact on child poverty and on young people's education, health and wellbeing', *House of Lords Library* (2021), https://lordslibrary.parliament.uk/covid-19-impact-on-child-poverty-and-on-young-peoples-education-health-and-wellbeing/.

21 Carl Cullinane et al., 'Briefing No. 1 - Lockdown Learning', *COVID Social Mobility & Opportunities study (COSMO)* (2022), https://cosmostudy.uk/publications/lockdown-learning.

22 See for example, Freddie Whittaker, 'Private schools over-inflated GCSEs during Covid, analysis suggests', *Schools Week* (2022), https://schoolsweek.co.uk/private-schools-over-inflated-gcses-during-covid-analysis-suggests/; Richard Adams 'London private school investigated over "blanket" A or A* grades in 2021 A-levels', *The Guardian* (2022), https://www.theguardian.com/education/2022/dec/24/north-london-collegiate-school-investigated-a-level-grades-2021-malpractice-allegations.

23 Gina Wilson, 'Statement: Impact of Covid-19 on Disabled Children', *CYPCS* (2021), https://www.cypcs.org.uk/news-and-stories/statement-impact-of-covid-19-on-disabled-children/.

24 '#LeftInLockdown – Pandemic Campaign and Research Overview', Disabled Children's Partnership, https://disabledchildrenspartnership.org.uk/leftinlockdown/.
25 Dan Rosenberg, 'Vulnerable families and school attendance – where are we now?', *Good Law Project* (2021), https://goodlawproject.org/update/cev-families-school-attendance/.
26 Sally Weale 'Call for "summer of play" to help English pupils recover from Covid-19 stress", *The Guardian* (2021), https://www.theguardian.com/society/2021/feb/13/call-for-summer-of-play-to-help-english-pupils-recover-from-covid-stress.
27 John Holt, *Escape from Childhood: the needs and rights of children* (E.P. Dutton, 1974), p. 1.

Chapter Three: Understanding children's rights

1 Informal survey on Instagram in March 2023 of 550 self-selecting participants.
2 Eugeen Verhellen, 'The Convention on the Rights of the Child: reflections from a historical, social policy and educational perspective' in Wouter Vanderhole et al. (eds.), *Routledge International Handbook of Children's Rights Studies* (Routledge, 2015).
3 Carol Harris , 'Waugh and child protection in the late 19th century', *Coram Story* (2021), https://coramstory.org.uk/explore/content/blog/waugh-and-child-protection-in-the-late-19th-century/.
4 Although it's hard to point to any direct reform leading from Dickens' writing, he undoubtedly contributed to the changing social attitude towards poverty, particularly the harsh treatment of women and children. However, if children were seen as the 'deserving poor' in the reformist movement, painted as innocent victims, their parents were not given the same support, often depicted as abusive, negligent, and alcoholic. In order for children to be 'saved', they had to be taken away from their parents and neighbourhoods to places where they could be fashioned into respectable citizens. Inability to materially care for children was seen as parental incompetence, a view that can still be found today in the separation of low-income families. For a discussion of this see chapter one in Karen Wells, *Childhood in a Global Perspective* (Polity Press, 2014).
5 UN Declaration on the Rights of the Child, CRIN (1959), https://archive.crin.org/en/library/legal-database/un-declaration-rights-child-1959.html.
6 There are also three additional optional protocols (one on the involvement of children in armed conflict; one on the sale of children, child prostitution, and children in pornography; and the final on

communications procedures), which were added between 2000 and 2014.

7 Priscilla Alderson, *Young Children's Rights: exploring beliefs, principles, and practice*, second edition, (Jessica Kingsley, 2008).

8 Harriet Grant and Pamela Duncan, 'England's playgrounds crumble as council budgets fall', *The Guardian* (2023), https://www.theguardian.com/environment/2023/aug/04/england-playgrounds-crumble-council-budgets-fall.

9 Christian Davies, 'Why I support the Children's Liberation Army of South Korea', *Financial Times* (2023), https://www.ft.com/content/f9ee435e-8ed7-420c-a7eb-0219f7228cdb.

10 Sarah Collard 'Children self-harming to escape prolonged confinement in cells, South Australian watchdog says', *The Guardian* (2023), https://www.theguardian.com/society/2023/jun/29/children-locked-in-cells-for-up-to-23-hours-at-south-australias-youth-detention-centre; Ben Smee, 'Five hundred days in solitary: Queensland teenager's case "a major failure of our system"', *The Guardian* (2023), https://www.theguardian.com/australia-news/2023/jun/26/500-days-of-solitary-ab-original-teen-spent-extraordinary-period-in-isolation; Ben Smee, 'Like Guantanamo', *The Guardian* (2023), https://www.theguardian.com/australia-news/2023/jun/06/like-guantanamo-the-children-locked-in-solitary-for-weeks-at-a-time-in-queensland-youth-prison.

11 Domestic violence is largely a hidden crime, and the majority of survivors do not report it to the police, for various reasons including fear of repercussions and worry that they will not be believed. Lorraine Radford et al., 'The prevalence and impact of child maltreatment and other types of victimization in the UK: findings from a population survey of caregivers, children and young people and young adults' in *Child Abuse and Neglect* 37 (10) (2013), pp. 801–13.

12 For example, 'Smacking young children has long-lasting effects', UCL (2021), https://www.ucl.ac.uk/news/2021/jan/smacking-young-children-has-long-lasting-effects.

13 RNZ, 'Number of parents smacking children drops by half in 15 years', *RNZ* (2021), https://www.rnz.co.nz/news/national/441474/number-of-parents-smacking-children-drops-by-half-in-15-years.

14 Aubrey Allegreti, 'Nadhim Zahawi says parents should be trusted on whether to smack children', *The Guardian* (2022), https://www.theguardian.com/society/2022/apr/21/england-should-follow-scotland-and-wales-and-ban-smacking-says-childrens-tsar.

15 A note on the word traffickers: because children cannot legally consent to any kind of sex act, anyone who profits from or pays for a sex act from a child, including photographs, is considered a human trafficker.

16 Katie McQue and Mei-Ling McNamara, 'How Facebook and Instagram

became marketplaces for child sex trafficking', *The Guardian* (2023), https://www.theguardian.com/news/2023/apr/27/how-facebook-and-instagram-became-marketplaces-for-child-sex-trafficking.

17 Claire Savage, 'Child social media stars have few protections. Illinois aims to fix that', *AP News* (2023), https://apnews.com/article/tiktok-influencer-child-social-media-illinois-law-65a837e2ba7151c91c17f69b08862022.

18 '"A lot of it is actually just abuse" - Young people and pornography report', Children's Commissioner (2023), https://www.childrenscommissioner.gov.uk/report/a-lot-of-it-is-actually-just-abuse-young-people-and-pornography/.

19 'General comment No. 25 (2021) on children's rights in relation to the digital environment', UN Committee on the Rights of the Child (2021), https://www.ohchr.org/en/documents/general-comments-and-recommendations/general-comment-no-25-2021-childrens-rights-relation.

20 Helen Dodd et al., 'Children's Play and Independent Mobility in 2020: results from the British children's play survey' in *International Journal of Environmental Research and Public Health* 18 (8) (2021); author's comment taken from: Sally Weale, 'UK children not allowed to play outside until two years older than parents' generation', *The Guardian* (2021), https://www.theguardian.com/society/2021/apr/20/gradual-lockdown-of-uk-children-as-age-for-solo-outdoor-play-rises.

21 *Play England 2023 Playday Report*, Play England (2023), https://static1.squarespace.com/static/609a5802ba3f13305c43d352/t/64ca676f4c818d6700d320ae/1690986358314/Street+Play+Report+July+2023+Final2.pdf.

22 Priscilla Alderson, *Young Children's Rights: exploring beliefs, principles, and practice*, second edition, (Jessica Kingsley, 2008), p. 73.

23 Miranda Fricker, *Epistemic Injustice: power and the ethics of knowing*, (Oxford University Press, 2007).

24 Debbie Allnock and Pam Mille, *No one noticed, no one heard: a study of disclosures of childhood abuse*, NSPCC (2013).

25 *The Art of Diapering*, Resources for Infant Educators (2022), https://www.youtube.com/watch?v=cJy35lL33pY.

26 Catherine Burke and Ian Grosvenor, *The School I'd Like: children and young people's reflections on an education for the 21st century* (Routledge, 2003), pp. ix–x.

27 Ibid., p. xvii.

28 Laura Lundy, 'Enabling the Meaningful Participation of Children and young People Globally: the Lundy model', Queen's University Belfast, https://www.qub.ac.uk/Research/case-studies/childrens-participation-lundy-model.html#.

29 The first three stages are the minimum requirements if we are to meet the right to participation outlined in Article 12 of the CRC.
30 Harry Shier, 'Pathways to participation: openings, opportunities and obligations', *Children and Society* 15 (2) (2001), pp. 107–17.
31 Harry Shier, 'Pathways to Participation Revisited: learning from Nicaragua's child coffee workers' in Barry Percy-Smith and Nigel Patrick Thomas (eds.), *A Handbook of Children and Young People's Participation: perspectives from theory and practice* (Routledge, 2010).
32 Ibid., p. 223.
33 Laura Lundy et al., 'Life Under Coronavirus: children's views on their experiences of their human rights', *The International Journal of Children's Rights* 29 (2021), pp. 261–85.
34 Afua Twum-Danso, 'A Cultural Bridge, Not an Imposition: legitimising children's rights in the eyes of local communities', *Journal of the History of Childhood and Youth* 1 (3) (2008), pp. 391–409.
35 Rachel Burr, 'Global and Local Approaches to Children's Rights in Vietnam', *Childhood* 9 (1) (2002), pp. 49–61.
36 African Charter on the Rights and Welfare of the Child, African Union (1990), https://au.int/en/treaties/african-charter-rights-and-welfare-child.
37 An example of this is the Trokosi system in Ghana, where girls are forced to live and work with priests in religious shrines, for the rest of their lives, to 'pay' for the sins of family members. This practice of handing girls as young as six into slavery is officially banned, but still happens. See for example, Rhonda Martinez, 'The Trokosi Tradition In Ghana: the silencing of a religion' in *History in the Making* 4 (1) (2011).
38 Karen Wells 'Making Gender and Generation: between the local and the global in Africa' in Imoh A. T.-D. et al. (eds.), *Childhoods at the Intersection of the Local and the Global* (Palgrave Macmillan, 2012).
39 Kevin MoClair, 'In America, Kids Come Last', Brown Political Review (2022), https://brownpoliticalreview.org/2022/04/in-america-kids-come-last/.
40 David Wallace-Wells, 'It's Not "Deaths of Despair." It's Deaths of Children', *The New York Times* (2023), https://www.nytimes.com/2023/04/06/opinion/deaths-life-expectancy-guns-children.html.
41 A. Glenn Mower Jr, quoted in Elizabeth Faulkner and Conrad Nyamutata, 'The Decolonisation of Children's Rights and the Colonial Contours of the Convention on the Rights of the Child' in *International Journal of Children's Rights* 20 (2020), pp. 66–88.
42 'Children's rights', Scottish Government, https://www.gov.scot/policies/human-rights/childrens-rights/.
43 'Children's Rights in Great Britain: submission to the UN Committee

on the Rights of the Child, Equality and Human Rights Commission (2020), https://www.equalityhumanrights.com/sites/default/files/childrens_rights_in_great_britain_0.pdf.

44 John Tobin, 'Incorporating the CRC in Australia', in Ursula Kilkelly, Laura Lundy, and Branagh Byrne (eds.) *Incorporating the UN Convention on the Rights of the Child into National Law* (Intersentia, 2021), pp. 11–46.

45 *Rights, Remedies and Representation: global report on access to justice for children*, CRIN (2016), https://archive.crin.org/sites/default/files/crin_a2j_global_report_final_1.pdf.

46 'Access to justice', UNICEF, https://www.unicef.org/eca/child-protection/access-justice.

47 *Rights, Remedies and Representation: global report on access to justice for children*, CRIN (2016), https://archive.crin.org/sites/default/files/crin_a2j_global_report_final_1.pdf.

48 Julie Taylor et al., *Deaf and disabled children talking about child protection*, NSPCC (2015) https://strathprints.strath.ac.uk/52256/1/Taylor_etal_NSPCC2015_deaf_and_disabled_children_talking_about_child_protection.pdf.

49 Phil Jones and Sue Welch, *Rethinking Children's Rights*, second edition, (Bloomsbury, 2018), pp. 19–20.

50 Some organisations like Save the Children have created simplified versions of the CRC in language that even young children can understand, see for example, Save the Children, https://www.savethechildren.org.uk/content/dam/global/reports/uncrc-child-friendly-version1.pdf.

51 Manfred Liebel, *Children's Rights from Below: cross-cultural perspectives*, (Palgrave Macmillan, 2012).

52 Sarada Balagopalan, 'Why historicise rights-subjectivities? children's rights, compulsory schooling, and the deregulation of child labor in India', *Childhood* 26 (3) (2019), pp. 304–20.

Chapter Four: Body politics

1 This expression is thought to have been popularised by Carol Hanisch in her 1970 essay 'The Personal is Political', which appeared in *Notes from the Second Year: women's liberation*, although she did not give the essay its title. It most likely came from *Notes from the Second Year*'s editors Shulamith Firestone and Anne Koedt. For more information see: Carol Hanisch, 'The Personal is Political' (1969), https://www.carolhanisch.org/CHwritings/PIP.html.

2 See for example, Berge et al., 'Intergenerational Transmission of Parent Encouragement to Diet from Adolescence into Adulthood', *Pediatrics* 141 (4) (2018).

3 Kimberlé Crenshaw, 'Demarginalizing the Intersection of Race and Sex: a Black feminist critique of antidiscrimination doctrine, feminist theory and antiracist politics', *University of Chicago Legal Forum* (1) (1989).

4 Nina Tame in Eliza Hull (ed.), *We've Got This: essays by disabled parents* (Scribe, 2023), p. 17.

5 Weaver, Matthew, 'Woman with Down's syndrome loses court of appeal abortion law case', *The Guardian* (2022), https://www.theguardian.com/society/2022/nov/25/heidi-crowter-woman-downs-syndrome-loses-court-of-appeal-abortion-law-case.

6 Isabel Mavrides-Calderón, @powerfullyisa Instagram, https://www.instagram.com/p/CvNKN8IurzX/?img_index=1.

7 Sarah Young, 'Who were the Queen's "hidden" cousins Nerissa and Katherine Bowes-Lyon?', *The Independent* (2022), https://www.independent.co.uk/life-style/royal-family/queen-cousins-nerissa-katherine-bowes-lyon-crown-netflix-b2168724.html.

8 'Children with disabilities: deprivation of liberty in the name of care and treatment', HRW (2017), https://www.hrw.org/news/2017/03/07/children-disabilities-deprivation-liberty-name-care-and-treatment.

9 Noel Titheradge, 'Children punched and hit over the head in care homes rated "good"', *BBC News* (2023), https://www.bbc.co.uk/news/uk-63792458.

10 'Safeguarding d/Deaf and disabled children and young people', NSPCC (2022), https://learning.nspcc.org.uk/safeguarding-child-protection/deaf-and-disabled-children; and 'Children with disabilities more likely to face violence, says UN-backed study', UN News (2012), https://news.un.org/en/story/2012/07/415382.

11 Zuyi Fang et al., 'Global estimates of violence against children with disabilities: an updated systematic review and meta-analysis', *The Lancet: child and adolescent health*, 6 (5) (2022), pp. 313–23.

12 2023 Anti-Filicide Toolkit, Autistic Self Advocacy Network (2023), https://Autisticadvocacy.org/anti-filicide/.

13 Gillian Smith et al., 'Rates and causes of mortality among children and young people with and without intellectual disabilities in Scotland: a record linkage cohort study of 796 190 school children', *BMJ Open*, 10 (7) (2019); and Andre Strydom, 'Learning from Lives and Deaths — people with a learning disability and Autistic people', https://www.england.nhs.uk/publication/learning-from-lives-and-deaths-people-with-a-learning-disability-and-autistic-people-leder-policy-2021/.

14 Petrit Krasniqi, Mathew Carr, Maddie Stevens, '"People don't understand": the impact of the cost-of-living crisis on children and young people with special educational needs and disabilities', *The Childhood Trust* (2023), https://www.childhoodtrust.org.uk/wp-content/

uploads/2023/06/The-Childhood-Trust-SEND-REPORT-June-2023.pdf.

15 'Living with: attention deficit hyperactivity disorder (ADHD), NHS, https://www.nhs.uk/conditions/attention-deficit-hyperactivity-disorder-adhd/living-with/.

16 Private conversation; see also Kerry Murphy, *A Guide to SEND in the Early Years*, (Featherstone, 2022).

17 'Understanding trauma and adversity', YoungMinds, https://www.youngminds.org.uk/professional/resources/understanding-trauma-and-adversity/.

18 *The Autistic Not Weird Autism 2022 Survey*, Autistic Not Weird (2022), https://Autisticnotweird.com/autismsurvey/#Autisticpeople. Interestingly, this figure remained consistent for respondents aged 19 and under, which shows that we can't blame 'old ways' of education: despite all we know now about what Autistic people need to thrive, school is still not set up for them to do so.

19 @sonshinemagazine Instagram (2022), https://www.instagram.com/p/CddwuzRoxms/?hl=en.

20 https://www.fawcettsociety.org.uk/unlimited-potential-the-final-report-of-the-commission-on-gender-stereotypes-in-early-childhood.

21 Lucy Pasha-Robinson, 'Children feel they are treated differently because of their gender, finds survey', *The Independent* (2018), https://www.independent.co.uk/news/uk/home-news/gender-difference-children-education-teachers-parents-family-survey-a8164321.html.

22 See for example: Alexandra Alter, 'Book Bans Rising Rapidly in the U.S., Free Speech Groups Find', *The New York Times* (2023), https://www.nytimes.com/2023/04/20/books/book-bans-united-states-free-speech.html; Sarah Shaffi, 'Third of UK librarians asked to censor or remove books, research reveals', *The Guardian* (2023), https://www.theguardian.com/books/2023/apr/20/third-of-uk-librarians-asked-to-censor-or-remove-books-research-reveals.

23 Alex Woodward, 'What is Florida's "Don't Say Gay" bill?', *The Independent* (2022), https://www.independent.co.uk/news/world/americas/us-politics/dont-say-gay-bill-florida-desantis-b2074720.html.

24 Gun Violence in Florida, *Every Town Research* (2020), https://maps.everytownresearch.org/wp-content/uploads/2020/04/Every-State-Fact-Sheet-2.0-042720-Florida.pdf.

25 Shon Faye, *The Transgender Issue: an argument for justice* (Allen Lane, 2021), p. 20.

26 Just Like Us, https://www.justlikeus.org/.

27 'what we do', akt, https://www.akt.org.uk/what-we-do.

28 Virginia Sole-Smith, *Fat Talk: coming of age in diet culture* (Ithaka, 2023).

29 'Changes Needed to Government Anti-obesity Strategies' Beat, https://www.beateatingdisorders.org.uk/about-beat/policy-work/changes-needed-to-government-anti-obesity-strategies/.

30 Eric Robinson and Angelina Sutin, 'Parents' Perceptions of Their Children as Overweight and Children's Weight Concerns and Weight Gain', *Psychological Science* 28 (3) (2017), pp. 320–29.

31 'Social media triggers children to dislike their own bodies, stem4 survey finds', stem4, https://stem4.org.uk/social-media-triggers-children-to-dislike-their-own-bodies-stem4-survey-finds/; Georgia Wells, Jeff Horwitz, and Deepa Seetharaman, 'Facebook Knows Instagram Is Toxic for Teen Girls, Company Documents Show', *Wall Street Journal* (2021), https://www.wsj.com/articles/facebook-knows-instagram-is-toxic-for-teen-girls-company-documents-show-11631620739.

32 Joshua Zitser, 'Insider created a TikTok account and set the age at 14 to test how long before a plastic surgeon's promotional video appeared. It only took 8 minutes', *Insider* (2021), https://www.insider.com/rhinoplasty-is-being-promoted-to-teenagers-nose-job-tiktok-2020-12.

33 Ciara Mahon and David Hevey, 'Processing Body Image on Social Media: gender differences in adolescent boys' and girls' agency and active coping', *Frontiers in Psychology* 12 (2021), https://www.frontiersin.org/articles/10.3389/fpsyg.2021.626763/full.

34 Helen Thai et al., 'Reducing Social Media Use Improves Appearance and Weight Esteem in Youth With Emotional Distress: Brief Report', *American Psychological Association* (2023), https://www.apa.org/pubs/journals/releases/ppm-ppm0000460.pdf.

35 Shi You et al., 'General Need for Autonomy and Subjective Well-Being: a meta-analysis of studies in the US and East Asia', *Journal of Happiness Studies* 19 (2017), pp.1863–82.

36 Nicolle Okoren, 'The wilderness "therapy" that teens say feels like abuse: "You are on guard at all times"', *The Guardian* (2022), https://www.theguardian.com/us-news/2022/nov/14/us-wilderness-therapy-camps-troubled-teen-industry-abuse; Kelly-Leigh Cooper, 'Troubled US teens left traumatised by tough love camps', *BBC News* (2021), https://www.bbc.co.uk/news/world-us-canada-57442175; Isa Medina and Amanda Montell, 'The Cult of the Troubled Teen Industry', *Sounds Like A Cult podcast* (2022), https://podcasts.apple.com/us/podcast/the-cult-of-the-troubled-teen-industry/id1566917047?i=1000575502277.

37 Bart Soenens and Maarten Vansteenkiste, 'A theoretical upgrade of the concept of parental psychological control: proposing new insights on the basis of self-determination theory', *Developmental Review* 30 (2010), pp. 74–99.

38 See for example, Daniela Salinas and Carin Neitzel, 'Relations Between Children's Levels of Responsiveness and Resistance, Maternal Interaction Behaviors, and Children's Social Behaviors With Peers in School', *Journal of Research in Childhood Education* 31 (1) (2017), pp. 84–102.

39 S. Nolas, C. Varvantakis, and V. Aruldoss, 'Political Activism Across the Life Course', *Contemporary Social Science* 12 (1–2) (2017), p.1–12.

40 Lorna Finlayson, 'I Was a Child Liberationist', *London Review of Books* 43, (4) (2021).

41 Jean-Michel Robichaud et al., 'The Impact of Environmental Threats on Controlling Parenting and Children's Motivation', *Journal of Family Psychology 34* (7) (2020), pp. 804–13.

42 See for example, Faith Orchard et al., 'Self-reported sleep patterns and quality amongst adolescents: cross-sectional and prospective associations with anxiety and depression', *Journal of Child Psychology and Psychiatry* 61(10) (2020); pp. 1126–37; Adam Winsler et al., 'Sleepless in Fairfax: the difference one more hour of sleep can make for teen hopelessness, suicidal ideation, and substance use', *Journal of Youth and Adolescence* 4 (2) (2015), pp. 362–78; Scientific American, 'Let Teenagers Sleep', *Scientific American* (2023), https://www.scientificamerican.com/article/let-teenagers-sleep/; Rebecca Robbins et al., 'Adolescent sleep myths: identifying false beliefs that impact adolescent sleep and well-being', *Sleep Health* 8 (6) (2022), pp. 632–39.

Chapter Five: Parenting as a radical act

1 John Watson, *Psychological Care of the Infant and Child* (W W Norton & Co., 1928); G. R. F. Ferrari (ed.), Plato: 'The Republic' (Cambridge University Press, 2000).

2 Joan Durrant, 'A Guide to Building Healthy Parent-Child Relationships: a positive rights-based approach', *Save The Children* (2011), https://resourcecentre.savethechildren.net/pdf/6182.pdf/.

3 See for example, Daryl Higgins, 'Three in five suffer corporal punishment, almost doubling risk of mental health disorders', Australian Catholic University (2022), https://www.acu.edu.au/about-acu/news/2022/june/three-in-five-suffer-corporal-punishment.

4 Jorge Curtas, 'Corporal Punishment and Elevated Neural Response to Threat in Children', *Child Development*, 92 (3) (2021), pp. 821–32.

5 See for example, Leonardo Bevilacqua et al., 'Adverse childhood experiences and trajectories of internalizing, externalizing, and prosocial behaviors from childhood to adolescence', *Child Abuse & Neglect* 112 (2021).

6 See for example, Emma Fulu et al., 'Pathways between childhood trauma,

intimate partner violence, and harsh parenting', *The Lancet: global health* 5 (5) (2017), https://www.thelancet.com/journals/lanpsy/article/PIIS2214-109X(17)30103-1/fulltext.

7 US: David Finkelhor et al., 'Corporal Punishment: current rates from a national survey', *Journal of Child and Family Studies* 28 (11) (2019); Australia: 'The Prevalence of Corporal Punishment in Australia', ACMS (2022), https://www.acms.au/the-prevalence-of-corporal-punishment-in-australia/#; UK: Connow Ibbetson, 'Smacking: parents who were physically punished as children are more likely to punish their children', YouGov (2021), https://yougov.co.uk/topics/society/articles-reports/2021/09/27/smacking-parents-who-were-physically-punished-chil.

8 'Emotional abuse', NSPCC, https://www.nspcc.org.uk/what-is-child-abuse/types-of-abuse/emotional-abuse/#what.

9 Alfie Kohn, *Unconditional Parenting: moving from rewards and punishments to love and reason* (Atria, 2005).

10 Dan Siegel, '"Time-Outs" Are Hurting Your Child', *Time* (2014), https://time.com/3404701/discipline-time-out-is-not-good/.

11 Ming-Te Wang and Sarah Kenny, 'Longitudinal Links between Fathers' and Mothers' Harsh Verbal Discipline and Adolescents' Conduct Problems and Depressive Symptoms', *Child Development* 85 (3) (2015), pp. 908–23.

12 Joan Durrant, 'A Guide to Building Healthy Parent-Child Relationships: a positive rights-based approach', *Save The Children* (2011), https://resourcecentre.savethechildren.net/pdf/6182.pdf/.

13 Graziela Zottis, 'Associations between child disciplinary practices and bullying behavior in adolescents', *Jornal de Pediatria* 90 (4) (2014), pp. 408–14.

14 adrienne maree brown, *We Will Not Cancel Us: and other dreams of restorative justice* (AK Press, 2020), p. 43.

15 bell hooks, *All About Love: new visions* (William Morrow, 2001), p.17.

16 Mark Sellman, 'Paedophiles using AI to create child abuse images', *The Times* (2023), https://www.thetimes.co.uk/article/paedophiles-using-ai-to-create-child-abuse-images-mrmxfd03s.

17 Fortesa Latifi, 'Influencer Parents and The Kids Who Had Their Childhood Made Into Content', *Teen Vogue* (2023), https://www.teenvogue.com/story/influencer-parents-children-social-media-impact.

18 Peter Gray, 'What Has Caused the Long Decline in Kids' Mental Health', *Psychology Today* (2023), https://www.psychologytoday.com/intl/blog/freedom-to-learn/202303/what-has-caused-the-long-decline-in-kids-mental-health.

19 Khalil Gibran, *The Prophet* (Knopf, 1923), p. 15.

20 Alison Gopnik, *The Gardener and the Carpenter: what the new science of child development tells us about the relationship between parents and children* (Farrar, Straus and Giroux, 2016), p. 20.
21 Ijeoma Oluo, *So You Want To Talk About Race* (Seal Press, 2018), p. 205.
22 Eloise Rickman, *Extraordinary Parenting: the essential guide to parenting and educating at home* (Scribe, 2020).
23 Myla and Jon Kabat-Zinn, *Everyday Blessings: the inner work of mindful parenting* (Hyperion, 1997), p. 5.
24 Ellen Chiocca, 'American Parents' Attitudes and Beliefs About Corporal Punishment: an integrative literature review', *Journal of Pediatric Health Care* 31 (3) (2017), pp. 372–83.
25 Quoted in Yolande Clark-Jackson, 'How gentle parenting is allowing Black parents to reframe old narratives', *Care* (2023), https://www.care.com/c/how-gentle-parenting-allows-black-parents-reframe-old-naratives/.
26 Stacey Patton, '*Corporal punishment in black communities: not an intrinsic cultural tradition but racial trauma*', American Psychological Association (2017), https://www.apa.org/pi/families/resources/newsletter/2017/04/racial-trauma.
27 Antonio Balmer, 'Childhood, Family, and the Decline of Capitalism', *Socialist Revolution* (2016), https://socialistrevolution.org/childhood-family-and-the-decline-of-capitalism/.
28 David Brooks, 'The Nuclear Family Was A Mistake', *The Atlantic* (2020), https://www.theatlantic.com/magazine/archive/2020/03/the-nuclear-family-was-a-mistake/605536/.
29 Instagram survey of 394 parents, self-selecting participants, 17th April 2023.
30 See for example, Tujia Seppala et al., 'Intragroup contact with other mothers living in the same neighborhood benefits mothers' life satisfaction: the mediating role of group identification and social support', *Journal of Community Psychology* 51 (3) (2022), pp. 1365–77; S. S. Luthar and L. Ciciolla, 'Who mothers mommy? factors that contribute to mothers' well-being', *Developmental Psychology* 51(12) (2015), pp.1812–23.
31 Radical Childcare (2018) *City Children's Charter*.
32 There is a conversation to be had here about how we can step in to support children — particularly children who hold multiple marginalised identities — without putting them and their families at risk. I suppose the answer, as with so many things, lies in social change that supports, funds, and cares for local communities and provides parents with help before things get to this crisis stage. Even though I'm in the UK, reading *Torn Apart* by Dorothy Roberts (where she details how child protective services in the US work to break up and terrorise Black families) has made me question how we can step in to help children when we witness genuine abuse in the short term.

Chapter Six: Loving pedagogy

1 UK: 'Childcare and early years survey of parents' GOV.UK (2022), https://explore-education-statistics.service.gov.uk/find-statistics/childcare-and-early-years-survey-of-parents; US: National Center for Education Statistics, https://nces.ed.gov/programs/digest/d19/tables/dt19_202.10.asp; Australia: 'Early childhood and transition to school', AIHW (2023), https://www.aihw.gov.au/reports/australias-welfare/childcare-and-early-childhood-education.

2 James Heckman et al., 'Perry Preschool Project', *Centre for Economics and Human Development*, https://cehd.uchicago.edu/?page_id=958.

3 Edward Melhuish and Julian Gardiner, 'Study of Early Education and Development (SEED): impact study on early education use and child outcomes up to age five years', *DFE* (2020), https://assets.publishing.service.gov.uk/government/uploads/system/uploads/attachment_data/file/867140/SEED_AGE_5_REPORT_FEB.pdf; and Edward Melhuish and Julian Gardiner, 'Study of Early Education and Development (SEED): impact study on early education use and child outcomes up to age seven years', *DfE* (2021), https://assets.publishing.service.gov.uk/government/uploads/system/uploads/attachment_data/file/1029529/SEED_Age_7_Impact_Report.pdf.

4 Tamsin Grimmer, *Developing a Loving Pedagogy in the Early Years: how love fits with professional practice* (Routledge, 2021), p. 6.

5 Matthew S. Liao, *The Right to Be Loved* (Oxford University Press, 2015); Liao, S. Matthew, 'The Right Of Children To Be Loved', *The Journal of Political Philosophy* 14 (4) (2006), pp. 420–40.

6 'The Bristol Baby Rights journey', Bristol Early Years, https://www.bristolearlyyears.org.uk/baby-rights/.

7 Nicole Bohic et al., 'Qualité de l'accueil et prévention de la maltraitance dans les crèches', *IGAS* (2023), https://www.igas.gouv.fr/IMG/pdf/2022-062r_tome_1.pdf.

8 See for example, K. Nystand et al., 'Toddlers' stress during transition to childcare', *European Early Childhood Education Research Journal* 29 (2) (2021), pp. 157–82.

9 Rachel Rosen and Jan Newberry, 'Love, labour, and temporality: reconceptualising social reproduction with women and children in the frame', in Rachel Rosen and Katherine Twamley, (eds.) *Feminism and The Politics of Childhood: friends or foes?* (UCL Press, 2018), pp. 118–19.

10 Alice Bradbury and Guy Robert-Holmes, 'Grouping in Early Years and Key Stage 1: "a necessary evil?"', *NEU / UCL*, https://www.teachingtimes.com/grouping-ks1_111217/, Sue Learner, 'Ability grouping in nurseries: "children reduced to pieces of data"', *Day Nurseries*

(2018), https://www.daynurseries.co.uk/news/article.cfm/id/1597201/ability-grouping-nurseries-children-data.

11 Nathan Archer, '"I have this subversive curriculum underneath": narratives of micro resistance in early childhood education', *Journal of Early Childhood Research* 20 (3) (2022), pp. 431–45.

12 *Who Cares About The Family?*, Mothers at Home Matter (2015), https://static1.squarespace.com/static/5ed9e68a9557e-c2f11733586/t/5efcb24e5edbbd4e09fa6f42/1593619027807/Who+Cares+about+the+Family+Jan2015+spreads.pdf.

13 Maureen Van Niel et al., 'The Impact of Paid Maternity Leave on the Mental and Physical Health of Mothers and Children: a review of the literature and policy implications', *Harvard Review of Psychiatry* 28 (2) (2020), pp.113–26.

14 Julia Goodman, 'Racial/Ethnic Inequities in Paid Parental Leave Access', *Health Equity* 5 (1) (2021), https://www.liebertpub.com/doi/10.1089/heq.2021.0001.

15 'Capitalism and Motherhood', Whole Mother Therapy (2022), https://www.wholemothertherapy.com/blog/capitalism-and-motherhood.

16 Richard Petts et al., 'Fathers' Paternity Leave-Taking and Children's Perceptions of Father-Child Relationships in the United States', *Sex Roles* 82 (2020), pp.173–88.

17 Petra Persson and Maya Rossin-Slater, 'When Dad Can Stay Home: fathers' workplace flexibility and maternal health', *NBER* (2019), https://www.nber.org/papers/w25902.

18 Mareike Buenning, 'What Happens after the "Daddy Months"? Fathers' Involvement in Paid Work, Childcare, and Housework after Taking Parental Leave in Germany', *European Sociological Review* 31 (6) (2015).

19 Elly-Ann Johansson, '*The effect of own and spousal parental leave on earnings*,' Working Paper Series IFAU —Institute for Evaluation of Labour Market and Education Policy (2010), https://ideas.repec.org/p/hhs/ifauwp/2010_004.html.

20 *Unlimited Potential: report of the commission on gender stereotypes in early childhood*, Fawcett Society (2010), https://www.fawcettsociety.org.uk/Handlers/Download.ashx?IDMF=17fb0c11-f904-469c-a62e-173583d441c8.

21 'In Sweden, it's possible to combine career with family life. Here's why.', Sweden (2022), https://sweden.se/life/society/work-life-balance.

22 Ivana La Valle and Megan Jarvie, 'Old challenges, new concerns: how Covid-19 has magnified inequalities in the childcare system', Coram, https://www.familyandchildcaretrust.org/how-Covid-19-has-magnified-inequalities-in-the-childcare-system.

23 Vanessa Clarke, Navtej Johal & Callum Thomson, 'Childcare: Full-time

nursery for under-twos nearly £15k a year, says report', *BBC News* (2023), https://www.bbc.co.uk/news/education-64865602

24 'The Early Years Miracle?', BBC *Analysis*, Radio 4 (2020), https://www.bbc.co.uk/sounds/play/m000f6tx.

25 Rachel Lawler, 'One in five early years workers considering leaving the sector', Early Years Alliance (2021), https://www.eyalliance.org.uk/news/2021/02/one-five-early-years-workers-considering-leaving-sector.

26 Alexandra Topping and Patrick Butler, 'Hunt's jobs drive will push mothers on benefits to work 30-hour week', *The Guardian* (2023), https://www.theguardian.com/society/2023/mar/22/jeremy-hunt-universal-credit-benefits-mothers-30-hour-weeks.

27 Michael Baker, Jonathan Gruber, and Kevin Milligan, 'The Long-Run Impacts of a Universal Child Care Program', *American Economic Journal: Economic Policy*, Vol. 11 (3) (2019), pp.1–26.

28 Janet Ericksen, 'Measuring the Long-Term Effects of Early, Extensive Day Care', *IFS Studies* (2018), https://ifstudies.org/blog/measuring-the-long-term-effects-of-early-extensive-day-care.

29 Ibid.

30 See for example, Jennifer M. Silva and Allison J. Pugh, 'Beyond the Depleting Model of Parenting: narratives of childrearing and change', *Sociological Inquiry* 80 (4) (2010), pp. 605–27.

31 Vanessa Olorenshaw, *Liberating Motherhood: birthing the purplestocking movement* (Womancraft, 2016), p. 4.

32 Shulamith Firestone, *The Dialectic of Sex: the case for feminist revolution* (Verso, 1970), pp. 93–94.

33 Peter Moss, 'Early education in Sweden – No comparison', *Nursery World* (2022), https://www.nurseryworld.co.uk/features/article/early-education-in-sweden-no-comparison.

34 Peter Moss, *Transformative Change and Real Utopias in Early Childhood Education: a story of democracy, experimentation, and potentiality* (Routledge, 2014), pp. 170–172.

35 Neil Leitch, 'Alliance slams "ludicrous, pointless and potentially dangerous" plans to relax childcare ratios', *Early Years Alliance* (2023), https://www.eyalliance.org.uk/alliance-slams-ludicrous-pointless-and-potentially-dangerous-plans-relax-childcare-ratios.

36 Joe Pinsker, 'Kill The Five-Day Work Week', *The Atlantic* (2021), https://www.theatlantic.com/family/archive/2021/06/four-day-workweek/619222/.

Chapter Seven: Deliberate harm

1 'Record Number of Emergency Food Parcels Provided', *The Trussell Trust* (2023), https://www.trusselltrust.org/2023/04/26/record-number-of-emergency-food-parcels-provided-to-people-facing-hardship-by-trussell-trust-food-banks-in-past-12-months/.

2 'Child poverty', UNICEF, https://www.unicef.org/social-policy/child-poverty.

3 This number takes into account family income after housing costs have been deducted: '*Households below average income: an analysis of the income distribution FYE 1995 to FYE 2021*', GOV.UK (2022), https://www.gov.uk/government/statistics/households-below-average-income-for-financial-years-ending-1995-to-2021/households-below-average-income-an-analysis-of-the-income-distribution-fye-1995-to-fye-2021#children-in-low-income-households.

4 'Poverty in Australia', Poverty and Inequality, https://povertyandinequality.acoss.org.au/poverty/. N.B. The figures are not directly comparable as definitions of poverty differ between the UK, US, and Australia.

5 'Child Poverty Facts and Figures', CPAG, https://cpag.org.uk/child-poverty/child-poverty-facts-and-figures.

6 '*UK Poverty 2022: the essential guide to understanding poverty in the UK*', Joseph Rowntree Foundation (2022), https://www.jrf.org.uk/report/uk-poverty-2022.

7 'Chapter 13 – Indigenous Australians', Parliament of Australia, https://www.aph.gov.au/parliamentary_business/committees/senate/community_affairs/completed_inquiries/2002-04/poverty/report/c13.

8 '3.7 Million More Children in Poverty in Jan 2022 without Monthly Child Tax Credit', Center on Poverty & Social Policy at Columbia University (2022), https://www.povertycenter.columbia.edu/news-internal/monthly-poverty-january-2022; Randall Akee, 'How does measuring poverty and welfare affect American Indian children', *Brookings* (2019), https://www.brookings.edu/articles/how-does-measuring-poverty-and-welfare-affect-american-indian-children/#:~:text=Given%20the%20best%20available%20data,almost%20the%20past%2030%20years.

9 Jemima McEvoy, 'The Richest Billionaire In Every State 2022', *Forbes* (2022), https://www.forbes.com/sites/jemimamcevoy/2022/04/05/the-richest-billionaire-in-every-state-2022/; 'High Income', The World Bank (2022), https://data.worldbank.org/country/XD.

10 Anna Gromada et al., 'Worlds of Influence: understanding what shapes child well-being in rich countries', *UNICEF* (2020), https://www.unicef-irc.org/child-well-being-report-card-16.

11 Brian Stauffner, 'Going to the Bank for Food, Not Money: the growing reality of hunger in "rich" countries', *Human Rights Watch* (2020), https://www.hrw.org/world-report/2020/country-chapters/global-4; Charlotte Edmond, 'These Rich Countries Have High Levels of Child Poverty', *World Economic Forum* (2017), https://www.weforum.org/agenda/2017/06/these-rich-countries-have-high-levels-of-child-poverty/.

12 Philip Alston, *Report of the Special Rapporteur on Extreme Poverty and Human Rights on his mission to the United States of America*, United Nations (2018), https://digitallibrary.un.org/record/1629536.

13 Philip Alston, *Visit to the United Kingdom of Great Britain and Northern Ireland: report of the special rapporteur on extreme poverty and human rights*, United Nations (2019), https://digitallibrary.un.org/record/3806308?ln=en.

14 Robert Booth, 'UN poverty expert hits back over UK ministers' "denial of facts"', *The Guardian* (2019), https://www.theguardian.com/society/2019/may/24/un-poverty-expert-hits-back-over-uk-ministers-denial-of-facts-philip-alston.

15 David Cameron, '*Welfare Speech*', GOV.UK (2012), https://www.gov.uk/government/speeches/welfare-speech.

16 George Osborne, '*Summer Budget 2015 Speech*', GOV.UK (2015), https://www.gov.uk/government/speeches/chancellor-george-osbornes-summer-budget-2015-speech.

17 From £26,000 to £20,000 (£23,000 in London): *Benefit cap: number of households capped to February 2022,* GOV.UK (2022), https://www.gov.uk/government/statistics/benefit-cap-number-of-households-capped-to-february-2022.

18 Mary Reader et al., *Does Cutting Child Benefits Reduce Fertility in Larger Families? evidence from the UK's two-child limit,* Larger Families (2022), https://largerfamilies.study/publications/does-cutting-child-benefits-reduce-fertility-in-larger-families-evidence-from-the-uk-s-two-child/.

19 '*Abortion statistics, England and Wales: 2021*', GOV.UK (2022), https://www.gov.uk/government/statistics/abortion-statistics-for-england-and-wales-2021.

20 'Forced Into a Corner: the two-child limit and pregnancy decision making during the pandemic', BPAS (2020), https://www.bpas.org/media/3409/forced-into-a-corner-the-two-child-limit-and-pregnancy-decision-making-during-the-pandemic.pdf; Lord Bishop of Durham, *Bishop of Durham Introduces Bill to Abolish Two-Child Limit*, The Church of England in Parliament (2022), https://churchinparliament.org/2022/07/08/bishop-of-durham-introduces-bill-to-abolish-two-child-limit/.

21 Good Morning Britain, *Jacob Rees-Mogg Says That He Opposes Abortion*

and Same-Sex Marriage, YouTube (2017), https://www.youtube.com/watch?v=WE6WC_BVZ4Q.

22 Mary Reader et al., *Does Cutting Child Benefits Reduce Fertility in Larger Families? Evidence from the UK's Two-Child Limit*, Larger Families (2022), https://largerfamilies.study/publications/does-cutting-child-benefits-reduce-fertility-in-larger-families-evidence-from-the-uk-s-two-child/; Ruth Patrick and Kate Andersen, *The Two-Child Limit & 'Choices' Over Family Size: when policy presentation collides with lived experiences*, The London School of Economics and Political Science (2022), https://sticerd.lse.ac.uk/dps/case/cp/casepaper226.pdf.

23 '*The Impact of Five Years of the Two-Child Limit Policy*', Child Poverty Action Group (2022), https://cpag.org.uk/sites/default/files/files/policypost/Heartbreaking_two_child_limit.pdf.

24 '*Universal Credit (Removal of Two Child Limit) Bill [HL]*', UK Parliament (2022), https://bills.parliament.uk/bills/3163.

25 Anna Davis, 'Teachers are buying students food, school uniforms and period products, new poll reveals', *Evening Standard* (2023), https://www.standard.co.uk/news/education/teachers-buying-food-period-products-poor-students-b1072211.html.

26 Tracey Jensen and Imogen Tyler, '"Benefits Broods": the cultural and political crafting of anti-welfare commonsense', *Critical Social Policy* 34 (4) (2015), pp. 470–91.

27 Joshua Lever, 'Benefits Street Episode 1', YouTube (2021), https://www.youtube.com/watch?v=GvKfcqpiEHw; Meghna Amin, 'Benefits Street star White Dee accuses Channel 4 of "exploiting" cast: "We were hung out to dry"', *Metro* (2022), https://metro.co.uk/2022/03/21/benefits-street-star-white-dee-accuses-channel-4-of-exploiting-cast-16313141/.

28 Donald Hirsh and Tom Lee, *The Cost of a Child in 2021*, CPAG (2021), https://cpag.org.uk/sites/default/files/files/policypost/Cost_of_a_child_2021.pdf.

29 '*UK Poverty 2022: the essential guide to understanding poverty in the UK*', Joseph Rowntree Foundation (2022), https://www.jrf.org.uk/report/uk-poverty-2022.

30 'Key Findings: British social attitudes in an era of crisis', *The National Centre for Social Research* (2022), https://www.natcen.ac.uk/news-media/press-releases/2022/september/british-social-attitudes-in-an-era-of-crisis/.

31 Anna Fazackerly, 'Headteachers in Tears at Stark Choice: keep staff or feed hungry pupils', *The Guardian* (2022), https://www.theguardian.com/education/2022/oct/22/uk-headteachers-in-tears-at-stark-choice-cut-staff-or-feed-hungry-pupils; Callum Mason, 'Colder Classes, Staff Cuts: why schools face a "catastrophic" Winter', *TES*

Magazine (2022), https://www.tes.com/magazine/news/general/energy-bills-cost-of-living-crisis-schools-face-catastrophic-winter.

32 EdBuild, https://edbuild.org/content/23-billion.

33 Adeshola Ore, 'Private School Funding in Australia has Increased at Five Times Rate of Public schools, Analysis Shows', *The Guardian* (2022), https://www.theguardian.com/australia-news/2022/feb/16/private-school-funding-has-increased-at-five-times-rate-of-public-schools-analysis-shows.

34 Joe Lepper, 'More Than 1000 Children's Centres Close Over Last Decade', *Children and Young People Now* (2022), https://www.cypnow.co.uk/news/article/more-than-1-000-children-s-centres-closed-over-last-decade.

35 Sarah Cattan et al., *The health effects of Sure Start*, The Institute for Fiscal Studies (2019), https://ifs.org.uk/publications/health-effects-sure-start.

36 https://www.disabilityrightsuk.org/news/2022/april/child-and-adolescent-mental-health-services-camhs-are-under-resourced-point-refusing.

37 Justine Smith, 'Revealed: the postcode lottery in child and adolescent mental health care', *The House* (2023), https://www.politicshome.com/thehouse/article/child-adolescent-mental-health-care-crisis.

38 Vanessa LoBue, 'How Parental Stress Can Affect a Child's Health', *Psychology Today* (2022), https://www.psychologytoday.com/gb/blog/the-baby-scientist/202203/how-parental-stress-can-affect-childs-health.

39 Vikki Spratt, *Tenants: the people on the frontline of Britain's housing emergency* (2022), Profile Books, p. 8.

40 Lisa Harker, 'Chance of a lifetime', Shelter (2006), https://assets.ctfassets.net/6sxvmndnpn0s/4LTXp3mya7IigRmNG8x9KK/6922b5a4c6e-a756ea94da71ebdc001a5/Chance_of_a_Lifetime.pdf.

41 Petula Dvorak, 'When "back to school" means a parking lot and the hunt for a WiFi signal', *Washington Post* (2020), https://www.washingtonpost.com/local/when-back-to-school-means-a-parking-lot-and-the-hunt-for-a-wifi-signal/2020/08/27/0f785d5a-e873-11ea-970a-64c73a1c2392_story.html.

42 Food Foundation, *New Data Show 4 Million Children in Households Affected by Food Insecurity* (2020), https://foodfoundation.org.uk/publication/new-data-show-4-million-children-households-affected-food-insecurity.

43 Anna Fazackerley, 'Schools in England warn of crisis of "heartbreaking" rise in hungry children', *The Guardian* (2022), https://www.theguardian.com/business/2022/sep/25/schools-in-england-warn-of-crisis-of-heart-breaking-rise-in-hungry-children.

44 Patrick Butler, 'Expand Free School Meals to Combat Rise in Malnutrition, say Health Experts', *The Guardian* (2022), https://www.theguardian.com/education/2022/nov/03/.expand-free-school-meals-to-combat-rise-in-malnutrition-say-health-experts.

45 Claire Crawford, Christine Farquharson, and Ellen Greaves, 'Breakfast clubs work their magic in disadvantaged English schools', IFS (2016), https://ifs.org.uk/articles/breakfast-clubs-work-their-magic-disadvantaged-english-schools.
46 GreggsOfficial, 'Greggs Foundation ... Meet some of our Breakfast Club kids ...' YouTube (2018), https://www.youtube.com/watch?v=NijU-243WFJI; *The Guardian*, 'Breakfast club at a Brixton primary school', YouTube, https://www.youtube.com/watch?v=w4ry69V24uc.
47 Jamie L. Hanson et al., 'Family Poverty Affects the Rate of Human Infant Brain Growth', *PLOS ONE* 10 (12) (2013).
48 Polly Curtis, *Behind Closed Doors: why we break up families – and how to mend them*, Virago (2022), p. 261.
49 Paul Bywater, 'The Child Welfare Inequalities Project: final report', *The Child Welfare Inequalities Project* (2020), https://pure.hud.ac.uk/ws/files/21398145/CWIP_Final_Report.pdf.
50 Davara L. Bennett et al., 'Child Poverty and Children Entering Care in England, 2015–20: a longitudinal ecological study at the local area level', *The Lancet Public Health* 7 (2022), pp. 496–503.
51 Dorothy Roberts, *Torn Apart: how the child welfare system destroys Black families--and how abolition can build a safer world*, Basic (2022), p. 24.
52 Family Matters, *The Family Matters Report 2021* (2021), https://www.familymatters.org.au/the-family-matters-report-2021/.
53 'National Agreement on Closing the Gap', Closing the Gap (2020), https://www.closingthegap.gov.au/national-agreement.
54 See for example, Borgen Project, https://borgenproject.org/drugaddiction/; 'Poverty: statistics', Mental Health Foundation, https://www.mentalhealth.org.uk/explore-mental-health/mental-health-statistics/poverty-statistics.
55 Sarah Reis, 'Domestic Abuse Is An Economic Issue', *CPAG* (2019), https://cpag.org.uk/news-blogs/news-listings/.domestic-abuse-economic-issue-%E2%80%93-its-victims-and-society
56 NWLM, 'What Does Abolitionist Activism Mean for Early Childhood Policies?', *National Women's Legal Centre* (2020), https://nwlc.org/what-does-abolitionist-activism-mean-for-early-childhood-policies/.
57 Maitreesh Ghatat and François Maniquet, 'Universal Basic Income: some theoretical aspects', *Annual Review of Economics* 11 (2019), pp. 895–928.
58 Moises Velasquez-Manoff, 'What Happens When the Poor Receive a Stipend?', *New York Times* (2014), https://archive.nytimes.com/opinionator.blogs.nytimes.com/2014/01/18/what-happens-when-the-poor-receive-a-stipend/.
59 CPAG, 'Education costs parents', *Child Poverty Action Group* (2023), https://cpag.org.uk/news-blogs/news-listings/

education-costs-parents-%E2%80%93-typically-least-%C2%A339-week-secondary-school-kids-.

60 Geoff Page, Maddy Power, and Ruth Patrick, 'School uniform costs are a source of financial and emotional stress for families living on a low income', *LSE British Politics and Policy blog* (2021), https://blogs.lse.ac.uk/politicsandpolicy/uniform-failings/.

61 Shulamith Firestone, *The Dialectic of Sex: the case for feminist revolution* (Verso, 1970), p. 85.

62 Northern Ireland: 'Money to Learn Education Maintenance Allowance, nidirect government services, https://www.nidirect.gov.uk/information-and-services/financial-support-school-or-college/money-learn-education-maintenance; Scotland: https://www.mygov.scot/ema; Wales: https://www.studentfinancewales.co.uk/further-education-funding/education-maintenance-allowance/what-s-available/; on the English protests see Jessica Shepherd 'EMA: Student protesters take to streets to fight for grant', *The Guardian* (2011), https://www.theguardian.com/education/2011/jan/19/ema-students-fight-for-grant.

63 Figures accurate May 2023, 'National Minimum Wage and National Living Wage rates', GOV.UK, https://www.gov.uk/national-minimum-wage-rates.

64 Sam Jones, 'Spanish minister proposes €20,000 "universal inheritance" from age of 18', *The Guardian* (2023), https://www.theguardian.com/world/2023/jul/05/spanish-minister-proposes-20000-universal-inheritance-from-age-of-18.

65 Craig Munro, 'Calpol most shoplifted item by "desperate" parents in London borough', *Metro* (2023), https://metro.co.uk/2023/04/20/calpol-most-shoplifted-item-by-desperate-parents-in-tower-hamlets-18646709/.

66 CPAG, 'The cost of having fun at school', *Child Poverty Action Group* (2022), https://cpag.org.uk/sites/default/files/files/policypost/The_Cost_of_Having_Fun_at_School.pdf.

Chapter Eight: What we learn from school

1 'Awarded Schools Across the UK', UNICEF, https://www.unicef.org.uk/rights-respecting-schools/the-rrsa/awarded-schools/.

2 Gina Schouten, 'Schooling' in Anca Gheaus, Gideon Calder, and Jurgen de Wispelaere (eds.), *The Routledge Handbook of the Philosophy of Childhood and Children* (Routledge, 2019).

3 Michel Foucault, *Surveiller et punir: naissance de la prison* (Editions Gallimard, 1991) as *Discipline and Punish: the birth of the prison* (Penguin 1991), p. 155.

4 BBC News, 'Is it rare for US teachers to spank unruly children at school?', *BBC News* (2022), https://www.bbc.co.uk/news/world-us-canada-56986827.

5 In 2019/20, there were 5,057 permanent exclusions for children in England, and 310,733 fixed-term suspensions. These figures are low in comparison with previous years as they include the start of the Covid-19 pandemic, when many children studied at home. Looking at data for previous years we see that exclusion rates have been growing year-on-year since 2012/13. See 'Permanent exclusions and suspensions in England: 2019 to 2020', GOV.UK (2021), https://www.gov.uk/government/statistics/permanent-exclusions-and-suspensions-in-england-2019-to-2020 and 'Permanent exclusions and suspensions in England: 2020 to 2021', GOV.UK (2022), https://www.gov.uk/government/statistics/permanent-exclusions-and-suspensions-in-england-2020-to-2021.

6 'What about the other 29? And other FAQs', *No More Exclusions* https://drive.google.com/file/d/15JxRG5jgsDCoq-T2gJFmLHvVdA5EPYFk/view.

7 'Social Impact', Wellspring, https://wellspringacademytrust.co.uk/social-impact/.

8 Martha McHardy, 'Why are school children rioting over toilet rule changes?', *The Independent* (2023), https://www.independent.co.uk/news/uk/home-news/school-toilet-riots-2023-cornwall-b2289449.html.

9 'Facts about Bullying', StopBullying.gov, https://www.stopbullying.gov/resources/facts; 'Australia's children', Australian Institute of Health and Welfare, https://www.aihw.gov.au/reports/children-youth/australias-children/contents/justice-and-safety/bullying.

10 'Review of sexual abuse in schools and colleges', Ofsted (2021), https://www.gov.uk/government/publications/review-of-sexual-abuse-in-schools-and-colleges/review-of-sexual-abuse-in-schools-and-colleges.

11 Sara Novak, 'Half of the 250 Kids Expelled from Preschool Each Day Are Black Boys', *Scientific American* (2023), https://www.scientificamerican.com/article/half-of-the-250-kids-expelled-from-preschool-each-day-are-black-boys/.

12 Walter Gilliam et al., 'Do Early Educators' Implicit Biases Regarding Sex and Race Relate to Behavior Expectations and Recommendations of Preschool Expulsions and Suspensions?', *Yale Study Centre* (2016), https://marylandfamiliesengage.org/wp-content/uploads/2019/07/Preschool-Implicit-Bias-Policy-Brief.pdf.

13 Sally Weale, 'Black people who were labelled "backward" as children seek justice for lifelong trauma', *The Guardian* (2023), https://www.theguardian.com/education/2023/feb/21/black-people-labelled-backward-as-children-seek-justice-for-lifelong-trauma.

14 Nazia Parveen and Tobi Thomas, 'UK schools record more than 60,000 racist incidents in five years', *The Guardian* (2021), https://www.theguardian.com/education/2021/mar/28/uk-schools-record-more-than-60000-racist-incidents-five-years.
15 'Agenda articles', *World Economic Forum*, https://www.weforum.org/agenda/2020/11/racism-united-kingdom-schools-black-children-inequality/.
16 'Who is Most Affected by the School to Prison Pipeline', *School of Education* (2021), https://soeonline.american.edu/blog/school-to-prison-pipeline/.
17 Jeffrey Boyake, *I Heard What You Said: a Black teacher, a white system, a revolution in education,* Picador (2022), p. 9.
18 See for example, 'Pupils repeatedly sent home from school over afro hair wins £8,500 payout', *Independent* (2020), https://www.independent.co.uk/news/education/education-news/afro-hair-discrimation-student-legal-action-payout-ruby-williams-urswick-school-a9323466.html and 'Sisters of African descent suspended from Victorian private school for not tying hair back', *The Guardian* (2022), https://www.theguardian.com/australia-news/2022/jul/29/sisters-suspended-from-victorian-private-school-highview-college-maryborough-for-refusing-to-wear-their-african-hair-tied-back.
19 Nazia Parveen and Tobi Thomas, 'Pimlico academy pupils stage protest over "discriminatory" policies', *The Guardian* (2021), https://www.theguardian.com/world/2021/mar/31/pimlico-academy-pupils-stage-protest-over-discriminatory-policies.
20 Carol Black, 'Children, Learning, and the "Evaluative Gaze" of School', *Carol Black* (2017), http://carolblack.org/the-gaze.
21 Pasi Sahlberg, *Finnish Lessons 2.0: what can the world learn from educational change in Finland?* (Teachers College Press, 2015).
22 Becky Taylor, 'Schools "teaching in 'ability' sets despite evidence this may cause harm"', *UCL* (2017), https://www.ucl.ac.uk/news/2017/sep/schools-teaching-ability-sets-despite-evidence-may-cause-harm.
23 Peter Gray, 'Why Our Coercive System of Schooling Should Topple', *Psychology Today* (2016), https://www.psychologytoday.com/intl/blog/freedom-learn/201612/why-our-coercive-system-schooling-should-topple.
24 Paul Hopkins, 'Primary school children get little academic benefit from homework', University of Hull (2022), https://www.hull.ac.uk/work-with-us/more/media-centre/news/2022/primary-school-children-get-little-academic-benefit-from-homework.
25 Erica Reischer, 'Can Reading Logs Ruin Reading for Kids?', *The Atlantic* (2016), https://www.theatlantic.com/education/archive/2016/06/

are-reading-logs-ruining-reading/485372/.

26 Mollie Galloway, Jerusha Conner, and Denise Pope, 'Nonacademic Effects of Homework in Privileged, High-Performing High Schools', *The Journal of Experimental Education* 81 (4) (2013), pp. 490–510.

27 'Key stage 2 attainment: national headlines', GOV.UK (2022), https://explore-education-statistics.service.gov.uk/find-statistics/key-stage-2-attainment-national-headlines/2021-22.

28 Jo Hutchinson and Mary Reader, 'The Educational Outcomes of Refugee and Asylum-Seeking Children in England', Education Policy Institute (2021), https://epi.org.uk/wp-content/uploads/2021/11/Refugee_asylum_working_paper_-EPI.pdf.

29 'Briefing: the children leaving school with nothing' UK Children's Commissioner (2019), https://www.childrenscommissioner.gov.uk/wp-content/uploads/2019/09/cco-briefing-children-leaving-school-with-nothing.pdf.

30 'Secondary education: school retention and completion', Australian Institute of Health and Welfare (2021) https://www.aihw.gov.au/reports/australias-welfare/secondary-education-school-retention-completion and 'Closing the Gap Report 2020: year 12 attainment', Australian Government (2020), https://ctgreport.niaa.gov.au/year-12-attainment.

31 Imran Tahir, 'The UK education system preserves inequality – new report', *IFS* (2022), https://ifs.org.uk/articles/uk-education-system-preserves-inequality-new-report#:~:text=Over%2070%25%20of%20private%20school,being%20more%20qualified%20as%20adults.

32 Donna Ferguson, 'Working-class children get less of everything in education - including respect', *The Guardian* (2017), https://www.theguardian.com/education/2017/nov/21/english-class-system-shaped-in-schools.

33 Peter Gray, *Free To Learn: why unleashing the instinct to play will make our children happier, more self reliant, and better students for life* (Basic Books, 2013).

34 Ken Robinson and Kate Robinson, *Imagine If…: creating a future for us all*, (Penguin, 2022).

35 'FAQs', Sudbury Valley School, https://sudburyvalley.org/faqs.

36 'Social and Emotional Development', Summer Hill School, https://www.summerhillschool.co.uk/social-and-emotional-development.

37 Charlie Shread and Marianne Osorio (dir.), *School Circles*, video documentary (2018).

38 Alfie Kohn, *Feel-Bad Education and Other Contrarian Essays on Children and Schooling* (Beacon Press, 2011).

39 Lots on this but see for example, Moses Kopong Tokan, 'The effect of motivation and learning behaviour on student achievement', *South African Journal of Education* 39 (1) (2019), pp.1–8; Richard M. Ryan and Edward

L. Deci, 'Self-Determination Theory and the Facilitation of Intrinsic Motivation, Social Development, and Well-Being', *American Psychologist* 55 (1) (2000), pp. 68–78.

40 Akilah. S. Richards, *Raising Free People: unschooling as liberation and healing work* (PM Press, 2020).

41 Dina Rickman, 'There are more illegal Jewish schools in a London borough than legal ones, council admits', *The Independent* (2016), https://www.independent.co.uk/news/uk/home-news/hackney-council-admit-there-are-more-illegal-than-legal-jewish-schools-in-borough-a7422526.html.

42 Molly Olmstead, 'How the Christian Home-Schooling Lobby Feeds on Fear of Public Schools', *Slate* (2022), https://slate.com/news-and-politics/2022/06/texas-shooting-conservative-christians-home-schooling.html.

43 Catherine Burke and Ian Grosvenor, *The School I'd Like: revisted: children's and young people's reflections on an education for the 21st century* (Routledge, 2015).

44 bell hooks, *Teaching to Transgress: education as the practice of freedom* (Routledge, 1994) p. 4.

Chapter Nine: A future built for children

1 Global CO2 Levels, 2° Institute, https://www.co2levels.org/.

2 'Mining Congress Journal, August 1966 – Air Pollution and the Coal Industry', *Climate Files*, https://www.climatefiles.com/coal/mining-congress-journal-august-1965-air-pollution-and-the-coal-industry/.

3 Bill McGuire, *Hothouse Earth: an inhabitants guide* (Icon Books, 2022).

4 Hannah Ritchie and Max Roser, 'CO2 emmisions', *Our World in Data* (2020), https://ourworldindata.org/co2-emissions.

5 Philip Shabecoff, 'Global Warming Has Begun, Expert Tells Senate', *New York Times* (1988), https://www.nytimes.com/1988/06/24/us/global-warming-has-begun-expert-tells-senate.html; Eric Holthaus, 'James Hansen's legacy: scientists reflect on climate change in 1988, 2018, and 2048', *Grist* (2018), https://grist.org/article/james-hansens-legacy-scientists-reflect-on-climate-change-in-1988-2018-and-2048/.

6 Nathaniel Rich, 'Losing Earth: the decade we almost stopped climate change', *New York Times* (2018), https://www.nytimes.com/interactive/2018/08/01/magazine/climate-change-losing-earth.html.

7 Armstrong Mckay et al., 'Exceeding 1.5°C Global Warming Could Trigger Multiple Climate Tipping Points', *Science* 337 (6611) (2022).

8 Brad Plumer and Nadja Popovich, 'Why Half a Degree of Global Warming Is a Big Deal', *New York Times* (2018), https://www.nytimes.com/interactive/2018/10/07/climate/ipcc-report-half-degree.html.

9 Naomi Klein, *This Changes Everything* (Penguin, 2015).

10 Riley Dunlap and Aaron McCright, 'Challenging Climate Change: the denial countermovement', in Dunlap and Brulle (eds.), *Climate Change and Society: sociological perspectives (*Oxford University Press, 2015), pp. 300–332.

11 Perry Sheffield and Philip Landrigan, 'Global Climate Change and Children's Health: threats and strategies for prevention', *Environmental Health Perspectives* 119 (3) (2011), pp. 291–8.

12 Nina Lakhani and Shah M. Baloch, 'Rich Nations Owe Reparations to Countries Facing Climate Disaster, says Pakistan Minister, *The Guardian* (2022), https://www.theguardian.com/world/2022/sep/04/pakistan-floods-reparations-climate-disaster.

13 Nicholas Rees et al., 'The Climate Crisis is a Child Rights Crisis: introducing the children's climate risk index', UNICEF (2021), https://www.unicef.org/media/105376/file/UNICEF-climate-crisis-child-rights-crisis.pdf.

14 Chi Xu et al., 'Future of the Human Climate Niche', *PNAS* 117 (21) (2020), pp. 11350–11355.

15 Sarah Chapman et al., 'Past and Projected Climate Change Impacts on Heat-Related Child Mortality in Africa', *Environmental Research Letters* 17 (7) (2022).

16 Chi Xu et al., 'Future of the Human Climate Niche', *PNAS* 117 (21) (2020), pp. 11350–11355.

17 Elizabeth Gibbons, 'Climate Change, Children's Rights, and the Pursuit of Intergenerational Climate Justice', *Health and Human Rights Journal*, 16 (1) (2014), pp. 19–31. Displaced children are also at higher risk of sexual assault and child marriage (a risk that is elevated by the reduction of already limited resources, conflict, and loss of education), see Christie McLeod, Heather Barr, and Katherina Rall, 'Does Climate Change Increase the Risk of Child Marriage? A Look at What We Know - And What We Don't - With Lessons from Bangladesh & Mozambique', *Columbia Journal of Gender and Law* 38 (1) (2019) pp. 96–145.

18 David Wallace-Wells, 'Ten Million A Year', *London Review of Books* 43 (23) (2021), https://www.lrb.co.uk/the-paper/v43/n23/david-wallace-wells/ten-million-a-year.

19 Fan He at al., 'Acute Impact of Fine Particulate Air Pollution on Cardiac Arrhythmias in a Population-Based Sample of Adolescents: the Penn State child cohort', *Journal of the American Heart Association* 11 (18) (2022).

20 'Young Campaigner Award: choked up', Shelia McKechnie Foundation (2022), https://smk.org.uk/awards_nominations/choked-up/; @choked-up_uk Instagram, https://www.instagram.com/chokedup_uk/

21 Emma Lawrence et al., 'The impact of climate change on mental health

and emotional wellbeing: current evidence and implications for policy and practice', *Grantham Institute Briefing paper No 36*, (2021), https://spiral.imperial.ac.uk/bitstream/10044/1/88568/9/3343%20Climate%20change%20and%20mental%20health%20BP36_v6.pdf.

22 Caroline Hickman et al., 'Climate Anxiety in Children and Young People and Their Beliefs About Government Responses to Climate Change: a global survey', *The Lancet* 5 (12) (2021), pp. 863–873.

23 Matt Kristoffersen, 'Collective action helps young adults deal with climate change anxiety', *Yale School of Public Health* (2022), https://ysph.yale.edu/news-article/collective-action-helps-young-adults-deal-with-climate-change-anxiety/.

24 Mary Chesney and Karen Duderstadt, 'Children's Rights, Environmental Justice, and Environmental Health Policy in the United States', *Journal of Pediatric Health Care* 36 (1) (2022), pp. 3–11.

25 Damon Centola et al., 'Experimental evidence for tipping points in social convention', *Science* 360 (6393) (2018), pp. 1116–1119; quote taken from David Noonan, 'The 25% Revolution — How Big Does a Minority Have to Be to Reshape Society?', *Scientific American* (2018), https://www.scientificamerican.com/article/the-25-revolution-how-big-does-a-minority-have-to-be-to-reshape-society/.

26 Gordon Brown, *Seven Ways To Change The World: how to fix the most pressing problems we face* (Simon & Schuster, 2021).

27 William MacAskill, *What We Owe The Future* (Oneworld, 2022).

28 Henry Shue, *The Pivotal Generation: why we have a moral responsibility to slow climate change right now* (Princeton, 2022).

29 Roman Krznaric, T*he Good Ancestor: how to think long-term in a short-term world* (Penguin, 2020).

30 Mac Macartney, 'The Children's Fire', (2018), https://macmacartney.com/portfolio/thechildrensfire/.

31 Future Generations Commissioner for Wales, https://www.futuregenerations.wales/.

32 David Runciman, 'A Tide of Horseshit', *London Review of Books* 37 (18) (2015), https://www.lrb.co.uk/the-paper/v37/n18/.david-runciman/a-tide-of-horseshit

33 Rachel Salvidge, 'Water Firms in England and Wales Lost 1tn Litres via Leaky Pipes in 2021', *The Guardian* (2022), https://www.theguardian.com/environment/2022/aug/19/water-firms-england-wales-litres-leaky-pipes-ofwat.

34 Oliver Milman, 'A 17-minute Flight? The Super-Rich Who Have "Absolute Disregard for the Planet"', *The Guardian* (2022), https://www.theguardian.com/environment/2022/jul/21/kylie-jenner-short-private-jet-flights-super-rich-climate-crisis.

35 Christiana Figueres and Tom Rivett-Carnac, The Future We Choose (Bonnier, 2021), p. 95.

36 Richard Schiffman, 'Climate Deniers Shift Tactics to "Inactivism"', *Scientific American* (2021), https://www.scientificamerican.com/article/climate-deniers-shift-tactics-to-inactivism/.

37 Mark Kaufman, 'The Carbon Footprint Sham', *Mashable* (2021), https://mashable.com/feature/carbon-footprint-pr-campaign-sham.

38 Katie Worth, 'Subverting Climate Science in the Classroom', *Scientific American* (2022), https://www.scientificamerican.com/article/subverting-climate-science-in-the-classroom/.

39 Rob Alex Fitt, 'Conservative Activists in Texas Have Shaped the History all American Children Learn', *Washington Post* (2020), https://www.washingtonpost.com/outlook/2020/10/19/conservative-activists-texas-have-shaped-history-all-american-children-learn/.

40 Timothy Gutowski et al., 'Environmental Life Style Analysis', paper for presentation at the IEEE International Symposium on Electronics and the Environment (2008), http://web.mit.edu/ebm/www/Publications/ELSA%20IEEE%202008.pdf.

41 Cristopher Callaghan and Justin Mankin, 'National Attribution of Historical Climate Damages', *Climatic Change* 172 (40) (2022).

42 'AR6 Synthesis Report: climate change 2023', IPCC (2023), https://www.ipcc.ch/report/sixth-assessment-report-cycle/; Fiona Harvey, 'Scientists deliver "final warning" on climate crisis: act now or it's too late', *The Guardian* (2023), https://www.theguardian.com/environment/2023/mar/20/ipcc-climate-crisis-report-delivers-final-warning-on-15c.

43 Rebecca Solnit, 'Big Oil Coined "Carbon Footprints" to Blame Us for Their Greed. Keep Them on The Hook', *The Guardian* (2021), https://www.theguardian.com/commentisfree/2021/aug/23/big-oil-coined-carbon-footprints-to-blame-us-for-their-greed-keep-them-on-the-hook.

44 Bayo Akomolafe, *The Times Are Urgent; Let's Slow Down*, https://www.bayoakomolafe.net/post/the-times-are-urgent-lets-slow-down.

45 Erica Chenoweth, 'Questions, Answers, and Some Cautionary Updates Regarding the 3.5% Rule', *Carr Center Discussion Paper Series* (2020), https://carrcenter.hks.harvard.edu/files/cchr/files/CCDP_005.pdf.

46 Isabelle Gerretsen, 'How Youth Climate Court Cases Became a Global Trend', *Climate Home News* (2021), https://www.climatechangenews.com/2021/04/30/youth-climate-court-cases-became-global-trend/.

47 Nicholas Rees et al., 'The Climate Crisis is a Child Rights Crisis: introducing the children's climate risk index', UNICEF (2021), https://www.unicef.org/media/105376/file/UNICEF-climate-crisis-child-rights-crisis.pdf.

48 Colombia: 'In historic ruling, Colombian Court protects youth suing the national government for failing to curb deforestation', *Dejusticia* (2018),

https://www.dejusticia.org/en/en-fallo-historico-corte-suprema-concede-tutela-de-cambio-climatico-y-generaciones-futuras/; Germany: Kate Connolly, '"Historic" German ruling says climate goals not tough enough', *The Guardian* (2021), https://www.theguardian.com/world/2021/apr/29/historic-german-ruling-says-climate-goals-not-tough-enough.

49 Dharna Noor, '"Gamechanger": judge rules in favor of young activists in US climate trial', *The Guardian* (2023), https://www.theguardian.com/us-news/2023/aug/14/montana-climate-trial-young-activists-judge-order.

50 Xiaoming Xu, 'Global Greenhouse Gas Emissions From Animal-Based Foods are Twice Those of Plant-Based Foods', *Nature Food* 2 (2021), pp. 724–732.

51 Although it's now easier than ever to find plant-based recipes or vegan options, changing our diets isn't easy. Food is deeply entwined with our cultures, our memories, and our sense of self. And I want to acknowledge that food isn't something that we all have equal access to, or equal autonomy over; if you rely on food-bank parcels, live in a 'food desert', have a very limited income, or have a family member with dietary restrictions, then it will be harder for you.

52 Sue Donaldson and Will Kymlicka, 'Children and Animals' in Anca Gheaus, Gideon Calder, and Jurgen de Wispelaere (eds.), *The Routledge Handbook of the Philosophy of Childhood and Children* (Routledge, 2019).

53 Aja Barber, *Consumed: the need for collective change; colonialism, climate change & consumerism* (Brazen, 2021).

54 @ajabarber Instagram, https://www.instagram.com/p/Ciw7H1woydD/.

55 Samantha K. Stanley et al., 'From Anger to Action: differential impacts of eco-anxiety, eco-depression, and eco-anger on climate action and wellbeing', *The Journal of Climate Change and Health* 1 (2021), pp. 1–5.

56 David Sobel, *Beyond Ecophobia: reclaiming the heart in nature education* (Orion, 1999).

57 Timothy Morton, *All Art Is Ecological* (Penguin, 2021).

Chapter Ten: Votes for children

1 In 2019 they won nearly 3 per cent of votes nationally, but only 0.2 per cent of seats in Parliament, and evidence from other elections — like those for local council seats, and past European Parliament elections — show it's highly likely that more people would vote for them under a proportional system.

2 David Runciman 'Democracy for Young People', *Talking Politics Podcast* (2018), https://t.co/3BgVugXdyF.

3 In the UK's 2019 general election, just 21 per cent of 18–24 year olds voted Conservative, compared to 67 per cent of over 70's.

Adam McDonnell and Chris Curtis, 'How Britain voted in the 2019 general election' YouGov (2019), https://yougov.co.uk/topics/politics/articles-reports/2019/12/17/how-britain-voted-2019-general-election.

4 Simon Kuper, 'Why the Tories Don't Care About the Future', *Financial Times* (2022), https://www.ft.com/content/37b43960-2a83-4c8b-bead-4bf84beae5b9.

5 Many countries have laws specifically stating that all adults have the right to vote, regardless of whether they have the mental capacity to grasp what they are doing (although it should be noted that some US states allow judges to strip voting rights from people with mental disorders who are deemed 'incapacitated' or 'incompetent', so this is not universal).

6 David Runciman, 'Votes For Children! Why We Should Lower the Voting Age to Six', *The Guardian* (2021), https://www.theguardian.com/politics/2021/nov/16/reconstruction-after-covid-votes-for-children-age-six-david-runciman.

7 Matthew Weaver, 'Cambridge Academic Defends Idea of Giving Six-Year-Olds the Vote', *The Guardian* (2018), https://www.theguardian.com/politics/2018/dec/13/cambridge-academic-defends-idea-of-giving-children-the-vote.

8 John Wall, *Give Children The Vote: on democratizing democracy* (Bloomsbury, 2022).

9 See for example, Ludvig Beckman, 'Children and the Right to Vote' in Anca Gheaus, Gideon Calder, and Jurgen de Wispelaere (eds.), *The Routledge Handbook of the Philosophy of Childhood and Children* (Routledge, 2019).

10 New Zealand's Human Rights Act sets the age of 16 as the point from which actions may be discriminatory, so the court noted its decision would apply only to those 16 and up, which raises questions around why only older children are included! Alys Davies, 'New Zealand Supreme Court rules voting age of 18 is discriminatory', *BBC News* (2022), https://www.bbc.co.uk/news/world-asia-63699786.

11 Christopher Osterhaus and Susanne Koerber, 'The Development of Advanced Theory of Mind in Middle Childhood: a longitudinal study from age 5 to 10 years', *Child Development* 92 (5) (2021), pp. 1872–88.

12 Ernst Fehr, Helen Bernhard, and Bettina Rockenbach, 'Egalitarianism in young children', *Nature* 54 (7208) (2008), pp. 1079–83.

13 See for example, East Kent Sudbury, https://eastkentsudbury.org.uk/, A. S. Neill Summerhill School, https://www.summerhillschool.co.uk/, and Sudbury Valley School, https://sudburyvalley.org/.

14 John Wall, *Give Children The Vote: on democratizing democracy* (Bloomsbury, 2022).

15 Lyman Stone, 'The Minimum Voting Age Should Be Zero', *New York*

Times (2021), https://www.nytimes.com/2021/09/01/opinion/politics/kids-right-to-vote.html.

16 Private conversation.

17 Matthew Lipman, 'Philosophy for Children: some assumptions and implications', *Ethics in Progress* 2 (1) (2011), pp. 3–16.

18 Erik Kenyon, Diane Terordye-Doyle, and Sharon Carnahan, *Ethics For the Very Young: a philosophy curriculum for early childhood education* (Rowman & Littlefield, 2019).

19 Kate Bacon and Sam Frankel, 'Rethinking Children's Citizenship: negotiating structure, shaping meanings', *The International Journal of Children's Rights* 22 (1) (2014), pp. 21–42.

20 Jens Qvortrup, *Childhood Matters: social theory, practice and politics* (Avebury, 1994).

21 Toby Rollo, 'Feral Children: settler colonialism, progress, and the figure of the child', *Settler Colonial Studies* 8 (1) (2018), pp. 60–79.

22 Zsuzsa Millei and Kirsi Kallio, 'Recognising Politics in the Nursery: early childhood education institutions as sites of mundane politics', *Contemporary Issues in Early Childhood* 19 (1) (2018), pp. 31–47.

23 Jessica K. Taft, 'What working children in Peru can teach us about intergenerational fairness', *Intergenerational Foundation* (2022), https://www.if.org.uk/2022/07/21/what-working-children-in-peru-can-teach-us-about-intergenerational-fairness ; Jennifer McNulty, 'Youth activism is on the rise around the globe, and adults should pay attention, says author', *UC Santa Cruz* (2019), https://news.ucsc.edu/2019/09/taft-youth.html.

24 Manfred Liebel, 'Adultism and Age-Based Discrimination Against Children' in Dagmar Kutsar and Hanne Warming (eds.), *Children and Non-Discrimination: interdisciplinary textbook* (CREAN, 2014), pp. 120–142.

25 'Iran: killings of children during youthful anti-establishment protests', Amnesty International (2022), https://www.amnesty.org/en/documents/mde13/6104/2022/en/.

26 Arita Holmberg and Aida Alvinius, 'Children's Protest in Relation to the Climate Emergency: a qualitative study on a new form of resistance promoting political and social change', *Childhood* 27 (1) (2019), pp. 78–92.

27 Kirsi Kallio and Jouni Hakli, 'Are There Politics in Childhood?' *Space and Polity* 15 (1) (2011), pp. 21–34.

28 Kirsi Kallio and Jouni Hakli, 'Tracing Children's Politics', *Political Geography* 30 (2011), pp. 99–109.

29 Ann Phoenix and Pamela Pattynama, 'Intersectionality', *European Journal of Women's Studies* 13 (3) (2006), pp. 187–192; Kimberlé Crenshaw, 'Demarginalizing the Intersection of Race and Sex: a Black feminist critique of antidiscrimination doctrine, feminist theory and antiracist

politics', *University of Chicago Legal Forum* 1989 (1) (1989), p. 8.
30 Katherine Brown Rosier, 'Children as Problems, Problems of Children' in Jens Qvortrup et al., *The Palgrave Handbook of Children's Studies* (Palgrave Macmillan, 2009), pp. 256–272.
31 Sevasti-Melissa Nolas, Christos Varvantakis and Vinnarasan Aruldoss, 'Political Activism Across The Life Course', *Contemporary Social Science* 12 (1–2) (2017), pp. 1–12.
32 Kirsi Kallio and Jouni Hakli, 'Are There Politics in Childhood?', *Space and Polity* 15 (1) (2011), pp. 21–34.
33 'Votes at 16', British Youth Council, https://www.byc.org.uk/campaigns/votes-at-16.
34 John McCormick et al., 'Scottish Independence Referendum: report on the referendum held on 18 September 2014', *Electoral Commission* (2014), https://www.electoralcommission.org.uk/sites/default/files/pdf_file/Scottish-independence-referendum-report.pdf.
35 Electoral Commission, 'Young voters in Wales need more support to engage in elections', The Electoral Commission (2022), https://www.electoralcommission.org.uk/media-centre/young-voters-wales-need-more-support-engage-elections.
36 Chiara Ricciardone, 'On the Authority of Children', *Amor Mundi* (2019), https://hac.bard.edu/amor-mundi/on-the-authority-of-children-2019-10-07.
37 *Feminism Is The Radical Notion That Women Are People* (Miami University Libraries, 2016), https://digital.lib.miamioh.edu/digital/collection/butlernow_p/id/46.
38 Craig Berry, 'The rise of gerontocracy? Addressing the intergenerational democratic deficit', *Intergenerational Foundation* (2012), https://www.if.org.uk/wp-content/uploads/2012/04/IF_Democratic_Deficit_final.pdf.
39 Sue Donaldson and Will Kymlicka, 'Children and Animals' in Anca Gheaus, Gideon Calder, and Jurgen de Wispelaere (eds.), *The Routledge Handbook of the Philosophy of Childhood and Children* (Routledge, 2019), pp. 282–293.

Conclusion: Widening circles of care

1 A transcript for the speech: Paul M. Logsdon, 'Transcript of Dr. King's Speech', Ohio Northern University (1997), https://www.onu.edu/mlk/mlk-speech-transcript.
2 Martha Nussbaum *Justice For Animals: our collective responsibility* (Simon & Schuster, 2023), p. 16.

Index